breakfast of
CHAMPIONS

breakfast of
CHAMPIONS

260 daily devotions
by Andy Elmes

Second edition. This edition published in 2013 by Great Big Life Publishing
Empower Centre, 83-87 Kingston Road, Portsmouth, PO2 7DX, UK.

First edition published by New Wine Publishing in 2011.

British Library Cataloguing in Publication Data

A catalogue record for this book is available from the British Library

Scripture quotations are taken from the following versions of the Bible:

NKJV   New King James Version. Copyright © 1982 by Thomas Nelson, Inc. Used by
         permission. All rights reserved.
NIV   The Holy Bible, New International Version. Copyright © 1973, 1978, 1984,
         2011 by Biblica, Inc. Used by permission. All rights reserved worldwide.
AMP   Amplified Bible Copyright © 1954, 1958, 1962, 1964, 1965, 1967 by the
         Lockman Foundation. Used by permission.
MESSAGE The Message Copyright © 1993, 1994, 1995, 1996, 2000, 2001, 2002. Used
         by permission of Navpress Publishing Group.
NCV   New Century Version Copyright © 2005 by Thomas Nelson , Inc . Used by
         permission. All rights reserved.
KJV   King James Version. Crown copyright.

ISBN 978-0-9928027-0-7

About the Author – Andy Elmes

Andy and Gina are the Senior Pastors of **Family Church**, a multi-congregational church located on the South Coast of England. Andy is a visionary leader who has grown the church from twelve people on its first day to now being a significant and influential church in the UK and beyond.

Andy is also the founder of **Synergy Network**, a fellowship of like-minded ministers who desire inspirational relationships and growth in their leadership, ministries and lives, independent of what type or style of church they lead. He is also the founder of **Great Big Life**, a ministry established to see people equipped and empowered not only to lead effectively in Church but also in every other section and sphere of life too.

Andy has a wealth of experience and wisdom to offer that comes from a very successful time in ministry. As well as planting churches, he has been involved in many forms of evangelism including travelling as an evangelist for many years across the UK and throughout the world.

A dynamic visionary, Andy helps people to see things outside of the box and, as a strategist, he helps others to set goals within their lives and ministries and move towards them quickly. His experience, combined with his life-coaching skills, makes him a valuable asset to any pastor or leader seeking personal development encouragement and to address change.

A highly sought-after conference speaker for events and conferences, Andy regularly shares on a whole range of subjects including leadership, motivation and evangelism. Andy's versatility allows him to communicate as a pastor, an evangelist, a teacher or coach reaching individuals of all ages and in a variety of settings. Andy is very natural and irreligious in his approach, using humour well and being very animated and often unconventional in his delivery. His desire is to lead people to Jesus and help them to discover all that is now available to them through what Jesus has done for them. His personal mandate is "to know the King and to advance His kingdom."

Originally from Portsmouth, this is where Andy and Gina, along with their five children, Olivia, Ethan, Gabrielle, Sophie and Christina, now reside and lead the different ministries from.

What others say

"Andy Elmes lives life to the full with contagious joy, constantly extending the kingdom of God. He communicates with one person as though he/she is the most important person on earth. A very engaging and humorous preacher, he hits the mark every time and large crowds of people remember his messages for years. Family Church is a reproduction of Andy's life, caring for the individual – full of faith, joy and vision. Andy is a great leader who is impacting thousands of lives around the world."

Ashley Schmierer
International President, Christian Outreach Centre global movement of churches

"This devotional, by my friend Andy, is likened to the US National Grid (power company); you can trust it to light up and empower not just your day, but your life. If there was one word that I would use to describe Andy, it would be 'genuine'! Throughout the years that that I have known Andy I have observed the integrity in his friendships, marriage, fatherhood and it shows in the pulpit and in this devotional. Andy's zest for life comes alive in the words that he pens down and lives by."

Pastor Danny Thornton
River of Life Family Church, Syracuse, New York USA

"Over the last couple of years I have consistently started the day with Breakfast of Champions. It has invariably inspired faith for the day, and been uncannily on target with things that are going on in my life. It's a great devotional and will challenge and stir you to greatness in the Kingdom. This book deserves to sell by the shed load – it is packed with life-changing, challenging, faith-giving truth to inspire you to greatness in the Kingdom!"

Pastor David Harland
City Coast Church, Brighton England

"I have known Andy for many years. He is a great friend, wise counsellor and pastor, tremendous evangelist and life coach! His life, messages and writings always inspire, equip and bring great wisdom for living. These devotions will equip you for life in your marriage, relationships, entrepreneurial business ventures and MUCH more. Read, apply, and enjoy a GREAT BIG LIFE!"

Terry Eckersley
Businessman and CEO, Woking YMCA

"I've known Andy Elmes for over 15 years and if there was a hallmark stamped on his forehead it would be, 'The Real Thing'. The contents of this book are not the words of a man who wants to say something, but the words of a man who has something to say. I highly recommend this book, it'll help you maintain a cutting edge in your life."

Ray Bevan
Senior Pastor of Kings Church, Newport, Wales

"Andy Elmes is a man committed to personal growth, and has a unique understanding of biblical change and transformation. He has faithfully, for many years, helped hundreds of leaders break their level of containment and move forward into purpose and freedom. If you want to do the same, I recommend you read and digest this book."

Derek Smith
Senior Pastor, Kings Church, Bolton

"It's been my privilege to be a friend of Andy's for several years now, and I have come to know and value his visionary and inspirational leadership. Andy has a wealth of experience to offer in so many ways, and I particularly value his regular 'devotionals' which, like me, so many have found to be very relevant and helpful in their daily lives. I'm sure this book will bring prosperity and success to all who read it. Well done, Andy."

Linvoy Primus
Professional footballer and co-founder of Faith & Football

Introduction

Welcome to *Breakfast of Champions*. A mid-week devotional written with the purpose of inspiring and empowering you to live the most effective, influential, God-filled life you can. Packed with wisdom and tips from his own colourful walk with God, Andy will inspire and challenge you to 'run your best race'. According to some, breakfast is the most important meal of the day. This can be the case spiritually as well. This devotional, served up alongside your Bible each day, will give your spirit the nutrition and fibre it needs to grow strong and healthy.

> *Never despise the day of small beginnings.*
> (Zechariah 4:10, KJV)

The history of *Breakfast of Champions* is a story worth telling, a story about how the seemingly little things we do can turn into great oak trees of accomplishments for God. While trying to pastor a football player who was playing abroad, Andy agreed to send him a verse and a thought on a midweek basis to encourage him, which he began to do. Over the next few months, he passed the thought on to a few other people ranging from pastors to sports and entertainment stars and business people, as he encountered need for it to encourage them.

Andy kept writing and sending these thoughts out on a daily basis, not knowing what was happening behind the scenes, thanks to the highway of the internet. One day he was too busy and did not send one. That afternoon, he received an email from a man in the Bahamas he didn't know, asking where it was and telling of how he, himself, daily forwarded it to business people in five other nations. Andy suddenly became aware that his simple devotional, with its bad grammar, was going all across the world and many were now using it as a daily devotional tool. Suddenly realising this, he had it adapted into a more professional-looking devotional that would be sent more on a mid-week basis via the internet, free to whoever wanted it.

Breakfast of Champions has continued to grow in its popularity with many new opportunities 'coming out of nowhere', including it having its own TV and radio slots on national Christian radio. God has opened so many doors for this devotional to have a voice. We are regularly amazed at the doors that open to it. But it was always written with one thought in mind, written to inspire you in your walk with God, written to encourage you to live a great big life *(John 10:10)*.

Due to so many requests, we have now taken what we feel are some of the best devotional thoughts from the first couple of years and compiled them into this book so that people can have a hard copy that they can keep, write on and go back to as they need.

This is Andy's first book and, we believe, the first of many to come. We hope you enjoy the wisdom, humour and challenges contained within its pages. On random days throughout the devotional, Andy throws in a further quote or nugget to chew over as well as prayers and challenges.

Our prayer is that this devotional will lead you ever closer to Jesus and cause you to walk in the inheritance He purchased for you by His own blood.

God bless,
The Great Big Life Publishing Team

Dedications

I would like to dedicate this, my very first book, to all the people that daily bless my life and help me to live it strong and with purpose.

Gina

Firstly to my precious wife Gina. You have stood by me, not just in the good times but in the tough and challenging times also. You believed in me when others did not and have been so patient with me when I was discovering who 'me' was. Gina, you have always encouraged and supported me to be all God was calling me to be, you have always stepped up with me to meet every new adventure and challenge that God has given us. You're God's special gift to me and I love and appreciate you so very much. We have stood in empty fields and sowed together, may we now dance in times of harvest together. Gina, you are the one I want to spend the currency of my days with; to sit with you, watching our children blossom into all that God has called them to be is a great reward indeed. Love you so much – remember the deal, "Love, life and laughter".

Olivia, Ethan, Gabrielle, Sophie and Christina

You guys are fantastic and I am so very proud of each of you. You all teach me so much and make my life so colourful. For the sacrifices you have made, as we have lived to put God first, I thank you. I know the harvests God has for each of you are great. You are all so very different, each with unique things that make you stand out. I am praying that each of you will love the Lord as I have loved Him and know His love as I have known it. So proud of you, team Elmes!

Dad

Thanks for always loving and protecting me and for telling me the truth when I needed it; for forgiving me and praying for me when I was 'out there' and for showing me what true courage looks like, especially in the toughest of times!

To my mates and co-labourers in the 'God dream'

To all my friends in the UK and around the world – thanks for your friendship, together we are making a difference. To Wayne and Nicky, Steu and Carla, Geoff and Jane – what an adventure we are having together; thanks for all the sacrifices you make, and for believing in and watching out for me and Gina and the kids. Are we having fun yet? LOL!

And, of course, God

Without Him, I would not be anything or have anything to give. I am eternally grateful for what He has done for me and for allowing me to be a part of His plans and dreams for my generation. May my life give Him the harvest He deserves.

Good Morning Champion,
Breakfast is Served!

breakfast of
CHAMPIONS

Whose forecast are you listening to?

And they gave the children of Israel a bad report of the land which they had spied out, saying, "The land through which we have gone as spies is a land that devours its inhabitants, and all the people whom we saw in it are men of great stature."

Numbers 13:32 (NKJV)

It never ceases to amaze me how many different weather forecasts you can get at one time as you sit and flick through the channels on your TV. You can sit there, any given morning, and hear forecasts that are so different it borders on ridiculous. At the end of the day, you have to choose whose forecast you are going to believe or make the one you are going to live the day by. And then how often do they get it so very wrong? Especially with the British climate! They can only do their best to predict what may be coming by the knowledge they have and the things they have learnt from what happened when things looked like this before. The only one who really knows what the weather is going to do is, of course, its creator, God.

In the same way, when it comes to your life and trying to get a forecast for that, there is never a shortage of so-called qualified forecasters professing to know everything about what's going to happen next. If you want to waste your time collecting them then, like weather forecasts, you will have no lack to choose from. But, at the end of the day, which one will you embrace as true?

When I listen to some of the forecasts for the years ahead coming from the media and so-called experts of the hour, I am so glad I have a superior option: that being God's ever-relevant, never-failing word. I have made the decision again this year that I am embracing God's Word and His promises as the forecast of what will happen to me and for me this year and, indeed, the rest of my life. I am turning away from every other man-made and self-concocted forecast to take hold of God's. How about you?

Our text today reminds us of the moment when the children of Israel were given a wrong forecast by certain leaders who were driven by fear not faith. They chose to make this false, man-made forecast the one they would embrace and ended up missing out on all that God had in store for them. As these men were prophesying and forecasting doom, God's men – Joshua and Caleb – were there too, forecasting victory. Sadly, the voices of fear and failure were given greater attention by the ears and hearts of Israel and they went with them.

Whose report, or forecast, are you going to believe? I will believe the report of the Lord! His Word is the only forecast you need. So, sit down, have a read and pay attention – you will be glad you did.

Don't forget, eat the right kind of bread

*The tempter came to him and said, "If you are the Son of God, tell these stones to become bread." Jesus answered, "It is written: 'Man does not live on bread alone, **but on every word that comes from the mouth of God.**'"*

Matthew 4:3-4 (NIV)

Good morning, Champion. Today we do not live by natural bread, or food, alone but it is also God's every word coming into our lives in a fresh way that causes us to grow in true strength and potential.

Natural bread profits the natural man but is unable to give you the needed nutrition and fibre that your spirit craves for. Only God's Word will satisfy that inner appetite. That Bible you own contains the living bread, the words of God, you really need. Each sentence, thought and principle is power-packed with spiritual nutrition able to produce in you and through you incredible things. Make sure you take time to eat and feast daily on the bread of God, not just the bread of man.

Don't even try and live by natural things alone. Jesus said that a man cannot do that because he needs the words of God to be all that he was designed and destined to be. Ever heard the business term 'GIGO'? It stands for 'garbage in, garbage out'. Listen, when you make sure you have a daily intake of the divine bread that is God's Word, the Bible, you change that principle to a more positive reality which is, 'God in, God out'. You will experience God's life, wisdom and power coming into every section of your life instead of the garbage you once knew.

Jesus modelled for us how the power and potential of the Word of God can keep you when He was tempted by Satan in the wilderness. That was a time of personal, physical (natural) weakness in the wilderness, yet He did not lose or quit. Why? He had eaten His daily spiritual bread.

In times of trouble or temptation, you too can have the right answers and power you need when you have taken time to eat and digest God's bread, not just man's. Champions take time to regularly eat the bread that God daily offers and, when they eat it, they are fit for life. His Word is, indeed, the breakfast of Champions.

I pray that you fall ever deeper in love with and desire more, with great appetite, the Word of God and may God give you today the daily bread you really need!

Faith takes you beyond the limitations in your life

"As surely as the LORD your God lives," she replied, "I don't have any bread – only a handful of flour in a jar and a little oil in a jug. I am gathering a few sticks to take home and make a meal for myself and my son that we may eat it – and die." Elijah said to her, "Don't be afraid. Go home and do as you have said. But first make a small cake of bread for me from what you have and bring it to me and then make something for yourself and your son. For this is what the LORD, the God of Israel, says: 'The jar of flour will not be used up and the jug of oil will not run dry until the day the LORD gives rain on the land.'"

1 Kings 17:12-14 (NIV)

Good morning, Champion. Reading this account is very eye-opening, even jaw-dropping. Imagine if a prophet or evangelist today treated a widow in distress like this? It would be all over the papers the next morning with headlines like, 'Greedy Evangelist Eats Widow's Last Morsel of Food'.

A brief overview of this account goes like this:

The prophet goes to this woman to get food because God sends him there specifically. When he gets there, he finds this widow getting ready to make one last meal for her and her boy. Then she had resolved to starve to death because of lack – thank God He had a better plan than that. She tells Elijah of her "seemingly little or last bit" and he says to cook it up and release it from her hand into his life, first promising her that it would then supernaturally multiply for her current great need and last long after he had gone.

She had to make the choice to place her faith in the words of the prophet of God and not in the very real evidence of her very present reality. When she released her "seemingly small bit", the miracle happened just as he had promised. Our lesson here is that with her, as with the disciples with their miracle with the bread and fish we read about in the gospels, they both saw the miracle – increase came when they were willing to let go of something that did not seem enough for the moment.

Question: When, exactly, did the miracle happen in the hands of this desperate lady and the disciples in *Luke 19*? It was not when they held the bread because that would have crushed them under a mountain of provision. No, it was when they let it go and released it in faith!

Don't see things as small or insignificant; see them as seeds for mighty miracles because, when God is on the case, anything can happen.

Faith to you today, Champion. He is the same today as He has always been. Go ahead and let go of something that does not seem big enough and watch what happens next.

Food for thought:

When we were saved, we attended our own funeral! We saw an old man die and a new one walk away. A man who is fully alive and in Christ will never die again.

What are you subscribed to?

From the fullness of His grace we have all received one blessing after another. **For the law was given through Moses; grace and truth came through Jesus Christ.**

John 1:16-17 (NIV)

The law, how to become right in God's sight by what you can do or achieve in your own ability, was given or 'delivered' by Moses but grace, becoming right with God based on what another has done on your behalf, and truth came through Jesus. Law and grace represent two very different covenants or agreements. The law, found in the Old Covenant, was always destined to be replaced by a new and better one, that which is active and relevant for those who believe today.

Here is the problem – you cannot have a subscription to both. You must choose which one you want delivered through the letter box of your life each day. What will it be? What do you want delivered? The law or His grace? Despite what some people teach, they cannot be mixed. Just as oil and water cannot be mixed, you have to choose one or the other. Remember, the law was only meant to lead you to grace and Jesus.

Who do you want to see walking up the garden pathway each morning? Do you want Moses to arrive carrying two stones that bring you into a daily lifestyle of legalism, producing hypocrisy, or would you prefer to have Jesus, holding out two open hands, revealing the marks of His crucifixion, that event which led to the finished work that released you from the law and positioned you in grace and mercy? You choose. I know who I am subscribing to.

Notice carefully: one was **given by** someone and the other **came through** someone. Jesus is grace and truth and when you receive Him you receive them! Remember, true grace is not sloppy. It is life-changing and, when understood correctly, it truly is God's unmerited, undeserved and unearned favour and forgiveness manifested in the life of the undeserving. It does everything that we, in our own strength and ability, could never accomplish.

I pray you welcome the life-changing footsteps of grace today and not the 'impossible-to-live-up-to' marching boots of the law that has, after all, been fulfilled and satisfied in Christ.

Grace to you, and loads of it!

Champion's Prayer:

Thank You, Jesus, that grace and truth come through You. Today, I subscribe to all that is mine by the finished work of Your cross. Thank You, today, that grace is my portion not wrath and judgement; thank You today that I have peace with God through You – Amen.

Why settle for a relationship with a shadow?

For the law, having a shadow of the good things to come, and not the very image of the things, can never with these same sacrifices, which they offer continually year by year, make those who approach perfect.
Hebrews 10:1 (NKJV)

Hebrews refers to the law as having, or being, the shadow of good things to come and not the image of them. Think about that: the law, which was only the temporary agreement made between God and man, was the mere shadow of God's master plan; that plan being Jesus and the grace that would come through Him to all who would believe.

Surely, it is a far better thing to have a relationship with an actual person than with their shadow? I have a shadow but my shadow is not me – it acts like me, moves like me and has the same rough shape as me but it is not me. If the light is right, my shadow will enter a room before me but, once again, it is not me. Its arrival will always be a warning, or an announcement, of my impending arrival.

The law, a relationship with God based on our doing, was only ever a shadow of the real thing which was to be relationship with God through what Christ would do on our behalf.

Gina (my wife) could choose to try and have a relationship with my shadow but she would not get much from it. Why? A shadow has no life – it's the substance that follows the shadow that contains the life! Whether she desired some DIY done, or simply to be loved, the shadow would not benefit her at all but the substance, the actual person that followed, would.

The difference between those who have a relationship with God and those who have mere religion is simply connected to this reality: those who have religion have, or are trying to have, a relationship with the shadow of something instead of the substance of the something itself – or, should I say, someone. Jesus is the substance, the master plan, the one you really need – don't settle for His shadow!

Food for thought:
God's design for your life is not that you attend church, but become it!

Don't go losing Jesus

After the Feast was over, while his parents were returning home, the boy Jesus stayed behind in Jerusalem, but they were unaware of it. Thinking he was in their company, they travelled on for a day. Then they began looking for him among their relatives and friends. When they did not find him, they went back to Jerusalem to look for him. After three days they found him in the temple courts, sitting among the teachers, listening to them and asking them questions.

Luke 2:43-46 (NIV)

Good morning, Champion. Imagine that? Mary and Joseph lost Jesus! Come on, that is a massive thing. It is not like losing your wallet or misplacing your car keys; this is Jesus, Son of God, the redeemer of humanity, entrusted to your parental care. They lost Him and didn't notice for a day, then took another three days to find Him again!

Imagine how they must have felt when they turned around and He was no longer there! As a parent I have done that a few times in shops and busy places – keeping an eye on five kids can be a real full-time job and every now and then one of them still catches us out and we lose them for a moment. The feeling is awful; the heartbeat rises, panic begins to kick in – yep, most parents have been there, right? Mary and Joseph lost Jesus but then did the right thing: they went back to where they had Him last and found Him again before carrying on with their journey.

My question is, "Have you ever lost Him?" I don't mean your salvation; I am talking about the close relationship, the intimacy that you once had with God. Have you ever turned around in the midst of busyness and wondered, "Jesus, where are You in all this?"

I know I have and, sometimes, I have 'lost Him' in the middle of the busyness of church business – how crazy is that? Losing Him while working for Him? Remember that Mary and Joseph lost Jesus during a religious feast. They were attending something that was all about God and lost God in the middle of it. It happens! But I have always known what to do – like Mary and Joseph, you stop, think ,"When was He last close?" and go back to that point and regain Him before carrying on any further with your life journey.

We can lose a few things in life and it not make much difference; but make sure you don't lose the main thing – Jesus. That intimate, daily walk with Him is the greatest thing that you have or could ever own! If you have misplaced Him, STOP and go back and get Him.

Don't go losing Jesus (cont'd)

After the Feast was over, while his parents were returning home, the boy Jesus stayed behind in Jerusalem, but they were unaware of it. Thinking he was in their company, they travelled on for a day. Then they began looking for him among their relatives and friends.

Luke 2:43-44 (NIV)

W e spoke yesterday about making sure that, in all of our doing, we do not 'lose Jesus'. Mary and Joseph never set out that day to lose Him and were in 'shock-horror' when they discovered they had. What was it that caused them to lose Him? I can think of a few possibilities and they are the very things that can often make us lose or run ahead of Him as well.

The Crowd

Thousands of people were leaving Jerusalem all at once. There must have been crowds everywhere; maybe it was the crowds that made it easy to misplace Jesus?

We all have crowds we need to deal with in everyday life: dealing with people, work, different situations that can arise and just being distracted by other things that are happening – the hustle and bustle of life. Crowds of one kind or another are always a part of life. Just determine in your heart that you are not going to leave Jesus behind because of them. As I said yesterday, I have done it – the busyness of serving Him in ministry has, at times, taken up the time I would use for walking with Him. The good news is He never lets you wander too far before you know He is missing.

Let's make sure we keep our priority knowing Him with us in the midst of what we do.

Presumption

The problem may have been their presuming, or supposing, Him to be with them in what they were doing. They never stopped to check He was still around or ready to go where they were going next.

Don't live faster than God and never just presume He is going where you are in a hurry to go. Check! Thinking that He agrees with what you are doing can be the issue – don't just rubber-stamp everything you are doing with, 'God is cool with this'. Take a moment to check. Also, presuming He has finished doing what He was doing, we can move on from things nice and fast but always make sure He has finished doing what He wanted.

I have noticed God does not move on until He has finished what He set out to do. Hope this gives you good food for thought today. Beware of the crowds of busyness, and take time to check He is with you where you are heading next. You can save yourself four days or more if you do.

More 'Don't go losing Jesus' (cont'd)

After the Feast was over, while his parents were returning home, the boy Jesus stayed behind in Jerusalem, but they were unaware of it. Thinking he was in their company, they travelled on for a day. Then they began looking for him among their relatives and friends.

Luke 2:43-49 (NIV)

Following on with the thought 'things that can cause you to lose Jesus', here are a couple more things that can be the cause of us 'losing Jesus' (that intimacy we were born again to have with Him).

Preoccupation

When your mind is too much on other things:

Agendas or ambitions can posses your attention and cause you to lose your focus sometimes. Be careful of distractions and things that take your mind off of where Jesus is in your life. They can come in all shapes and sizes and most often they look good, not bad. For Joseph, I think it was about getting home quickly because he knew he had a busy day in the carpenter's shop the next day (like you do, when you have been away). His mind was so set on what had to happen next that he left the most important thing behind. Joseph had thought to himself, "Right, the festival is over – let's get home, busy day tomorrow". He set his face homeward and was moving at a great rate of knots. We all have the potential to get caught up or preoccupied in, or by, our busy lives.

Abdication

When you presume it is someone else's job to watch Jesus for you:

Joseph and Mary probably were each guilty of thinking that the other one was watching Jesus, and it turned out neither of them were! The lesson for us here is clear: it is not another person's job to watch your relationship with Jesus for you. That, my friend, is our individual, personal responsibility. We don't believe any longer in a traditional priest mentality as they did in the Old Testament when they only related to God through Moses. Those days are over and we all now have a personal responsibility to watch where Jesus is in our lives ourselves, with ministers positioned by God in our lives to assist us but not do it for us.

Today, I am taking responsibility for my personal walk with Jesus and I am going to maintain the success of our journeying together, not abdicate it to another. How about you?

Champion's Prayer:

Lord Jesus, thank You that I am reminded that my relationship with You is my responsibility. Forgive me for the times I have been preoccupied with other things and for when I have tried to make it the responsibility of another. Today, Jesus, I want to walk close with You and not to lose You in the busyness of the many crowds of life – Amen.

He is real easy to find again

When they did not find him, they went back to Jerusalem to look for him. After three days they found him in the temple courts, sitting among the teachers, listening to them and asking them questions. Everyone who heard him was amazed at his understanding and his answers. When his parents saw him, they were astonished. His mother said to him, "Son, why have you treated us like this? Your father and I have been anxiously searching for you." "Why were you searching for me?" he asked. "Didn't you know I had to be in my Father's house?"

Luke 2:45-49 (NIV)

We have spoken a lot this week concerning not 'losing Jesus' and have considered some of the things in our everyday life that can cause us to do so. I want to now talk about what to do if you do wake up one day and ask yourself, "Where is He in all of this?" The answer is simple: do what Mary and Joseph would have done and track back your steps to when you knew He was close with you last. That is what we do when we lose anything else, isn't it? When you realise you have mislaid your wallet or purse you think back over the journey of your day till you remember when it was last with you. Do the same here. It works.

Here are two keys to re-finding Jesus that we learn from *Luke 2*. The NIV version says Jesus responded, *"I had to be in my Father's House."*

Your pursuit of Jesus will always take you to the Father's house, church, not away from it. Don't buy into lies that say you just need some time out from church because that is how you lose Him further. Jesus is still all about His Father's house and we should be also. When we are, it's certainly harder to lose sight of Him. Love the Father's house! In the NKJV translation it says that Jesus responded, *"Did you not know that I must be about My Father's business?"*

If you want to feel close with Jesus again then make sure that your life is about the Father's business too and, when you do, you will turn around and find Him next to you again because that is what He is always about – His Father's business!

Be where He is and be involved in what He is involved in. Remember what He said in *Matthew 16:18*, He would "build His Church". The Church is the only thing He committed to build on the earth and He is still in the centre of its development today. Let's build it with Him because when we do, it's amazing how close He can feel. Why? Because we are about the Father's business with Him.

Champion's Challenge:

If you feel far from Jesus or like you have lost Him or the intimacy you once knew with Him, be like Joseph and Mary. Stop. Get Him back. Then carry on.

What a difference a day makes

Then King Nebuchadnezzar was astonished; and he rose in haste and spoke, saying to his counsellors, "Did we not cast three men bound into the midst of the fire?" They answered and said to the king, "True, O king." "Look!" he answered, "I see four men loose, walking in the midst of the fire; and they are not hurt, and the form of the fourth is like the Son of God."

Daniel 3:24-25 (NKJV)

Morning, Champion. If you look for Jesus in the whole Bible you will see Him, or a type or shadow of Him, in every single book. Throughout the Old Testament He pops up. One of the greatest examples of this is here, in *Daniel 3*, when He appears in the fire with the three men who stood up for God before Nebuchadnezzar. If you get chance this weekend to read *Daniel 3,* go ahead and do so – it's a great chapter.

Shadrach, Meshach, and Abed-Nego had taken a stand to only worship God; they had rejected the political correctness of their day and stood out in the crowd for it. As with Daniel, they had been set up by other envious leaders; boxed into a corner where it was down to them worshipping a golden statue erected as a god to see if they would live or die. They refused and were thrown into a furnace that had been heated seven times hotter because of the king's annoyance with them. The king, thinking he had sorted the problem, glanced into the furnace and saw the three men perfectly well and also another person. The reason He was *"like the Son of God"* was because He **was** the Son of God, Jesus!

When you take a stand to live a life where you 'turn up and stand up for God', He will turn up and stand up for you – in the good places **and** in the challenging ones too. We do not face a physical furnace but we do face other furnace-like challenges in life: the fire of people's opinions who don't like God, the fire of mockery and threats of what we could lose and the fires of trials and persecutions. Stand for Him and He will turn up for you!

As with Daniel in the account of the lion's den, the day ended a lot different to how it began. The day began with the three men being thrown into a fire for what they believed and a nation that would not recognise their leadership or their God. The day ended with the people who had set them up being thrown into the furnace, and with the three men being promoted and their God becoming famous in the land and honoured by the once unbelieving king. **"What a difference a day makes – 24 little hours". Live a life where you stand up for Him and He will cause a bad day to turn into a great one**!

If you face a furnace today, of one sort or another, stay in faith – step into it knowing God is for you and that God can **and will** save the day. Then wait for everything to turn around for your benefit when the fourth man arrives! It may take a day, like it was for the three men, or maybe it will take a little longer – keep trusting, the fourth man will be there in perfect time.

God bless you. Live for the one true King – the one who comes and joins you in the furnace.

Hear God speaking through everyday life

This is the word that came to Jeremiah from the LORD: *"Go down to the potter's house, and there I will give you my message." So I went down to the potter's house, and I saw him working at the wheel. But the pot he was shaping from the clay was marred in his hands; so the potter formed it into another pot, shaping it as seemed best to him. Then the word of the* LORD *came to me: "O house of Israel, can I not do with you as this potter does?" declares the* LORD. *"Like clay in the hand of the potter, so are you in my hand, O house of Israel."*

Jeremiah 18:1-6 (NIV)

Good morning, Champion. I love this account of God sending Jeremiah somewhere very practical, and that had to do with everyday life, to teach him something of great significance. Because Jeremiah had open ears to God, whenever and wherever, he was able to hear God speak to him from more than just religious scrolls: through everyday life things too.

In this account, we see that God wanted to communicate something very important to the prophet and He could have used a lot of words, and maybe a bit of thunder and lightning, but chose to speak through something that was very normal and common to daily life: a potter at work, making and re-making pots.

Sometimes we are all guilty of boxing God into our well-formatted prayer lives when the truth is that God is not speaking to us for half an hour a day but throughout the day. The issue is not: **is God speaking**, Champion, but rather: **are we listening**? Have we got ears to hear like Jeremiah when God wants to say or communicate something to us using something from everyday life, like a potter at work?

God is ever-speaking, so let our hearts be ever-listening. Think about Jesus in the Gospels where we see that He too communicated the deepest of things to His followers using everyday things to make His point, things such as vines, mountains, sheep and farmers to name a few. He used these everyday things to communicate divine truth to them. Yes, we must also bear in mind that everything we hear must line up with the truth of the Word of God but the reality is that God wants to speak to you today, outside of your well-formatted devotional time slots, and will use everyday things to help you understand deep revelation if you have ears to hear.

Be listening today for the ever-speaking God to say something to you. Maybe, as with Jeremiah, it will be through something very simple and 'everyday'.

Bless you, Champion, and have a great day.

Hear God speak through your everyday life

God told Jeremiah, "Up on your feet! Go to the potter's house. When you get there, I'll tell you what I have to say." So I went to the potter's house, and sure enough, the potter was there, working away at his wheel. Whenever the pot the potter was working on turned out badly, as sometimes happens when you are working with clay, the potter would simply start over and use the same clay to make another pot. Then God's Message came to me: "Can't I do just as this potter does, people of Israel?" God's Decree! "Watch this potter."

Jeremiah 18 (The Message)

Good morning, Champion, let us consider again the God who speaks to us through everyday things. I have heard so many Christians say things like, "God does not speak to me." Again, I want to underline that when we have communication problems with God it is normally more to do with us not listening than Him not speaking. Maybe He is speaking through an everyday situation and you never imagined He would make things so simple?

God has taught me leadership lessons in and through so many things, even when I have been walking my dog. He has taught me how to structure my church leadership while sitting at a harbour watching ships of different types go by and He has taught me concerning a person yielding their whole life to Him when I was cutting a pizza. He has taught me lessons on spiritual fitness while I was on the cross-trainer at the gym and church unity by a game of *Monopoly*. Believe me, the list goes on.

I really want to encourage you today to keep reading the Word, keep praying like you do but dare to listen for God speaking outside of those established routes and routines because maybe what you need to hear for that situation you are in is somewhere He wants you to go. Go out for a walk; get off of the couch; let God take you to a potter's house where He can show you something.

Remember in *John 15*, Jesus took His disciples next to a simple everyday vine to help them understand the deep truths of their union with Him. He stood there, pointed at the visual lesson and then said, "Me vine, you branch and my Father is the vinedresser" and they instantly understood everything about connecting with God in just a couple of moments. God still wants to teach us that way too, if we are willing to listen. I find it truly amazing the way that God can use anything to teach you something and the only thing we need to do is hunger to learn and have ears that are wide open to hear!

Champion's Prayer:

Thank You today, Father, that You are speaking to me. Let my ears be open to hear what You are saying. Speak to me through Your Word but also through people and even the everyday things I see and hear. Today, I tune into Your voice and wait for Your instruction – Amen.

He is the potter, we are the clay!

This is the word that came to Jeremiah from the LORD : "Go down to the potter's house, and there I will give you my message." So I went down to the potter's house, and I saw him working at the wheel. But the pot he was shaping from the clay was marred in his hands; so the potter formed it into another pot, shaping it as seemed best to him. Then the word of the LORD came to me: "O house of Israel, can I not do with you as this potter does?" declares the LORD. "Like clay in the hand of the potter, so are you in my hand, O house of Israel."

Jeremiah 18:1-6 (NIV)

We see Jeremiah instructed to go and watch a potter to hear God's message to him, visually portrayed before him. God knew that, for the prophet to catch the fullness of the message in his heart, it had to be communicated in more than words. So, as we have said, be ready for God to do the same for you.

As Jeremiah watched the old potter taking clay and forming it into what he had first imagined in his mind, when he saw him shaping and reshaping and removing bits that marred the clay, suddenly the penny dropped and the realisation that 'He is the potter and I am the clay' set in. The word of the Lord to Jeremiah that day was this: if the potter can make and mould as he sees best then the Divine Potter should be allowed to make and mould your life as He sees best.

Guess what? I believe that message is still relevant to us today. Sometimes we can all be like clay that thinks it knows better than the potter and sometimes we all need a bit of remoulding to have the bits that have the potential to mar taken out. The potter removes those bits otherwise, when it is in the kiln, the pot will split. God wants to get the bits out of us because then, when the kiln of life burns hot, we will not crack but remain intact and be proven. Yes, we all need that reminder sometimes, just as Jeremiah did. He is the potter and we are the clay and as the clay is in the hands of a potter, so are we in His.

The good news? You can trust the potter's hands. You may not understand why He is remoulding a certain part of your life but, Champion, you can trust Him because He has no intention of harming, only thoughts of perfecting. He is not out to make something embarrassing or to cause pain but rather something beautiful and something that will be yet another trophy of grace – let the Potter get His hands all over you again today, He knows what you have the potential to be.

Champion's Prayer:

Father, I thank You that today my life is in Your hands. I trust You to make and mould me into all that You know I can be. I know You will not cause me harm but rather, with Your loving hands, cause me to take my correct form – You are the potter, I am the clay – Amen.

Credited to, not worked for

What does the Scripture say? "Abraham believed God, and it was credited to him as righteousness." Now when a man works, his wages are not credited to him as a gift, but as an obligation. However, to the man who does not work but trusts God who justifies the wicked, his faith is credited as righteousness.

Romans 4:3-5 (NIV)

The very essence and true power of grace is that it is always totally unmerited, undeserved and unearned. It is something freely given to the person who believes, not to the person who tries to earn or achieve it.

The text today reminds us again that Abraham had righteousness, or right standing with God, credited to him when he believed, not when he achieved. He did not work or labour for it but qualified himself for it by his faith, by simply believing and trusting God.

Champion, we also, as Abraham, are credited with the righteousness of God when we realise, as Abraham did, that none of our labour is good enough or ever enough to qualify us for it. Only when we choose to simply trust and rely in God's grace – unmerited, unearned favour – and faithfulness does He credit to us all of the righteousness we could ever need.

This can be difficult for some to grasp because we have been raised in a society and world that teaches a wage-based way of thinking: "When we work hard or do enough we then get what we desire or deserve." This way of thinking puts the emphasis on our doing: we do and then we get. True grace really messes this system up and actually works in the complete reverse to it – that is why so many cannot grasp the simple beauty of grace. Abraham did nothing yet had everything he needed credited, given freely, to him by God. It was not a wage for something he had done but grace, something freely given by God. See the truth here: it was God giving him what he did not deserve and could never earn. His righteousness, as ours today through Christ, was not a wage given for a good job done or a life well lived!

Be reminded today that the way we gain righteousness and partake daily in the grace of God is still the same – we should not try to earn or gain something from God according to a wage mindset; rather we should daily come and receive by faith alone from the good hand of God what we could have never earned or qualified ourselves for. Remember, the Bible says that we when we belong to Jesus, we are the seed of Abraham and heirs of the same promise. *(Galatians 3:29)*

Food for thought:
Till a person has lived beyond themselves, they have not truly lived.

What are you hiding in your heart?

I seek You with all my heart; do not let me stray from Your commands. I have hidden Your word in my heart that I might not sin against You.

Psalm 119:10-11 (NIV)

The heart is a vitally important place in your life because it is in the heart that we all have the potential to both store and hide stuff. As with so many things, this can be a negative or positive reality, depending on what each person is choosing to store or hide within theirs.

The writer declares that he has hidden God's Word in his heart. Let's face it, there can be no better thing to both store and hide in your heart than the living word of God! What's stored in your heart will eventually be heard on your lips and manifested in your life. Your heart is like the cistern of a toilet: when your life gets 'flushed' by the hand of circumstance, what is in the heart always comes out – often shocking or blessing those who may be watching at that moment.

Make sure that today you are storing God's Word in your heart. As it says in Colossians, *"let the word of God dwell in you richly" (Colossians 3:16).* Then, whenever you need wisdom or truth you will have a ready supply deep within your life. Just remember, we all have the potential to store and hide other stuff, so be honest with yourself and make sure you are not. Hey, if you need to have a good spring clean of the wardrobe or pantry of the heart, go ahead and do it. Let's not make our heart store what does not do it good – things like bitterness, unforgiveness and envy can be easily hidden in the cloisters of your heart and remain unseen by others for years. But, believe me, those things and others like them are toxic and will do your heart no good at all. In fact, they will slowly rot your heart, affecting everything good that is sharing the storage area.

As the writer knew, when we hide His Word in our hearts, it will keep us from sinning too. Why? Because we always live out of what we have stored in it – desires, ambitions and dreams are all birthed from what we allow to remain and hide in our heart. Every sin that we can commit, small or large, starts as an undealt-with seed – like a thought in the mind that is then allowed to be stored and germinated in the heart.

If you don't want a tree of sin in your life, don't let its seedling grow in your heart. Rather, pack that heart with the seeds of God's Word and then go ahead and watch what grows.

Champion's Challenge:

Have an honest think about what you are carrying around in that heart of yours. If there are things that will not profit or will cause damage, then get them out. Replace them with things that will make your heart strong. Things like faith, hope and love.

Master the mouth

When we put bits into the mouths of horses to make them obey us, we can turn the whole animal. Or take ships as an example. Although they are so large and are driven by strong winds, they are steered by a very small rudder wherever the pilot wants to go. Likewise, the tongue is a small part of the body, but it makes great boasts. Consider what a great forest is set on fire by a small spark.

James 3:3-5 (NIV)

Here we see James comparing the mastering of our mouths to a couple of significant things. Firstly, to a strong horse. He uses the analogy that when you have the control of a horse's mouth, you have control of where it can and can't go. Next, he uses the example of a great ship and its rudder, again making the point that when you have control of that small part called the rudder, you actually have control over the whole vessel and you also hold the power to cause it to set sail where ever you so desire.

James is speaking strongly concerning the mouth and the need for its mastering, reminding us that it has the potential to take us to places we don't want to go, as well as places we do. The mouth is such a small part of the body, yet has incredible power given to it. When I look back over my life, I see that my tongue got me into a whole lot of trouble but has also brought me into a lot of good when I allowed God to control it.

It can be used positively or negatively, according to our choice. It has the power to disqualify as well as qualify. Remember the sad account of the children of Israel on the edge of the promised land and how they managed to talk themselves out of everything that God had promised that they could have – incredible things that were just footsteps away?

Let us be ever cautious concerning where we allow our tongue to take us – it is such a small part of who we are physically but has the power to start a whole lot of trouble!

Wow, think on that today, Champion – that little, pink thing that lives in your mouth has the potential to take you to great places. But, out of control, has the power to ruin you and leave you where you never wanted to be.

Use it wisely, Champion – master the mouth and you can determine where your life will set sail for next.

Are you speaking words that build or tear down?

From the fruit of his mouth a man's stomach is filled; with the harvest from his lips he is satisfied. The tongue has the power of life and death, and those who love it will eat its fruit.

Proverbs 18:20-21 (NIV)

L et us again consider 'the mouth', specifically looking again at what lives inside of it – the tongue. We saw yesterday that if it is left unmastered and untamed it has the potential to cause our lives to sail to places we really do not want to go. Today, let us see what *Proverbs* has to say about it.

First of all, it reveals that a man's stomach, or life, is filled by the fruit of his mouth and that your lips are what produce harvest in your life. Again, the question here is whether your words are producing a positive harvest or a negative one: a harvest you love or a harvest you hate. Let's underline again, that choice is down to you. It's all about how you choose to use your tongue.

Secondly, the Word of God warns us that the tongue actually has the power of life and death and that with it we can kill or cause life to spring up.

Think about it today: your words have the power to build people up or destroy them. Your words can empower leaders, dreams and visions or rip them down. I believe many of us may have used our mouth for demolition before knowing Jesus but now we must use our 'mastered mouths' to bring life and hope and to build up, not tear down.

Lastly, let's consider our confession; the words we choose to speak over our own lives each day can bring life and death to our own situations. What are you speaking or confessing daily over your life, Champion? Are you speaking words of life that build strong hope and future or words of death and unbelief that tear down those Godly promises in your life? The best words you can use are the ones that agree with God's words.

Use your tongue to speak God's words and promises over you, your family and everybody else in your world. Make the decision, today, that your words will bring life and hope to all that hear them, including you!

Champion's Challenge:

Today, look for someone who is in need of encouragement. Spend a few minutes speaking words of hope and life into them and the situations they are facing. Keep speaking till you see a flame of hope light up in their eyes. Build someone up with your words!

Your words are creative seeds

And God said, "Let there be light," and there was light. God saw that the light was good, and He separated the light from the darkness. God called the light "day," and the darkness He called "night." And there was evening, and there was morning — the first day.

Genesis 1:3-5 (NIV)

In the first chapter of *Genesis*, which some have aptly titled *The Book of Beginnings*, we see God busy creating. Throughout this chapter, we see Him making things: forming the sun and moon, establishing day and night and dividing the land and sea. In fact, He makes everything we today know as the earth and life. Notice this though, God does not lift a finger or move a foot but rather He speaks things into being. He says, "*Let there be...*" and things come into existence.

When you read on a little bit further in *verse 21*, He speaks of the creation of man and how he was made in His own image and likeness. Think about this. He created us in His image and likeness. I believe that, in our design, He gave us also the potential to create without using our hands and it is vital that we understand this reality: that our spoken words create things too.

We saw yesterday that, according to Proverbs, our words have the potential of life and death so let's think more about the **life** part this morning. Your words of life, spoken in faith, have the potential to create incredible things, both in life and in people. Every word we speak is like a fertile seed that can produce a harvest because God made our words to have creative potential to them.

Think of it this way: your tongue is a seed dispenser and, daily, when you speak, you are sowing seeds that will produce a harvest. Again, I find this sobering that we get to choose the type of harvest we create by the words, or seeds, we select to speak. When we realise this truth, great things can begin to happen in the situations we may face and the people we are in contact with.

Remember when Jesus taught the disciples concerning moving mountains? He said, "Speak to the mountain". Are you speaking God's life-filled promises into those mountain-like situations, Champion? If not, start again today. Get the promise or opinion of God for it and begin to speak it out with your God-given authority.

I tell you the truth, if anyone says to this mountain, "Go, throw yourself into the sea," and does not doubt in his heart but believes that what he says will happen, it will be done for him.
Mark 11:23 (NIV)

Food for Thought:
What you sow, you mow.

Use acceptable language

Let the words of my mouth and the meditation of my heart be acceptable in Your sight, O LORD, my strength and my Redeemer.

Psalm 19:14 (NKJV)

We have been looking at the mastering of the mouth this week and yesterday we saw how our words have the potential to create things because we were made in the image of God. We also looked at how our tongues can create harvests and move mountains when we understand the life and power contained in the words we speak.

What a great verse this is: "*Let the words of my mouth … be acceptable in Your sight*". What sort of words do you think God finds acceptable? Do you think He is listening out for words of faith being spoken out and words of truth? Yes, both of these but also, I believe, He delights in the words we speak that bring life to our personal situations and especially to other people's lives. When God hears us speaking words of life and hope to people, I believe He likes that a lot.

It's amazing the power our words can have on other people, isn't it? Words of encouragement can repair low self-esteem in a life that has maybe been crushed by the harmful words of so many others. Words of faith, hope and wisdom can bring a smile to the face of a person whose heart may be so heavy, confused and hopeless.

Godly, well chosen, life-inspired words can build people up, give hope, bring joy and strengthen the lives of those who hear. We may have all used our tongues to make people feel small in the past but that should not be happening now. Our words should make people feel bigger, better and more hopeful than they were before they bumped into us.

Your challenge again today, Champion, is to go find someone and encourage them with the words of your mouth and don't stop until their eyes light up and their mouth smiles back at you in response.

Remember, God's words made you live. Let your words cause life in someone else.

Champion's Prayer:

Father, let my words release hope, let my words build people up, not tear them down, let my words bring life to those needing it. Holy Spirit, help me to control my mouth. Help me to say what I need to and to not say what I don't. May my words please You – Amen.

He backs up His Word

Therefore, holy brethren, partakers of the heavenly calling, consider the Apostle and High Priest of our confession, Christ Jesus.

Hebrews 3:1 (NKJV)

We have spoken a lot about our mouths and the words we choose to speak. My final thought is concerning your confession. When you make His words and promises your property and speak them out as your confession, powerful things will start to happen in and around you.

God has graciously given us His Word to use and when we allow it to dwell richly in our hearts, and be found daily upon our lips, it is then that we begin to see the manifestation of His promises in our lives and situations. Why? Simple. He is faithful and backs up His Word! He will not back up our insecure, soul-based statements. He will not back up words of doubt, unbelief and fear. He will not back up whining or pleading but He will always respond to His Word richly implanted in the heart and spoken out of our mouth with faith.

Be challenged today, Champion, to be ever placing His Word in your heart and letting it live on your lips. God watches over His Word to perform it and promises it will not return void but will accomplish what it was sent for. When we confess His Word concerning our salvation, He is the High Priest of that confession and backs it up, saving us completely. But also, when we speak His promises concerning other areas of our lives, He is the High Priest of those confessions too and will back them up also.

Here's the timeless recipe of faith: don't look at the size of the problem but rather find God's promise concerning it and begin to confess those promises over the situation. Don't listen to or speak out the whimpers of your soul but let faith arise that, today, Jesus remains the High Priest of the (God-inspired) words we speak, just as He promised.

Find that 'God-word', Champion, the one that perfectly fits your situation and begin to confess that out in faith and watch what happens.

Food for thought:

The faith walk is more about what you do with your lips than your feet. Make sure what's in your heart is on your lips!

How do you get out of an all-time low?

Joseph's master took him and put him in prison, the place where the king's prisoners were confined. But while Joseph was there in the prison, the LORD was with him; he showed him kindness and granted him favour in the eyes of the prison warden.

Genesis 39:20-21 (NIV)

I was listening to the radio on the way to the office and heard a band called The Wanted singing today's title in a song. They asked this question, "How do you get out of an all-time low?" They then sang about a whole lot of things that would not help you but never mentioned the One who would, Jesus. Listen, when you are in a 'low time', God is there and really is your *"very present help in time of need" (Psalm 46:1).*

Think about Joseph. Here we see him sitting in prison when he had done nothing wrong but also we see he was not alone. Read it again: both the Lord and His grace were present. Remember Joseph's story? His journey had started with big God-given dreams and promises and almost straight away he woke up in a low – abandoned in a pit – because his brothers could not handle what God had promised. But as you read on, you see God's favour kept lifting him up and moving him forwards. Here, we now see Joseph in a prison. He could have thought, "What is this about, what about the dreams?" In some ways this was an 'all-time low' for him.

Yet he was not crushed or disappointed – why? Because he knew something that I am going to share with you. Here it is: this was just one chapter in a very, very good book – not the best chapter, granted, but like the other chapters it would come and it would go. He knew that God had promised him that the story would end looking a lot different to a prison cell; he trusted God above what he was feeling or currently experiencing (that's faith).

Champion, that is what we all need to do when we find ourselves in 'an all-time low'. Remember, God and His favour are present with us and that this is just a single chapter in a very good book – your life. We then turn a couple of pages in Joseph's life-story and he is no longer in a prison but instead the Prime Minister of the nation, saving the brothers who abandoned him in that earlier chapter of his life. That's God, my friend. If you keep believing, He will keep moving you to the next and better chapter.

Remember, His plans are to prosper you, to give you a hope and a future *(Jeremiah 29:11),* but that does not mean that sometimes the road is not a little bumpy!

Not everyone will 'get it'

"Here comes that dreamer!" they said to each other. "Come now, let's kill him and throw him into one of these cisterns and say that a ferocious animal devoured him. Then we'll see what comes of his dreams."

Genesis 37:19-20 (NIV)

Here we see the very strange reaction, or response, of Joseph's brother to the dreams and promises God had given to him. Maybe a little later, when he was sitting abandoned in the bottom of a pit, he may have thought to himself, "You know, in hindsight, maybe I shouldn't have shared the full content of that dream with them, maybe I should have left out the 'you will bow before me' bit?"

Okay, granted, the content of the dream was a bit full on, but no way did it deserve the violent response it got – come on, these were his brothers, right? They faked his death and threw him in a pit! Listen Champion, sometimes, when God gives you a big dream or promise, your spirit receives it with joy but that does not mean that others will receive it that way too.

You may have great faith for that 'big dream or miracle' but the truth is that those around you may not. That's the sad reality – you need to be careful who you share your 'God-given stuff' with. Sometimes, when God gives a big dream or a plan, those who seem closest to us can become our biggest obstacles or doubters. Their caring wisdom can cause unneeded hurdles on your road of faith. All I can say is, when you know that you know what you have received is from God, let those care-based questions cause a greater persuasion, not doubt. Others will be more subtle: they will say, "That's so good" with their mouth but the look in their eyes or that slight smirk on their cheek will reveal what they are really thinking.

Again, if you know the dream or the plan is God-inspired, learn to live above those things. Then there are the idiots who have zero control over the functioning of their mouth – don't need to say too much about them, right? Just smile back but don't listen to or absorb what they are trying to sow. I suppose the lesson Joseph gives us is: **be careful who you share your God-given dreams, plans and promises with**. As someone wise once said, "Don't feed piggies your pearls". Let them keep eating what they are used to. People in your world will respond differently to your dreams according to a number of things, like, "Do they know God? Do they have faith? Is their love for you shadowing God's given route for you?"

All I am saying is protect what God gives, don't cast it before those you shouldn't. Be a person who seeks wise counsel but know, in your life, who gives wise counsel. Hey, we serve a big God who gives big dreams and promises. Have a heart that is ever open and ready for God to drop a big dream into your life. **Warning: most of them don't make sense – that's where faith comes into it!**

Waking up in your best dream

And Joseph said to his brothers, "Please come near to me." So they came near. Then he said: "I am Joseph your brother, whom you sold into Egypt. But now, do not therefore be grieved or angry with yourselves because you sold me here; for God sent me before you to preserve life."

Genesis 45:4-5 (NKJV)

L et's stay with Joseph for one more morning.

Think about his life, the book of his days – it was such an adventure, a roller coaster of faith. There were many mornings he would wake up and say, "Where am I?" When I travel a lot, speaking in many different places, towards the end of the travels every now and then I find myself waking up in a hotel and having to think, "Where am I?"

Joseph's life must have been so much like that: one morning he opens his eyes and he's at home with his adoring father Israel; another morning he wakes up and he's in a filthy pit; another morning a palace; another morning a prison. Wow! It must have been weird waking up sometimes not knowing what you would see. But one day he woke up and saw the walls of the bedroom of a man who was the second-in-charge of the nation: that man was HIM!

Why was that such a good morning? Because, that morning, he found himself walking in the reality of the harvest of the dream he first saw all of those chapters and years before.

When he was just a lad, God had given him a dream that he would be raised up to rule and to be a part of God's plan to lead a whole nation. That dream was the same one that got him into sooooo much trouble. But this morning would be the morning his brothers would come and bow before him, looking for assistance and not knowing who he was; this morning his dad would find out he was alive and he would be reunited; this morning would be the one when he would say to those who harmed him, "What you meant for evil, God used for good".

I don't know what room of your life-journey you woke up in this morning. Good, bad, challenging? But I can tell you, if you are daring to follow God's plan for your life, you will wake up in a room one day that you have seen before – you saw it in that dream God gave you.

Once again, I say the now is just a chapter in a great big book. That book, my friend, is your ever-unfolding life. Your author, God, has set the ending up to be real good!

Don't live to give God a bargain – give Him the best

But the king replied to Araunah, "No, I insist on paying you for it. I will not sacrifice to the LORD my God burnt offerings that cost me nothing."

2 Samuel 24:24 (NIV)

King David was looking for a threshing floor to build an altar to God for worship so that he could break the plague that was on his people (read *chapter 24* if this needs more explanation).

He approaches Araunah to ask if he can buy what he needs and Araunah offers him everything he needs for absolutely nothing (read *verses 21-23*). Many of us would have thought, "What a mega bargain. I got that cheap!" But not David. He actually refuses not to pay. Why? Because of his revelation of worship, he knew that worship was all about giving your best, not what you have left or got cheap.

Whenever David worshipped the Lord or gave Him anything, he always gave Him the very best he had – whether it was time, energy, song or finance. His worship was always based on God's worth to him. That is why he never held back. God meant everything to him.

How about us? Would we take the bargain offer? When it comes to us worshipping the Lord with who we are and what we have, will we give the bare minimum or what is considered normal, or will we be extroverts of worship, like David?

I suppose the only thing we need to really consider to determine the measure of our worship response by is what God gave to us in Jesus. Did He hold back or give us second best or what was left? No, Jesus was the very best and He gave Him for us which, again, leaves us now with a due response.

Purpose in your heart that, like David, you won't give God songs, offerings, service or anything that costs you nothing. As you do, you set yourself up for a very blessed life. Don't hold back; give the King the worship He deserves and not what you got cheap or had left over. When giving to God, always remember this principle: if you feel a seed leave your life, you will always feel the harvest when it comes back to you.

Champion's Challenge:

What can you give to God today that costs you something? Is there something you can do? Somewhere you can go? Something you can give? I challenge you to do or give something that costs you something more than normal.

As we are, so is He

Love has been perfected among us in this: that we may have boldness in the day of judgment; because as He is, so are we in this world.

(1 John 4:17 NKJV)

Ever heard this verse before? What an awesome reality and responsibility. I like the way the NIV says it: "*In this world we are like Jesus*". There are actually two ways of looking at this. You can look at it from the viewpoint that it is written from, which is: as He is there, in heaven, so we are here, on earth, regarding our state of righteousness and authority on the earth. Or you could turn it around and see the reality of it the other way too: as we are here so He is there!

Before you start sending me letters saying I am a heretic, let me clarify. I am not saying that He follows our lead or gets His power and what He needs from us, I am just considering the daily reality of this being a fact when it comes to the issue of unsaved people watching us.

Think about it – they don't know Jesus like we do, they have never experienced Him and the chances are that He has been terribly misrepresented to them by religious people and the media. So how can people know what Jesus is really like in Heaven? The answer is very simple: by looking at and watching us.

Remember, the Bible clearly teaches that He is the head and we are the body! Wow, think about that – we are His physical body on this earth. When we understand this, it should cause us to want to show the world sameness between the head and the body rather than some sort of Frankenstein's monster whose head is so very different to its body.

So we are Him on this earth and people will know what He is like by the way we choose to live. Okay, that raises some good challenges. When people bumped into Jesus on the streets of Jerusalem two thousand years ago, would they experience the same when encountering us today? Let's get specific. Imagine what a great welcome you would have got when you met Him – unforgettable! Do people get that same welcome when they come to your church? They would have experienced a great attitude, power and – especially – life. Imagine the life that flowed out from Him as He walked through Israel. We need to make sure that we never act dead because the head is not dead but rather the source of life abundant; "*as He is*", so we should be.

When designing our lives, and indeed our churches, to "*glorify Him*", the best thing we can do is make sure it looks, sounds and feels like Him so that when people encounter us they get a taste of everything that He, the head, really is. I have said to my church leaders that nothing but life should ever come from our stage or meetings – none of this dirgy, dead stuff but life! Remember, people are watching and, as we are here, that is what they will consider Him to be there.

Keep short accounts?

Therefore, putting away lying, "Let each one of you speak truth with his neighbour," for we are members of one another. "Be angry, and do not sin": do not let the sun go down on your wrath, nor give place to the devil.

Ephesians 4:25-27 (NKJV)

Interesting advice: don't let the sun go down on your wrath. Put another way, 'keep short lists or accounts' when it comes to dealing with people and what they may have done to you.

Remember, love covers a whole multitude of sins and, according to *1 Corinthians 13*, keeps no record of wrongs! The bottom line is that you live in a real world with real people and every now and then someone is going to do something that has the potential to hurt and offend you. It's how you respond to them or to what they have done that determines your future freedom and defines your true level of maturity in God.

I was playing golf once in Wales on a very well known, prestigious course and was intrigued by a small sign I saw concerning the replacement of divots, pieces of turf lifted by a golfer during play. It gave this advice: "If the divot is replaced within five minutes of the damage being done, by the end of the day it will have begun to restore and mend itself. Leave it more than five minutes and it can then take 15 weeks to repair itself!"

Life is like a game of golf. There will always be someone who takes a slice out of you, sometimes on purpose, sometimes by mistake. As with golf, some people have a good swing on life and others don't. The ground of your life always has the potential to get a bit dug up by the bad life swings of others – that's life.

The question is: what will you do about it? Will you forgive them quickly and start to heal straight away or keep them on some holding list for a while till you feel like payment for their wrong swing has been fully paid? Most often it is not them that suffer when we are not fast to forgive but, like the wellbeing of the golf course I spoke of, it is us.

Champion, learn to get that bit of uprooted turf back in place as quick as you can; keep short lists; make sure all is settled in your heart by the time the sun goes down! You may not be able to control someone taking a chunk out of your heart every now and then but you **can** determine how long it takes your heart to heal.

Food for thought:

Forgiveness is to set a prisoner free and then realise the true prisoner was actually you.

Lessons from the golf course

Stand therefore, having girded your waist with truth, having put on the breastplate of righteousness, and having shod your feet with the preparation of the gospel of peace

Ephesians 6:14-15 (NKJV)

Yesterday, we used a golf analogy – the replacement of divots – to learn something profound about forgiveness. Let's continue with a golf theme and talk about some more life lessons that I learned from playing golf. I do not claim to be a good golfer but I certainly found some great parallels between the game of golf and life that help me in my daily Christian walk.

A correct stance is vital

Before you even attempt to hit a ball in golf, you have to make sure you are standing correctly. If you want to hit straight balls, you have to have a correct stance. This is a great parallel to our Christian walk because if we want to 'hit good shots', we need to make sure our stance is correct. Make sure you are standing daily in the finished work of Christ; standing tall in His victory and completeness. Always remember that you are standing in the revealed truth that you are now a new creation and old things have truly passed away. You are not who you used to be!

It is good also to make sure that you have a well balanced stance and that you're not leaning heavily on one side. For example, learn to balance your ideals and your realities in life well. You will save yourself much pain if you can balance these and the healthy tension created between knowing how to embrace your ideals and your realities will produce an ever forward-moving life. Another good one is to check that you have a good balance between God's Word and His Spirit in your life. As it was once said so well, "Too much Word and you will dry up. Too much Spirit and you will blow up. Enough of both and you will grow up."

Have a good grip on life

As with a golf club, you need to make sure your grip on life is correct. It needs to be loose enough so that you can have a sense of humour and enjoy the journey but firm enough so that you have good control and get things done well and with excellence.

Keep your eye on the ball

Here is a classic piece of 101 golf advice: keep your eye on the ball, not on what's ahead later or what's going on around you now. Stay focused and concentrate on what you're doing. What's the ball of the moment for you, Champion? What needs your attention right now? You know you have a big old course left to finish and many more shots left in the game but what ball has God given you to hit today? Focus your eyes and your swing on that and hit it well.

More lessons from a golf course

"As iron sharpens iron, so one man sharpens another."

1 Corinthians 15:33 (NIV)

"Do not be misled: 'Bad company corrupts good character'."

Proverbs 27:17 (NIV)

L et's go back to the golf course this morning to learn some more lessons that will help us to play this game of life well.

Who you choose to play with can improve, maintain or ruin your game

I believe in the power of positive mentorship. If you want to play better golf, you hang out with those who can play well or better than you. As you do this, you continually 'get tips' that help you to play better. This is the same with your Christian walk. The verses above show us that who we choose to walk with has an effect upon us, either negatively or positively. Walk with people who will sharpen your life. Always keep a teachable spirit, one that is ever ready to learn something new about the game, and you always will.

Who you choose to walk with can determine your future. Another great saying I heard once was, "Show me your friends and I will prophesy your future."

It's a lonely game to play alone

As with golf, life was never meant to be played alone and is too lonely when you do. Life, like golf, is best played with others. John Donne once said, "No man is an island, entire of itself . . . any man's death diminishes me, because I am involved in mankind." How true that is. One of God's greatest gifts to you in life is friendship: relationships built on various levels. Make sure you are developing and committing to healthy relationships as they have a way of bringing out the best in you and your game. Make sure you are in a healthy church, not just attending but building friendships. This is a part of God's will for your life.

Know what to do when you're stuck in the sand

When playing golf, it's inevitable that one day you will end up in a sand bunker when you never meant to. It's a part of the game. But it's your response, or what you do next, that determines how soon your normal game is resumed. Again, this is so like life; every now and then you can find yourself stuck in a rut or wedged into a sandpit-like moment. Here's some good advice someone once gave me when I was actually in one: "Don't thrash around digging yourself deeper in. Stand back, think and then make a precise shot to get yourself out". Hey, Champion, don't exhaust yourself making more sand fly; stop, think, then do something precise.

Even more lessons from the same golf course

"This is the day the LORD has made; let us rejoice and be glad in it. O LORD, save us; O LORD, grant us success."

Psalm 118:24-25 (NIV)

L et's make one more visit to the golf course to learn some more great lessons that can help us to play life well.

It's about getting the most out of each game

Make sure you are enjoying today's game, not just enduring it, waiting for another. Play the best you can today but also take time to enjoy the walk through it. Remember, today is God's gift to you as well as a promised tomorrow and it is He who will give you success in it. Even if today is not your best game, it's still a great opportunity to improve your game. At the very least, today has the potential to teach you something that can improve how you play tomorrow. Know there is likely to be another game tomorrow and in that one you can put into practice all you learnt today if you are a wise player.

Warn others when you hit one wrong

If ever you have played golf, you probably would have, at one time or another, heard someone unexpectedly shout, "Fore!" This interpreted for non-golfers means, "Oh no! I just hit a ball wrong! Watch out, it could hit you any second." At this point, everyone near cowers and covers their heads to protect themselves. Every person has a bad day every now and then – that's life. When you do, and you have hit a ball wrong, make sure you are not putting others in harm's way. Have the courtesy to warn those around you and, of course, if you accidently hit someone, make sure you have the courage to apologise and take responsibility for your actions or words.

Watch your scoring

Ever played sport with a 'one, two, lose a few' player? They cheat and their score card changes according to how badly they're playing or how well you are! Have you ever played that way? One great final parallel between life and golf is "To yourself be true".

Don't overestimate or underestimate how you're doing in your life and your walk with God, get the score right. Otherwise, it's a sad thing when you do improve as it will be lost in the exaggeration of your last scoring and that will be a shame as we all like to see our score get better regularly, don't we? Be true about who you are, where you're at, what you believe and, most of all, to God. Then watch your score get better as you daily play the incredible game of life.

Faith is never that reasonable

Now faith is being sure of what we hope for and certain of what we do not see. This is what the ancients were commended for. By faith we understand that the universe was formed at God's command, so that what is seen was not made out of what was visible.

Hebrews 11:1-2 (NIV)

Always remember, Champion, you are called to live by faith *(2 Corinthians 5:7)* and it is faith that both pleases God *(Hebrews 11:6)* and activates His promises in your life and in those situations you may be facing. One of the problems with faith is that it is never very 'reason-able' or 'able to be reasoned'. God has not called you to be reasonable, by which I mean He doesn't want you to be continually trying to reason how and if what He has promised will come true. He has called you to have faith to simply believe with childlike trust that He does not lie and will always come through on His promise.

It is when we're forever trying to reason things out with earthly understanding that we get ourselves all worked up or, worse, into the territory of fear. It's time to stop doing that because, if God has promised you something, you do not need to be able to reason it out for it to be true. Just simply believe it.

Think about today's scripture. It talks about creation and the universe being formed out of things not visible. Try and work that one out! Most of what God creates and does for us does not make sense because He does not live under the gravity of reason that we do. Remember, He instructs us to only believe because all things are possible to those who do so *(Mark 10:27)*.

God has called us to be 'faith-full', or full of faith, and not 'reason-able'. Faith in God will often defy what you have reasoned to be possible.

The question here is: "Do you want to live, today, in that which is reasonable or in that which faith in an unconditional God can produce?"

Go on Champion, get a Word from His Book for your situation, a Word which is higher than you can naturally reason and then choose to be faithful. Be full of faith towards His promise and see what an unlimited, zero-gravity God can do.

Champion's Prayer:

Father, thank You that You have given me a brain and the ability to reason but help me, Lord, not to reason when I simply need to believe. Help me to rediscover that child-like faith You want me to have. Help me to live beyond my ability to reason in that place called faith – Amen.

He is willing and able!

"Now to Him who is able to do exceedingly abundantly above all that we ask or think, according to the power that works in us."

Ephesians 3:20 (NKJV)

We need to remain ever conscious of the fact that our God is able – whatever the situation, circumstance or need we may be facing – our God is so able! He is not subject to the things that limit us; He is free and outside of the restraints and gravities we so often know as normal and the fact is, He really can do anything, for anyone, at any time. Live ready for Him to do something awesome for you today!

Want some more good news? As well as able, He is willing. It is important to know that both of these ingredients are present today for us. Amazingly, God being is able is not enough – nothing would change unless He was also willing. Likewise, if He was willing but did not have the ability, nothing would change for us either.

Let me give you an example. What if I was willing to give you a million pounds? That would be nice, wouldn't it? But if I was not able to give you a million pounds then nothing would change for you, except you being blessed by my good intentions. God is both able and willing towards you today. Remember when the leper came to Jesus and said, "Lord, if you are willing, I can be healed."? Jesus replied, "I am willing." Today, He's saying that same thing to you in your very real need or situation – "I am able and I am willing!"

Now, that's a great thought that should cause faith to rise within you – not only is Your heavenly Father willing but He is also so able. He has all ability to do whatever is needed for you, Champion! We live on a single planet – He made the universe. When we pray, we must remember that He does not live in a four bedroom house down the road, He holds the universe, that which man has only partially been able to discover, in the span of His hand!

So today, when you pray, speak to Him knowing that He is both willing **and** able concerning you and what you face. When you understand those two realities, anything can happen at any given moment. It's like combining two powerful chemicals that react when mixed together.

Champion's Challenge:

Today, begin to confess this simple, yet very powerful, truth over your life: "My God is both able and willing towards me."

He is bigger than your imagination!

Now to him who is able to do immeasurably more than all we ask or imagine, according to his power that is at work within us.

Ephesians 3:20 (NIV)

Yesterday, we looked at the fact that God is both willing and able towards you. He wills to do you good and has the ability to back it up as well but to what degree or amount? According to *Ephesians* the degree is, "*Immeasurably more than all we ask or imagine*". Other translations say, "*beyond what you can dream*" and "*above what you can imagine or ever think*". I like the New King James version. It says "*exceedingly, abundantly.*"

What great words they are – exceedingly, abundantly. Those are words of overflow and not words of lack or 'just enough'.

The key point to grasp is that He can do so much more than you can imagine! Face the truth, God is not the same size as your imagination. He goes far beyond it. I am so glad that it does not say that God is able to do what we imagine He can in our wildest dreams. It says He is the God of "*and beyond.*" He goes **beyond** what we have the potential to imagine in our wildest of thoughts. When you use your imagination concerning what He can do for you and take it to the furthest point possible, when you stretch your imagination till it creaks because it has no more stretch left, God meets you there and says, "Is that it? Or do you want some more?"

Don't downsize or limit God today by thinking He can only do what you can imagine or think. The truth remains that the end of your wildest dreaming is often His starting point! Dare to dream big concerning His plans for you. Take your imagination to its very boundaries concerning what He is able to do in and with your life but then stop and remind yourself, He still intends to go far, far beyond.

Imagine what some of the heroes of faith like Abraham, Moses, Gideon and David thought when they looked back over their lives when they were old. I am certain they would have looked back and thought to themselves things like, "That life I just lived was exceedingly, abundantly, far above any life I could have ever dreamed for myself. The things I saw were so off the chart of anything I ever could have dreamed." I pray that the declaration of your life will be, "Thank you God of 'and beyond'."

Do this today and, when you look back over the years of your life, you will never be disappointed.

Let faith arise and believe big because He is dreaming big for you!

Think bigger thoughts

God can do anything, you know—far more than you could ever imagine, guess, or request in your wildest dreams! He does it not by pushing us around, but by His Spirit working gently and deeply within us.

Ephesians 3:20 (The Message)

S o far this week we have established that God is both willing and able towards you and me and the situations we may be facing. We also established that when we reach the end point of our ability to imagine and dream concerning His plans for us, He is just getting started and lives in the realm called 'exceedingly, abundantly, above and beyond what we can imagine or dream.' By faith, Champion, decide to start to live more in His thoughts for you rather than your own. Why? Because His are so much bigger!

"For My thoughts are not your thoughts, Nor are your ways My ways," says the Lord. "For as the heavens are higher than the earth, So are My ways higher than your ways, And My thoughts than your thoughts."

Isaiah 55:8 (NKJV)

For years, I thought this was just a belittling statement made to let me know my place in the order of things. I felt that what God meant went something like this, "I am God up here and you are Andy, mere human, down there and my ways are high and yours are low. My thoughts are great and yours are little because I am God and you are my creation and that's how it is". Then, one day, I realised it was actually an invitation. It was God saying, "Yes, my thoughts are so much higher and bigger than yours, so why don't you come up and join me in mine?" From that day, I have been committed to exchanging my limited thoughts for His unlimited ones in all areas of my life.

If you dare to exchange your thoughts, He will always lift your dreams and plans to a higher place because, as the heavens are higher than the earth, so are His thoughts. The choice is ours again today. Will I live in thoughts that are based on my mere earthly potential or reasoning, what I am able to achieve by my ability or with the help of a few friends, or do I begin to dream and think bigger and higher, according to what can happen because God is with me and is the author of my destiny?

Hey Champion, think big, think high, release your redeemed imagination to imagine what really can happen when the God who formed a universe is on your side. Live extra large because you only walk the pathway of this life on earth but once! And, as Paul revealed, you now have the mind of Christ *(1 Corinthians 2:16)*.

A Power at Work in You

Now to Him who is able to do exceedingly abundantly above all that we ask or think, according to the power that works in us.

Ephesians 3:20 (NKJV)

According to *Ephesians 3*, God is doing what He does in accordance to His power, or Spirit, working in us. Remember today, that His Spirit is at work both within you and through you and it is this divine reality that makes impossible things, things beyond your dreams, possible in your world today. He is 'able to do' because His full potential is now resident within your life – remember, His Spirit is not just with you but **in** you! He is not relying on your ability alone but rather it's now a new dynamic combo of your body and His life.

And I will pray the Father, and He will give you another Helper, that He may abide with you forever – the Spirit of truth, whom the world cannot receive, because it neither sees Him nor knows Him; but you know Him, for He dwells with you and will be in you.

John 14:16-17 (NKJV)

What great news! God has amazing plans and intentions for your life; plans so far above what you could ever imagine and He has also placed His Spirit in you to make those dreams come into full manifestation and reality. Surely nothing is impossible with that God-plan at work? So remember, there is a power working in you today that is beyond you! Like Paul, you can now *"do all things"*.

"I can do all things through Christ who strengthens me."

Philippians 4:13

You are no longer a mere man but a God-filled temple *(1 Corinthians 3:1-4 and 16)*. So choose not to live like a mere man one day longer – make the choice to be a temple, a place where God's Spirit is resident, not a hotel where He visits every now and then.

Have a great day filled with God dreams and a confidence of His internal ability.

Champion's Prayer:

Father, thank You for Your power now at work in me, thank You that my potential is not limited by my own ability but now Your power now lives in me and flows through me. Enable me to walk into this day, expectant, knowing that anything could happen – Amen.

The spirit of prophecy lives in you!

And it shall come to pass in the last days, says God, That I will pour out of My Spirit on all flesh; Your sons and your daughters shall prophesy, Your young men shall see visions, Your old men shall dream dreams. And on My menservants and on My maidservants I will pour out My Spirit in those days; And they shall prophesy.

Acts 2:17-18 (NKJV)

Here is the classic promise concerning the Spirit that was spoken of by Peter just after the initial outpouring of the Spirit at Pentecost. He was referring to the prophecy of Joel *(Joel 2:28-32)* found in the Old Testament. Jesus had now fully risen from the dead and, as promised, had poured out His Spirit on the Church and the good news for us today is that He has never called the Spirit back to heaven. This means that the same Spirit that filled those early believers still fills our lives today – the same Spirit!

It says that when the Spirit is present – poured out – people would begin to "*dream dreams*" and "*see visions*" and that they "*shall prophesy*" – speak out God's plans and Word and proclaim things that are to come. Are you a manservant or maidservant of the Lord? If so, then start to prophesy more into your life and the world God has given you influence in. Begin to listen to what the Spirit of God is saying deep within you concerning the situations you are facing. Begin to speak the Word of the LORD regarding those things that are overwhelming you and that seem physically impossible to handle.

People have made prophecy weird and spooky and seemingly un-doable by normal, everyday folk but that is not how God designed it. Jesus is the Spirit of prophecy and He resides within your life. This means that, in any given situation, He has something better to say about the outcome. Oh, that we would have ears to hear, faith to believe and confidence to proclaim the intentions of God over the things we daily face. It is written, *"AND THEY WILL PROPHESY"*

So, you do not have to be a prophet to prophesy, just a servant of the Lord and a son or daughter of His kingdom. Today, if there is something in your world that needs to turn around, then don't stay silent but begin to prophesy by finding God's Word for the situation in the Bible and then by speaking the Word and the plans of God over it. Remember that spoken words of faith can still move mountains in the twenty first century.

Bless you today. Don't stay silent, have yourself a naturally prophetic day.

It's a good job He's sitting down

Day after day every priest stands and performs his religious duties; again and again he offers the same sacrifices, which can never take away sins. **But when this priest had offered for all time one sacrifice for sins, he sat down at the right hand of God.** *Since that time he waits for his enemies to be made his footstool*

Hebrews 10:11-13 (NIV)

Our high priest, Jesus, is seated today, unlike the Old Testament priests mentioned in the opening verse who could never sit down for long because their job was never done or ever completed. They daily stood, offering the blood of animals as payment for the sins of the people. The blood of animals could never remove sin or make such a payment that would fully satisfy the demand of the law. It took the blood of our high priest, Jesus, to fulfil the law completely.

He came as the Lamb who would take away – not cover – the sin of the world: past, present and future, including mine and yours. Remember, John the Baptist greeted Him with those exact words because that is what He was: God's perfect Lamb whose blood would fully pay the bill we owed.

It's important to hear these words, "*He sat down,*" because that statement declares to us that what He came to do, He did and what He wanted to achieve by sacrificing His life, He achieved. He sat down because the job was done, not because He was 'taking a break'. His very own words at the cross were, "*It is finished*". He has accomplished, by His death, burial and resurrection, everything He needed to. Remember, He was not achieving anything for Himself because He needed nothing. Everything He accomplished was for us: our salvation, our healing and our freedom.

Don't wait for Him to get up to finish anything. He did it all perfectly two thousand years ago.

The next time He gets up will be to come and collect what belongs to Him, and that's us! Make sure today you are living in the finished work of Christ and not waiting for Him to finish something He has already completed. It's because of a job well done, a completed one, that He is seated today.

A boxer may have to rise from being seated to fight another round but not Jesus. It was a knock-out. He has beaten the devil and is waiting for him to be made into a footstool.

Please, stay seated

And God raised us up with Christ and seated us with him in the heavenly realms in Christ Jesus, in order that in the coming ages he might show the incomparable riches of his grace, expressed in his kindness to us in Christ Jesus.

Ephesians 5:6-7 (NIV)

According to *Ephesians*, Jesus is not the only one seated in heavenly places today. We too are seated with Him. Why? Because everything He did two thousand years ago, He did *for us* and *as us*. He was substituting Himself for us when He received judgement, punishment and death. When we, by faith, receive Him as Saviour, we enter into the completeness of everything He did on our behalf. We become, as the New Testament refers to it, *"in him"*. By placing our faith in Him as Saviour, we are identifying with Him not just in His death but also in His resurrection.

He was humanity's representative, taking upon Himself everything that was rightfully ours – punishment for sin, sickness, spiritual death, suffering – to bring us into everything that was rightfully His – righteousness and life. So, by faith, a believer was **in Christ** when He died and was buried and he or she was **in Christ** when He rose again. So, today we are **in Him** by faith alone and it is that which positions us in heavenly places and qualifies us for the incomparable riches and grace promised in these verses.

Imagine, if I were to put a bookmark in my Bible, everywhere the Bible went, the bookmark would go too, whether good or bad. Why? Because it is 'in the Bible'. Everything that Bible experienced, the bookmark would be a part of. By faith, we identify with Jesus in everything: His death, His burial and His resurrection to newness of life with water baptism being a visual example and testimony of this truth.

We do not need to be judged, punished or put to death on a cross for sin. Why? Because we were in Him when He did all of that **for us** and **as us**. Think about it. Were you there when Adam and Eve were thrown out of the garden of Eden? Did you eat a bite of the forbidden fruit? No, you had no part in this first sin and yet you were born sinful and separated from God. Why? Because you were in the first Adam. When we become born again, we become instantly **in Christ** – the second Adam – and His resurrection life and position becomes ours, as does His very position of righteousness.

Have a think about it. Before we can walk or stand in God correctly, we need to be seated correctly in His finished work!

More than a champion

Yet in all these things we are more than conquerors through Him who loved us.

Romans 8:37 (NKJV)

It would be a great enough thing to know that you are a Champion, or a conqueror, through Christ but that is not what *Romans 8* says that we are. It distinctly says that we are more than that!

I don't know what you think about yourself but you need to know what God thinks about you today. He declares over your life, and every situation that you face, that you are not just a Champion but much more. Independent of your current feelings or situations, that is what you are and you will walk in the power of that when you dare to agree with Him.

The best example, or analogy, of this that I have ever heard is that of the prize fighter and his wife. The prize fighter gets into the ring and fights his greatest fight and wins. He is then given the pay cheque for the victory he just fought for. He gets showered, washing off the blood and sweat from the gruelling battle that just took place. He then gets dressed and goes home. When he walks through the door, his wife greets him with her lips puckered for a kiss and her hand out for the cheque he just won and he gladly hands it over. She is more than a conqueror! She did nothing but gets to live in, and enjoy the benefits of, a victory she never personally achieved.

Listen, Champion, Jesus has fought the battle that had to be fought and won. It was a perfect win, a total knockout and He now invites us to live in the victory – the pay cheque – of that fight. Don't keep trying to fight a battle that has already been won but make up your mind that you're going to be, "*more than*" and live in the victory of your prize-fighting King Jesus.

Because of His perfect victory two thousand years ago, we now walk in the benefits of His win. Today, you are not just a Champion or conqueror but you are more than a conqueror. So, let that determine how you choose to live out your life today. Remember, we walk in the very footsteps of an eternal winner.

Having disarmed principalities and powers, He made a public spectacle of them, triumphing over them in it.

Colossians 2:15 (NKJV)

Just when you thought it was all over

Then he opened their minds so they could understand the Scriptures. He told them, "This is what is written: The Christ will suffer and rise from the dead on the third day, and repentance and forgiveness of sins will be preached in his name to all nations, beginning at Jerusalem."

Luke 24:45 (NIV)

Here is another really interesting account. It is when two of the disciples are walking down the road from Jerusalem to Emmaus with Jesus but did not have a clue it was Him. It's now Sunday morning, the Sunday after the most horrific weekend they could have imagined. Over the weekend, they had watched their Lord and friend falsely accused, butchered, hung on a tree till he was dead and then buried in a tomb. They had lost all hope and were questioning what it was all about. Suddenly, Jesus turns up in disguise and starts asking about the weekend and what all the fuss was about. With amazement, they start to tell him about what had happened to their Jesus not knowing it was actually Him.

Jesus then starts to share from the scriptures with them and speaks of what all the prophets had foretold regarding the weekend they had just experienced. Still they did not click on concerning His true identity. He then spoke of this prophecy that spoke specifically of the purpose of the death and about the third day; it clearly said that on the third day He would rise again to life. Maybe grief had shadowed this truth from them but they should have remembered the amount of times He had personally told them about heaven's three day plan *(Matthew 16:21)*. Have a look through the gospels; He spoke of it often because He wanted them in the loop with events that would unfold.

Champion, He is the God of the third day! The God of the resurrection. Things you may being going through may look negative, they may even resemble the Friday of that weekend where everything looks like it is over and it is dead and buried. You need to remember, Champion, He is the God of the third day and in all things regarding your life, and even your death, He has a third day plan. He is the God of the resurrection who brings things to life and causes things to live again, who makes a way where and when there seems to be no way. In that situation you are facing today that looks like a car wreck with no possible future or that miracle you are believing for that is based on His Word and promises to you, don't walk away from the tomb yet. As somebody once said, "It may seem like Friday night but Sunday is on the way."

He always had a third day plan. When the disciples forgot, He never did because, as all the prophets foretold, it was always in the story line. How precise is this one in *Hosea*?

After two days he will revive us;
on the third day he will restore us that we may live in his presence.
Hosea 6:2 (NIV)

Have you got heartburn?

Now it came to pass, as He sat at the table with them, that He took bread, blessed and broke it, and gave it to them. Then their eyes were opened and they knew Him; and He vanished from their sight. And they said to one another, "Did not our heart burn within us while He talked with us on the road, and while He opened the Scriptures to us?"

Luke 24:30-32 (NKJV)

Let's continue this morning with the thought of these two men on the road to Emmaus. We saw, yesterday, how Jesus walked with them but they did not know it was Him; how they had lost hope and were downcast because they had forgotten the promise about the third day and promise of resurrection. Jesus unfolds the scripture to them but they still do not realise it is Him.

Then they pull in for the night and invite Him to stay, which He does. During the course of the night, He breaks bread and hands it out and, at this moment, reveals Himself to them as their Jesus who they thought was dead. How appropriate that it was when He broke the bread, just like He had done the night before His death.

At this moment they see Him but He then disappears. Then one of them says to the other these great words, *"Did not our heart burn within us while He talked with us"*. They were conscious that they had both experienced a spiritual heartburn while in His presence earlier, not natural indigestion but a burning within that was based on love.

For all of us who have known Him and walked with Him, there should be a burning within when we read about Him and are in His presence. The absence of this 'love burn' can indeed tell us if we have religion or relationship, whether we have drifted from and need to get close again.

How about you, Champion? What happens within you when you are in His presence, in His house or with His people? What happens in you these days when you read the Word? Is He revealed? Does something burn within? If not, it's time to get that heartburn back.

Yes, we have His presence in us now through new birth but I am speaking specifically about what happens to you in worship and the devotional, the audience of one, section of who you are. If the heartburn is not there, stop and get it back!

Champion's Prayer:

Heavenly Father, if I have lost that burning within, would You please ignite it again. Let me have again that spiritual heartburn that lets me know when I am in His presence that keeps me living in love with Him. Thank You – Amen.

Storm management

Therefore whoever hears these sayings of Mine, and does them, I will liken him to a wise man who built his house on the rock: and the rain descended, the floods came, and the winds blew and beat on that house; and it did not fall, for it was founded on the rock.

Matthew 7:24-25 (NKJV)

If you are alive, then you will experience difficult storms in life. None of these storms need ruin or crush you but it is important to understand how to manage them. One way of managing storms is to first find out where they are coming from or what is causing them, then you can know precisely how to deal with them effectively. This week, let's look at some storms that we can all face at one time or another.

The storms of life

Storms of life. These are the ones that are nothing to do with spiritual attack or the devil's schemes and so on but rather just those things that come to both the righteous and the unrighteous simply because of being alive; they are the storms of life. I compare these storms to the one we read about in *Matthew 7*. In this account, there are two men who choose to build on very different foundations; notice that the same storm then hits both of them but only one building remained intact, the wise man's, because he built on a solid, rock-like foundation – God. The other man, who built upon quick and easy other alternatives, watched as the storm came and took with it everything he had built. What a horrible moment that would have been for him.

Listen, in challenging times, where fear and uncertainty are daily dished out from every media outlet possible, don't fear but rather have confidence. These storms may blow and the waves may even hit the sides of our lives but, when we daily stand with Godly wisdom and principles with faith, we will prevail.

Let me underline this again: life has storms – financial, relational, all manner of storms – they affect the saved and unsaved. The difference is that Jesus is in the midst of our storms, with us, and as we commit to daily stand by faith and wisdom we will not be moved or crushed!

Food for Thought:
Great leaders choose to inspire desire in the hearts of their followers; they are not travel agents for guilt trips.

Storms of disobedience

But the LORD sent out a great wind on the sea, and there was a mighty tempest on the sea, so that the ship was about to be broken up. And he said to them, "Pick me up and throw me into the sea; then the sea will become calm for you. For I know that this great tempest is because of me."

Jonah 1:4 and 12 (NKJV)

Here is an interesting storm that we don't often talk about; a storm arranged by God because a man was being disobedient.

You may say, "Wait a moment, God sends storms on people? I've heard all the faith preaching, God doesn't do that, does He? I thought God loved people."

Well, it's obvious when you read this chapter that it was indeed God that sent this storm. Not because He did not love Jonah – in fact it was because He did. He loved him too much to let him run away from the destiny He had for him. Notice that Jonah did not die and, apart from a smelly covering of whale sick, he was left unharmed by the storm. But he was repositioned back into what God had for his life.

God has got great plans for us. When we rebel or run from them, God, because He loves us, will author or allow certain things to happen to get us back into position. Again, let me say, not because He does not love us but because He **does** so much! Let me underline also, to avoid any confusion, these storms do not come to kill or harm but to reposition!

The good news is, these storms are easily sorted. If you know that what you're experiencing is the result of you running or rebelling from or against what God has planned for your life, simply stop and repent; choose His way and watch the storm cease and your life come back into all that God has for it. These storms are not common ones but they are storms that happen sometimes and, like Jonah, you know when you are in one and what has caused it. You need, like Jonah, to just do something about it!

Champion's Challenge:

If, while reading this, you became aware of something in your life that could well be disobedience, don't waste another moment. Take that to the Father and say, "Sorry." then get up and live in His direction for that area of your life. As you do, the storms will cease, just as they did for Jonah.

Storms of opposition

Now it happened, on a certain day, that He got into a boat with His disciples. And He said to them, "Let us cross over to the other side of the lake." And they launched out. But as they sailed He fell asleep. And a windstorm came down on the lake, and they were filling with water, and were in jeopardy. And they came to Him and awoke Him, saying, "Master, Master, we are perishing!" Then He arose and rebuked the wind and the raging of the water. And they ceased, and there was a calm. But He said to them, "Where is your faith?"

Luke 8:22-25 (NKJV)

We are talking about storms. Here we read of another storm, a storm that was not 'just life' or the product of disobedience – rather it was sent by the enemy to stop, or oppose, Jesus and the disciples. To fully understand this storm, you need to read on a bit and see where the boat was headed.

They had set sail from the busy shores of Galilee to the secluded region of the Gadarenes. In this region there was a farmer and some pigs and a tormented man filled with a legion of demons. The purpose of the boat trip was to liberate this one tormented man who had been isolated and forgotten by society – he had been stuck away in a quiet place so he wouldn't have to be seen as he had a life out of control and lived naked and tormented in the graves of the dead. Though others did not see him, or want to see him, God did and sent Jesus on a mission trip for the benefit of one.

When the devil clicked on that Jesus was heading to liberate his masterpiece of torment, he sent a storm to oppose, or stop, them. Jesus rose up, dealt with the storm and sailed on to this desperate man. He then told the disciples they could have dealt with it too.

Whenever you have freedom in your sights, especially the freedom of others, you will experience storms of opposition. These are the storms you have authority over and can rebuke, so get up in the boat of your life and tell these storms to cease in Jesus' name!

Then sail on, Champion, and bring freedom to that person or situation that needs it. Let me underline: Jesus has given you authority over storms of opposition, things sent to stop or delay you – remember, no thing, or storm, fashioned against you will prosper in Jesus' name.

These are the most common storms that Church leaders face and it is good to recognise their reality but never submit to their threats. They have been sent to stop or delay you, don't let them. And, as a leader, I have learnt the bigger the storm, the bigger the freedom the other side of it. When I sense a storm of opposition I actually get a bit excited and have learned to not look at it but beyond to the soon-coming outbreak of freedom that is moments away.

Having confidence in storms

And now I urge you to take heart, for there will be no loss of life among you, but only of the ship. For there stood by me this night an angel of the God to whom I belong and whom I serve, saying, 'Do not be afraid, Paul; you must be brought before Caesar; and indeed God has granted you all those who sail with you.'

Acts 27:22-24 (NKJV)

Here we read of the account of a serious storm that hit while Paul was aboard a ship as a prisoner. It was a storm so violent that it caused the ship to be smashed to pieces off the island of Malta. In the midst of this storm, while everyone, including the captain, was freaking out with fear, Paul – who had been spending time with God while the storm raged (wise thing to do) – stands up and begins to speak and his words bring real confidence in the midst of this panic.

With confidence, he gives a prophetic forecast for the ship and its passengers: for the ship, no hope; for the passengers, as it says a little later, not even a hair on their heads will be harmed.

Where did this confidence come from? Firstly, God had spoken to him. Whenever you are in a storm and others are freaking out, you go and get the Word of God regarding the outcome. This will always cause peace in you and in those who choose to listen to you. Secondly, Paul knew, and told, how his mission was not over so he could not be harmed. That's great confidence – when you know you have not finished your race, then a storm can throw what it likes. You are safe, as are those who journey with you!

I was on a plane a couple of years back and, shortly after take-off it had to do an emergency landing as an engine had failed. Alarms went off, baggage flew out of overhead stores, people began to scream, especially the woman behind me! Without thinking, I turned to her and said, "Don't worry, you will be okay. I am on this flight and I know God." She instantly stopped screaming (probably in shock at what I had said!), and my calm became hers. And I really did have a calm because I knew my race had not yet been run.

You too can have confidence in the storm when you have the Word of God and know your race has not fully been run.

Storm management and 'Finally'

What the wicked dread will overtake them; what the righteous desire will be granted. When the storm has swept by, the wicked are gone, but the righteous stand firm forever.

Proverbs 10:24-25 (NIV)

This week, we have spoken about storms. Let me conclude by highlighting some of the thoughts we have covered.

If you are alive, then storms will be a part of your life journey, especially when you live for the wellbeing of others. To navigate them correctly, you need to know where they are coming from and what to do so you can know how to handle them effectively.

Sometimes there are the storms that are 'just life'. With faith and Godly wisdom, you will prevail. Other times, disobedience can cause things to come to reposition us. Then there are the ones which are more spiritually initiated; storms of opposition that come to stop or delay your freedom or the freedom you carry for others. These are the most common storms in the life of the person who lives to see Jesus set others free.

When we, like Paul did in yesterday's message, take time to pray about the storm we may be experiencing, we will always have God's wisdom concerning what sort of storm it is and how we are to navigate our lives successfully through it. When we walk with Jesus daily, we have confidence because we know that we know that He is in the boat with us. No matter how loud the storm seems, He is with you. Maybe the lesson the disciples learned in their storm experience was this: instead of trying to wake Jesus up, simply realise that, if He is not flipping out, they didn't need to either.

Hey, Champion! If God is in peace and at rest, you can be too – according to Jesus, it just takes a little faith to do so.

Finally, be encouraged by today's verse. Hey, different storms come and then storms go, the wicked get washed away but the righteous, like the wise man who built his life on the rock, remain standing strong!

Food for Thought:

A cornerstone determines how high a structure can go, how big it will be, how straight it will be and how much pressure it can withstand. Make sure Jesus is your cornerstone.

Bask in the bigness of God

Peter sent them all out of the room; then he got down on his knees and prayed. Turning toward the dead woman, he said, "Tabitha, get up." She opened her eyes, and seeing Peter she sat up.

Acts 9:40 (NIV)

This was a very serious situation where Peter had been brought by some people to raise a woman named Tabitha from the dead. This was 'need a miracle' territory! Notice what he did before he dealt with or even faced the largeness of the problem – he prayed! Then he turned and dealt with the miracle-needing situation.

Before he looked at the seemingly impossible mountain, he spent time 'basking in the bigness' of his God, the God who says that all things are possible to those who believe. This empowered him with all the confidence he needed to turn around, look at the situation full on and do what was seemingly impossible.

Hey, Champion, when you find yourself in a time of challenge or a moment when you are needing a miracle here is some good advice someone once gave me: the very first thing you need to do is take time to bask in the bigness of God. This will enable you, as it did Peter, to correct your perception concerning how big the problems and situations really are and also remind you how big your God is in the very midst of that moment of challenge.

When you take time to bask in the bigness of God, everything else is then reduced to its true, beatable size. The reality is that when you are needing or desiring a miracle you have the choice to bask in the bigness of one of two things: either the bigness of the problem or in the God who is bigger than any problem – your choice. You have to choose one or the other as you cannot bask in the bigness of both.

Bask, as Peter did, in the bigness of your God!

Champion's Prayer:

Father, help me today to bask in Your bigness, to not waste time basking in the problem but in the answer which is Your promise concerning it. Father, today I remember You placed the stars in their place and hold all things together by Your Word. I close my eyes and consider how massive You are and open them knowing my once large mountains have shrunk – Amen.

Basking in the bigness of God (who happens to be the creator of the universe)

And Abram said, "You have given me no children; so a servant in my household will be my heir." Then the word of the LORD came to him: "This man will not be your heir, but a son coming from your own body will be your heir." He took him outside and said, "Look up at the heavens and count the stars – if indeed you can count them." Then he said to him, "So shall your offspring be."

Genesis 15:3-5 (NIV)

I think we all know this great account, it's where God promises Abraham children and descendants too numerous to physically count. A promise made to a man and a woman who, naturally speaking, had no chance of ever having kids.

To Abraham, God's promise initially looked physically impossible because his wife had always been barren and also because of the stage of life they were both at. Their bodies were well beyond the age of being able to produce children naturally. They needed a miracle if this was to ever happen.

Abraham was so busy and distracted by looking at how big the problem or challenge was. Now look what God does. He steps into Abraham's doubts and invites him to step outside. Why? Because He knew that Abraham just needed a perception adjustment. He just needed to spend a moment basking in God's bigness. Abraham goes outside and God instructs him to look up into the unpolluted sky. As he does, he sees stars so numerous he could not even begin to count them. It was probably then that the penny dropped, "The One who had promised me the child is the One who has set each of those stars in place." At that moment, God became so much bigger than the seemingly impossible challenge facing him and it was then that Abraham's faith arose to embrace the promise.

As Abraham basked in the bigness of God under that open heaven, every big challenge and impossibility he faced suddenly became very small.

Hey Champ, if you are having trouble believing for something big, do what God invited Abraham to do and go out in your garden tonight and look up.

See the stars filling the universe and remind yourself, as you bask in His bigness, that the One who promised you victory made all that you can see and all that lies beyond that which you can't!

Make sure your behaviour fits the moment

That night all the people of the community raised their voices and wept aloud. All the Israelites grumbled against Moses and Aaron, and the whole assembly said to them, "If only we had died in Egypt! Or in this desert! Why is the LORD bringing us to this land only to let us fall by the sword? Our wives and children will be taken as plunder. Wouldn't it be better for us to go back to Egypt?"

Numbers 14:1-3 (NIV)

When you read these verses you could be mistaken in thinking that something awful had just happened when, bizarrely, it was quite the opposite. They had just returned from looking at the land the Lord had promised them. It was indeed as He had promised, a land flowing with milk and honey and they were even loaded down with goodies from it.

Yes, there were a few obstacles that would need to be removed but think about it; if God had given them the land then He had already guaranteed the victory over those obstacles. Joshua and Caleb had come back with a faith-filled response and with behaviour to match. Sadly, the other spies came back filled with dread and woe and unbelief. If you read on, their behaviour caused the children of Israel, except Joshua and Caleb, to miss out on what God had set up for them as a massive blessing. What should they have been doing? They should have been excitedly packing, getting supplies ready and mobilizing Israel for the big crossover. Instead, they behaved with unbelief, sowing fear and doubt, starting rumours and causing a mutiny that totally dishonoured God. Their behaviour disqualified them from God's blessing!

A good lesson to learn here is to always let your behaviour be fitting for the moment at hand! Whenever you are standing on the edge of a God-promised miracle, there will always be a healthy tension. It is in these moments that we need to choose to behave in accordance with what God has promised and not in accordance with soul-based panic and unbelief – unless you intend to miss out. When right behaviour and a God-appointed moment stand in unity together, you will always experience the manifestation of what God has promised. When you read on concerning Joshua and Caleb, you see they got what was promised. Why? They watched their behaviour!

HOMEWORK

Why not read through **Numbers 13** and **14**? There is a lot to learn in these two chapters about faith and having a correct attitude. Remember, your attitude will always determine your altitude.

Put your praise at the front

And when he had consulted with the people, he appointed those who should sing to the LORD, and who should praise the beauty of holiness, as they went out before the army and were saying: "Praise the LORD, For His mercy endures forever." Now when they began to sing and to praise, the LORD set ambushes against the people of Ammon, Moab, and Mount Seir, who had come against Judah; and they were defeated.

2 Chronicles 20:21-23 (NKJV)

I just want to encourage you again today, Champion, regarding the power of your praise. Whatever challenge or situation you may be facing, either right now or at another time, always remember to put your praise right at the front of the armies of your life.

In these verses, we see Jehoshaphat do something very wise which can be wisdom for us again today if we choose to learn from it. He appointed the praise to be at the front and not in the middle or at the back. When they began to praise from the front, God set ambushes against their enemies and great victories were had. How about you? Do you want God to set some ambushes for the enemy of your soul and set you up for a nice big win? Then get your praise out in the front of your life again today.

- Put it in front of every other activity and praise Him first!

- Put it in front of every other plan of attack and praise Him first!

- Put it in front of every other ability and resource you have because nothing else you have in the arsenal of your life is as powerful as your praise.

Praise belongs at the very front of who we are and what we desire to do. Praise is the overflow of a forgiven soul and a declaration of faith in a never-failing God. Praise changes the atmosphere of any battlefield of your life. So go on, get your praise on! Appoint it to be positioned at the front and then march forwards expecting a victory.

Food for Thought:

The stone of your faith embedded in the foreheads of your giants is what will cause them to fall.

Check for a pulse

This is what God the Lord says – He who created the heavens and stretched them out, who spread out the earth and all that comes out of it, who gives breath to its people, and life to those who walk on it:

Isaiah 42:5 (NIV)

In any good movie, when someone gets hurt, the first thing they do is check the person's pulse to get a good picture of how serious things really are.

This morning let's start with an experiment. Take your forefinger and put it on the wrist of your opposite arm, move it around till you feel a pulse – got one? Good. Here are two good thoughts concerning what you have found:

- You are already better off than some people! Remember, we need to always keep all challenges and momentary situations we may be facing in their true perspective. Yes, they may be very real and even very painful situations you are going to have to walk through but think about this: some do not even have the option to have a challenge today. When you choose to look at it this way, you realize you are actually doing alright and if your pulse is a nice strong pulse then you are doing a whole lot better than a whole lot more other people who are struggling with poor health today. Maybe this day is better than you first thought?

- Remember, God is the one who gives you that pulse today. It is a sign of life and the evidence of blood being pumped around your body, enabling you to live another day. Don't ever get so impressed with yourself or what you have achieved that you leave God out of the applause. The bottom line is that if He was not faithful to give you a pulse daily then nothing else in your life would work well or mean very much at all.

I spoke to a young man today who is destined to be successful and I asked him if he prayed and he replied, "Yes."

I said, "When you pray each morning, feel for your pulse and that will remind you that everything we have and could ever have is because God has, again, faithfully given us the gift of life."

We probably all need to have a go at that – especially in tough or very successful times – and then give credit where credit is due. Have a great day, and remember the Lord your God in it – for He is the one who gives you breath and indeed life to all who walk the earth.

"Pride ain't no friend of mine"

Or do you think that the Scripture says in vain, "The Spirit who dwells in us yearns jealously"? But He gives more grace. Therefore He says: "God resists the proud, but gives grace to the humble."

James 4:5-6 (NKJV)

It's common knowledge that "God goes against the wilful proud; God gives grace to the willing humble."

James 4:5-6 (The Message)

It is good for us to remember that pride is no friend to our life. It will actually cause you to know the resistance of God's hand rather than the lifting grace of it.

I don't know about you, but I do not want to live my life with God resisting me but I certainly do want to experience His grace daily assisting me. The key is very simple: keep pride out of your heart and let humility – not false humility – reign in all the corridors of your being.

Pride and arrogance are the forerunners to stuff we really do not want.

Pride goes before destruction and a haughty spirit before a fall. Better to be of a humble spirit with the lowly, than to divide the spoil with the proud.

Proverbs 16:18-19 (NKJV)

There is nothing wrong in taking a healthy pride in what you do but that is so different to the unhealthy pride that tries to stand arrogantly in the face of God and His wisdom and knowledge. Remember, it was pride that deceived Satan concerning who he really was and was the very doorway to him getting kicked out of heaven.

Satan had a pretty good job – he was head worship leader, given the privilege of reflecting the worship of heaven towards God on a daily basis. One day, he decided he did not want to pass it on but own it. At that very moment, destruction came to collect him! May we all, today, again purpose to walk humbly before our God, not being scared to celebrate who He has made us to be but ever conscious of what we would be and where we would be without Him!

Champion's Prayer:

Father, I'm sorry for any unhealthy pride in my life. I understand that it can block things You want to do for me and through me. I cast it aside and stand before You in humility knowing that it's because of You that I live, move and have my being – Amen.

"Pride ain't no friend of yours"

Pride goes before destruction and a haughty spirit before a fall

Proverbs 16:18 (KJV)

First pride, then the crash – the bigger the ego, the harder the fall.

Proverbs 16:18 (The Message)

But Naaman became furious, and went away and said, "Indeed, I said to myself, 'He will surely come out to me, and stand and call on the name of the LORD his God, and wave his hand over the place, and heal the leprosy. Are not the Abanah and the Pharpar, the rivers of Damascus, better than all the waters of Israel? Could I not wash in them and be clean?" So he turned and went away in a rage.

2 Kings 5:11-12 (NKJV)

A real sobering thought this morning is that pride can actually keep you from miracles that God has for you!

We read here the pride-filled response of a Commander of the Syrian armies, a man by the name of Naaman. Yes, a very important man but a man with a big problem: he had leprosy! He may have been a high-ranking army commander but he was also a man dying on his feet with an incurable body-eating disease, which meant, just like anyone else with leprosy, he needed a miracle from God.

This much-needed miracle was not a problem. He sent for Elisha to come and help. Elisha sent a note, a prescription, for him from God concerning what to do to get healed. When he read the prescription he got offended instead of excited! Why? Simple, because of his pride.

- He was offended that Elisha did not personally come but rather sent a note.

- He was offended at what God expected him to do to get cured.

- He was offended at where he was expected to do it and felt he knew better.

Read it again and listen to that tone of pride that may have made him feel important but sadly left him separated from the God-intended miracle for his life. Pride always has a distinctive sound and tone to it. Always be careful when you hear it and be sure to deal quickly with it when you do. He turned away in a rage – why? Because he felt what God had asked him to do violated who he was in some way.

Can you see how pride can keep you from things that God has for you? God did not want to violate Naaman but make him better. But God also had a plan to heal him of his unhealthy infectious pride at the same time which, like leprosy, was not doing him any good.

To be continued . . .

Humility always wins!
"Pride ain't no friend of yours" (cont'd)

And his servants came near and spoke to him, and said, "My father, if the prophet had told you to do something great, would you not have done it? How much more then, when he says to you, 'Wash, and be clean'?" So he went down and dipped seven times in the Jordan, according to the saying of the man of God; and his flesh was restored like the flesh of a little child, and he was clean.

2 Kings 5:13-14 (NKJV)

After storming off in a huff, a servant of Naaman helped him to understand what his pride would equal in his life, which was basically a very painful and embarrassing death. Naaman responds this time with a humble heart and does what was prescribed and the result was exactly what had originally been promised. Notice that God did not play with or barter with Naaman's pride but simply waited for his response to change. As soon as it did, the promised miracle was released.

What was the problem with the Jordan?

The problem was that it was a public place which meant this great commander had to de-robe himself to get what God had promised. When he took his robes and armour off, a couple of things would happen:

- He would be the same as everybody else. There would be no uniform or ranking to separate him. But, really, that is how we are, isn't it? We all stand before God the same, ever needing Him to do things for us.

- He had leprosy which meant people would have seen he had a need. But maybe he did not want people to know he was needy?

First, we need to understand that we are all the same and God does not regard the uniforms or titles of men. Secondly, we all have needs and every one of us is depending on God for one thing or another.

I am so glad Naaman dealt with his pride and did not leave and die but rather humbled himself and lived. He learned that day that his pride may have made him feel important but it could not get him what he needed from God. Equally, our pride will only ever block us from what God desires to do. Ever walk with humility before your God, Champion.

Take Him up on His invitation

If any of you lacks wisdom, he should ask God, who gives generously to all without finding fault, and it will be given to him.

James 1:5 (NIV)

What a great invitation to anyone lacking wisdom! Come on, let's face it, at one time or another, in one way or another, we all regularly lack wisdom, right? The Bible simply says that when we lack wisdom and need some more for any given situation we have only to approach God and ask for it. Then He promises to do two incredible things when dispensing it to us.

Give it generously (in great abundance)

I love that – it does not say a little bit or just enough, but liberally. That's God all over – He is the God who always loves to do exceedingly and abundantly (*Ephesians 3:20*). When you ask God for wisdom, He won't give you a trickle but an ocean.

Give it without finding fault

This is actually what makes approaching God when in need of wisdom a thing that is so possible. We need to understand this part so that we can have a confident approach to God in our times of need.

I don't know about you, but inside of me there used to be something that would say, "Well, I got myself into this situation – if I go to God and ask for help, He is going to look over His glasses, point His finger and probably give me a big lecture on how I should have done it better in the first place!" Thinking like that would never empower me to want to run to Him for help when in need, yet this text reveals that things are so very different to that: when I come to God needing wisdom, He does not judge or find fault but rather gives me what I need to both turn the current situation around, and to also live differently so it does not happen again. Your God is approachable.

Let's face it, like Solomon knew, the greatest thing we can ever ask God for is wisdom because when we have Godly wisdom, we can then have everything else. When I listen to myself pray these days, I hear myself more than ever asking God for wisdom. Why? Because I know He freely gives it to those who ask and His pure wisdom always makes the difference to every situation I may find myself in.

Hey, my life is a whole lot bigger these days which means I need a whole lot more wisdom – how about you? Ask Him for some more today, knowing He will give it in abundance without reproach or a good telling off.

Who are you listening to?

And He was transfigured before them. His face shone like the sun, and His clothes became as white as the light. And behold, Moses and Elijah appeared to them, talking with Him. Then Peter answered and said to Jesus, "LORD, it is good for us to be here; if you wish, let us make here three tabernacles: one for You, one for Moses, and one for Elijah." While he was still speaking, behold, a bright cloud overshadowed them; and suddenly a voice came out of the cloud, saying, "This is My beloved Son, in whom I am well pleased. Hear Him!"

Matthew 17:2-5 (NKJV)

Jesus had taken three of His disciples – James, Peter and John – to this place on a high mountain where He was transfigured before them. As if this was not enough to make a great memorable moment, Moses and Elijah also pitched up. The three disciples start to think about making three tabernacles for the great men now present before them, completely missing the point that these great biblical icons were present for a reason: God the Father wanted to make a point!

Think about the three men present before the disciples, Elijah, Moses and Jesus. Moses represented the Law, then there was Elijah and he represented the prophets and Jesus was God's one and only Son and represented God's new covenant master plan. He was the one sent to be the sacrificial lamb who would restore the broken friendship between God and man.

Moses and Elijah were very important characters from the Old Testament and vital figures concerning the Old Covenant. But notice what the Father said, "Here is my Son. Hear Him". On this day, the Father validated the voice, leadership and ministry of His Son Jesus. Why? Because He represented a new covenant and the soon-coming new day between God and man – a day when grace and mercy would reign where law and legalism had once ruled.

Here's my question: who are you listening to and following today? Are you giving ear to the law and the prophets from the Old Testament or the Messiah and Redeeming King from the New Testament? The old covenant had its place but was always destined to be replaced by the new, according to the desire and eternal redemptive plan of God.

Remember, Jesus is still God's master plan today and He has a very different sound to that of the law and the prophets. The sound of God's master plan is one of freedom, reconciliation and life. Make sure today, like John and Peter and James, you *"hear Him"*.

The power of response

It happened that as He made His way toward Jerusalem, He crossed over the border between Samaria and Galilee. As He entered a village, ten men, all lepers, met Him. They kept their distance but raised their voices, calling out, "Jesus, Master, have mercy on us!" Taking a good look at them, He said, "Go, show yourselves to the priests." They went, and while still on their way, became clean. One of them, when he realized that he was healed, turned around and came back, shouting his gratitude, glorifying God. He kneeled at Jesus' feet, so grateful. He couldn't thank Him enough – and he was a Samaritan. Jesus said, "Were not ten healed? Where are the nine? Can none be found to come back and give glory to God except this outsider?" Then He said to him, "Get up. On your way. Your faith has healed and saved you."

Luke 17:11-17 (The Message)

In this account we can learn some great lessons concerning the power of response in our lives and, hopefully, be challenged concerning developing our personal responsibility or, put another way, 'ability to respond'.

In this passage we see three responses and all of them are pretty amazing. First, Jesus' response to the need of these ten men. Leprosy had taken away their lives and shut their worlds down both physically and socially. Jesus steps in and miraculously gives them their lives back – Jesus was indeed responsive to their cry for help.

The next response we see is the response of the one who returned. He was a Samaritan, which meant, out of the ten that were healed, he would have been considered the least likely one to come back to say thanks. You can hear the gratefulness and passion in his words of thanks.

But it's the final one which really caught my attention and that was the lack of due response from the other nine who had all received miracles that day from Jesus.

Think about the figures for a minute. Only 10% of the lepers responded in a way fitting with what had happened to them. Only one in ten responded appropriately. Were they evil men? I don't think so. I think they just swiftly got back into the normal lives that their illness had separated them from and forgot to respond correctly by coming back to Jesus and saying thanks. They understood what it was to respond when in need; they called out to Him, *"Master, have mercy on us!"* but they just forgot to respond correctly when God answered their cry. Champion, always make sure you say thanks to God!

Let's make sure that we are responsive to God when we should be. Also, in our other relationships, and in life itself, being responsive will always bring increase into your world and make things that you have even more fruitful. My observation and experience has been that both God and life give 'stuff' to responsive people. Let's make sure that today we are responding correctly.

Being responsive keeps things alive

One of them, when he realized that he was healed, turned around and came back, shouting his gratitude, glorifying God. He kneeled at Jesus' feet, so grateful. He couldn't thank him enough – and he was a Samaritan.

Luke 17:15-19 (The Message)

W e are looking at responsibility: our 'ability to respond correctly'.
Being responsive is vital for all of the relationships in our life if we want them to be all that they were designed to be. Especially our relationship with God. He wants a responsive relationship with us. It was never meant to be a quiet, one-way road but rather a daily, interwoven relationship, with us responding to Him and Him responding back – that's true Christianity.

Other relationships in our world need us to remain responsive too. For example, as a pastor I deal with an element of marital breakdown. The sad thing is that many marriages break down simply because one or both parties involved stop responding with 'due response'.

Every healthy marriage starts with what resembles a picture of 'volcanic' response: a man and a woman stand at the front of a church, like Lady Guinevere and Prince Charming, with no shortage of desire or response taking place! At the reception that follows, the atmosphere is charged with the thought of responses yet to come – God designed it that way. The day is filled with excitement, expectation and joy-filled responses by both parties. Sadly, for many, if you were to press fast forward to about ten years down the road, you get the picture of a man behind his newspaper at the kitchen table giving automated responses to his wife who is desperately wanting back the response and attention from that 'responsive stallion' she once knew. Instead, she hears the automated statements from behind a paper, "That's good, dear . . . sounds nice, dear." and the vibrancy of the marriage has begun to fade.

Good news! If he was to suddenly realize what had happened and remember what he once had – and the promises that were made and dreams they started their journey with – and that morning, with fresh revelation, he walked past the paper, spun her around, looked her in the eyes and sang to her their favourite love song, that marriage would begin to come alive again, instantly! Remember, all we added back into it was this thing called **response**! When we respond correctly, things come alive and stay alive and greater things are attracted to our lives. This principle is relative to every relationship in our world.

God bless, have a great day and men, go sing to your wife.

God's Word is waiting for you to respond to it

For all the promises of God in Him are Yes, and in Him Amen, to the glory of God through us.
2 Corinthians 1:20 (NKJV)

Responding correctly or being responsible – 'response-able' – even affects our relationship and experience with God's Word, the Bible. You can choose to treat the Bible like any other old book in your library and get nothing more than information from it or you can treat it like God's ever-living Word, relevant to every situation you may face, and get the revelation and wisdom for life that God wants you to have from it on a daily basis. God's Word was always meant to be responded to. Remember what James said of our response to God's Word? "Don't just be a hearer of it but a doer also" (*James 1:22*). When we respond with faith to what we read, we activate its incredible potential in our life and daily destinies.

Have you ever wondered why there are so many *'Amen's'* in the Bible?

Amen is a Hebrew word. It is, in itself, simply a statement of response. Amen means: so be it, it is sure, yes I agree or, if you're from Portsmouth like me, bring it on, right here, right now! It's an activating statement. Like the phone call that activates the potential of your newly-delivered credit card so it is with your "Amen" when you read. The Bible requires a response from you when you read it if you want to release what's in it for your life and situations.

Today, don't just read the Bible, have a conversation with it. When you read a promise of God that is applicable to your life or situation, release that promise with a response: "Yes Father, in Jesus' name, that promise is yes and amen to my life too." There are over eight thousand promises that are "Yes" and "Amen" to you but they remain just words on the page till you release them with a faith-filled response.

Today, read the Word and release your response: AMEN – "So be it, it is certain, bring it on!"

So Champion, today, again make the decision to respond to God, respond to the people God has given you and respond to His word as living truth waiting to be activated in your life. If the lepers had not responded to Jesus' words and instruction but just sat there and listened, nothing would have happened. It was when they responded by doing what He said, *"Go show yourselves to the priest"* that their miracle was released into their lives.

BE RESPONSIVE.

It's about your response, not His intentions

*For with God nothing will be impossible." Then Mary said, "Behold the maidservant of the LORD!
Let it be to me according to your word." And the angel departed from her.*

Luke 1:37-38 (KJV)

Yesterday, we shared on the importance of responding to God's Word and how and when to do it. When we give response to it rather than just read it, we can release its potential and power into our lives and situations.

So much about walking in our God-given destiny is about us responding correctly to God and His Word. You walking in God's plan for your life is actually more about your response than His intentions. Understand that God's intentions for you are settled. He is not confused *(Jeremiah 29:11)*, but the fact is that His intentions for us are activated in our lives when we respond to Him correctly. The Bible is a big, old catalogue of people's responses that allows us to see the fruit of the lives of those who responded to God both correctly and incorrectly. Their responses should inspire us with ours. Let's look at one.

Mary

She is a young teenage girl when God appears in her life and makes His intentions known, "I want to bring the Saviour of the world through your life". This was a big shock for her but notice that she did not become pregnant with 'the God plan' till the moment she responded with that great statement, *"Let it be to me according to your word."* It was after she made that response that she became pregnant with 'the God plan'. God did not violate her and He won't violate you. He lets you know His intentions and waits for your response to activate them. Just like with Mary, God has a whole bunch of stuff in heaven that He wants to 'get to the earth' and He is looking for someone like you to bring them here through. Will that be you today? Will you allow your life to be the womb that God can use to birth something great?

All the great Christian heroes we read of are just people, like you and me, that heard the heart of God and, like Mary, realised that nothing is impossible for God, then had the courage to say, *"Let it be to me according to your word"* and that means, "Your intentions."

Mother Theresa's great response saved thousands of children from poverty and death – that was a God intention.

Reinhard Bonnke's great response saw millions of Africans saved and set free – that was a God intention.

How about you? What is God saying about His intentions for your life and how are you going to respond to what He wants to do through you?

Faith is a pleasing response

And Jesus, walking by the Sea of Galilee, saw two brothers, Simon called Peter, and Andrew his brother, casting a net into the sea; for they were fishermen. Then He said to them, "Follow Me, and I will make you fishers of men." They immediately left their nets and followed Him.

Matthew 4:18-20 (NKJV)

L et us consider again the power our responses have by considering the response of these young men who started the day as fishermen and ended the day as disciples of Jesus, who would change the world. What was it that changed their whole lives in a moment of time? Yes, it was about God making His intentions known to them but it was equally about them responding in faith to God's Word and stepping out into the unknown. Faith is a due response and, remember, it is a response that always brings God pleasure *(Hebrews 11:6)*.

It was a day like any other. They are busy doing what they had always done when Jesus turns up and drops God's divine intention for their lives into their laps. There is no two-day seminar with PowerPoint and Q&A over an evening meal – just a single moment where a response was needed to activate a brand new life offer. They could have turned to Him and said, "That's great, but a bit scary; thanks, but no thanks", and Jesus would have turned and walked on. They didn't do that but instead they perceived that this was a God moment and responded to it with faith, not reason, and went with it.

Remember, this is exactly what Abraham and so many of the other Bible heroes did. Abraham was also living a normal everyday life when God's intentions turned up, seemingly out of nowhere, and he had a choice whether or not to respond to them correctly. A whole new life started for him as he stepped out by faith into a whole new map-less pilgrimage.

God's intentions will always come to pass and if you say, "No" He will simply use someone else. The annoying thing about this is that you get to see it happen and have to deal with the fact that it could have been you because that was originally your offer.

Don't miss your God moments. I believe that God prepares our hearts for these moments of challenge prior to His arrival. We do not know what is going to happen but we know something is about to. Make sure you are ready, like the disciples and Abraham, for God to arrive out of nowhere and offer you some of His great intentions. When you, by faith, respond correctly to God, you always end up with more than you imagined or actually came for. Just as that returning leper experienced; he came to get healed, he left healed and saved.

Then He said to him, "Get up. On your way. Your faith has healed and saved you."

Luke 17:19

Worship is a due response

And one of them, when he saw that he was healed, returned, and with a loud voice glorified God, and fell down on his face at His feet, giving Him thanks. And he was a Samaritan.

Luke 17:15-16 (NKJV)

When I close my eyes and think of this lone leper returning to thank Jesus for what He had done for him, I get a lovely picture of it simply being, what we call today, worship. Yes, it's true he was a Samaritan and that meant he was the least likely of the ten to ever worship Jesus for who He was but that makes it even more powerful. Jesus deserving worship is not a cultural thing but an 'everyone who has had their lives changed by Him' thing. I have been challenging you to daily give God due response in your life. Worship, like faith, is exactly that: a due response, something that He deserves. He is not only due our worship but the very best of it.

Remember, worship is 'worth-ship', the placing of your worth on someone or something. When you take time in your day to worship God, you put your worth on Him; and yes, He so deserves it! A great key to remember is that we should not worship Him firstly for what He does but for who He is. If you only worship Him for what He does, your worship life will be like a roller coaster. It will be up and down according to the varying situations in your life. But if you worship Him firstly for who He is, you can have consistency in your worship that only ever then increases when He does you good in one way or another.

God so loves your worship because it is something that you choose to give away. It can't be snatched or demanded; rather it is freely given from one to another. Every human has worship in them to give away and you see many give it to different things and people on a daily basis. Some give their worship to football teams and others to cars or pop stars. It is good for us to enjoy other things but always make sure that the best of our worship, our greatest shout of adoration, is reserved for our King, Jesus.

Today, give God what He is due. Give Him your worship; don't just give it because He has done something for you, give it to Him firstly for who He is.

Champion's challenge:

Take some time today to get yourself alone and spend this time worshiping God for no reason at all other than the fact that He is worth it.

What are you willing to lose to gain what you say you want?

During the fourth watch of the night Jesus went out to them, walking on the lake. When the disciples saw him walking on the lake, they were terrified. "It's a ghost," they said, and cried out in fear. But Jesus immediately said to them: "Take courage! It is I. Don't be afraid." "Lord, if it's you," Peter replied, "tell me to come to you on the water." "Come," he said. Then Peter got down out of the boat, walked on the water and came toward Jesus.

Matthew 14:25-31 (NIV)

Here we read the great account of Peter asking to do something that he really wanted to do and notice that Jesus did not put him off but rather simply told him to come. The next move was down to Peter because he now had to decide how much he really wanted what he had asked for. For him to get what he said he wanted, he would have to lose some things. Hey, that is faith.

- He would have to lose his mind. This was completely illogical and so foreign to everything he had ever been taught. Imagine his mind screaming out, "People don't walk on water! Do they?" He had to lose what he believed or reasoned to be true to get what he said he wanted. That's faith!

- He had to lose his security. The boat was a secure place and the ocean was not. He needed to learn that the most secure place you can know is the one that God has called you to. Still like Abram leaving Haran he had to leave what made him feel secure to take hold of what he said he wanted. That's faith!

- He had to lose his fears. Notice the first thing Jesus said to the disciples when He approached them dealt with the issue of fear. For Peter to get what he said he wanted, he had to lose, or step out of his very real and well-established fears. That's faith!

Remember, he had asked Jesus if he could walk on the water with him. It was Peter that really wanted to do what he did and Jesus just invited him to go ahead and stand on His Word and see the impossible become possible. We then see him actually get out of the boat and that says to me that his request to walk on water was not a bunch of idle words but that he really wanted what he had asked for. He wanted this so badly that he was willing to lose some things to get it.

How about you, Champ? How much do you want what you are asking God for? Are you ready to lose some things to gain it?

What are you willing to lose to gain what you say you want? (cont'd)

And as she was going to get it, he called to her and said, "Please bring me a morsel of bread in your hand." So she said, "As the LORD your God lives, I do not have bread, only a handful of flour in a bin, and a little oil in a jar; and see, I am gathering a couple of sticks that I may go in and prepare it for myself and my son, that we may eat it, and die." And Elijah said to her, "Do not fear; go and do as you have said, but make me a small cake from it first, and bring it to me; and afterward make some for yourself and your son. For thus says the LORD God of Israel: 'The bin of flour shall not be used up, nor shall the jar of oil run dry, until the day the LORD sends rain on the earth.'"

1 Kings 17:11-14 (NKJV)

Here we read of the account of when Elijah the prophet went to a widow that the Lord sent him to. The Lord had told Elijah that this widow woman would feed him, for he had been fed supernaturally by ravens till this point. He turned up and asked the woman for water and food and she responded by informing him of the severity of the life-threatening recession she was currently in. Did that stop the prophet asking for food? No, he wasn't greedy but he knew in his heart that God had an incredible recession-busting plan for this poor woman and, as with everything about God, it would involve, you guessed it, faith!

Did she really want to see that recession broken? Did she want herself and her son to live on past that last meal? How much did she want that? Enough to lose something that seemed the only thing she actually had left?

This seems to portray God in a harsh light. Was God being cruel? No. The prophet told her clearly what would happen if she would trust God and, just as with Peter getting out of the boat, a promise from God was given but the choice was still hers.

We too always have a choice to step out on the promises of God or stay in that which we reason to be safer. Maybe it was the desperation of the moment she was in that pushed her to go for it. Maybe it was the hungry look in the eyes of her son? Whatever it was, she did it. She dared to lose something that seemed to be what she needed to gain what she really wanted. Read on because God came through as promised and she had provision for herself and her child until the rains came or, put another way, till the recession ended.

What God asks us to do sometimes may be perceived as Him being mean but it is more likely to be Him giving us an invitation to a bigger and better moment. As with the widow, we all have to look at what we have then look at what He is promising and **then** make a choice. Will we lose something by faith to gain something that is promised?

What are you willing to lose to gain what you say you want? (Even more cont'd)

Sitting down, Jesus called the Twelve and said, "If anyone wants to be first, he must be the very last, and the servant of all."

Mark 9: 35(NIV)

Let us continue with this thought as I sense God really wanting to underline it in our lives. What are you willing to lose in order to gain what you are saying you **really** want?

This wisdom of Jesus does not make too much sense if you try to understand it according to the taught wisdom of an unsaved, ungodly world but it makes perfect sense in the Kingdom of God. Remember, we are now citizens of God's Kingdom. If we want to function correctly and prosper in God's Kingdom, as we are promised we can, we need to dare to live by Kingdom wisdom not just earthly sense. The Kingdom of God says to receive, you must give; to become great, you become least; to **increase** who you are, you must **decrease** who you are. This principle introduces us to the very workings and mechanics of what faith is.

There are many examples of people who said they wanted something only to find they needed to apparently lose something important to them to gain it.

- **Naaman the Syrian general in *2 Kings 5*** said he really wanted a miracle, to be healed of leprosy, and God complied with this by giving Naaman an easy set of instructions to follow to receive fresh, new skin. Naaman had to lose his pride to gain what he had said he wanted.

- **The rich young ruler in *Matthew 19*** said he wanted to be a follower of Jesus and to be perfect. Jesus never discouraged him but simply told him what he would have to lose to gain what he claimed he wanted. The loss would involve what he had always attached his security to and, in this case, it was his wealth. He felt this was too high a price to gain what he thought he so earnestly desired. Obviously, he did not want what he was asking for as badly as he thought he did. Maybe he should have thought about the cost before asking?

The Bible is full of people willing to give up whatever was necessary to gain what their heart truly desired. Sometimes, before telling God what we want, we should take a moment to see if we are ready to lose something important to gain it. Give that some thought and then go ahead and get out of the boat!

Champion's Challenge:

Are you ready to lose something to gain what you say you really want? How ready are you to lose that something?

Don't labour in vain

Unless the LORD builds the house, its builders labour in vain. Unless the LORD watches over the city, the watchmen stand guard in vain.

Psalm 127:1 (NIV)

This *Psalm* gives us all a good reminder to make sure that God is involved in what we are building with our life lest, after spending our lives building this thing, we find out it was actually worthless and all in vain , a total waste of time.

Each of us is busy building a number of things today: careers, families, ministries to name but a few. The key to long-term success is to make sure that God is the cornerstone and is right in the centre of it all and that you are building with Him, not without Him.

How do we do that? We must value taking the time to include Him in what we are doing. Think of walking with Him as working with a business partner and consult Him concerning what you are going to give your life to build. Seek His wisdom and input and, when you do, you will be amazed at the time you can save and the hidden ditches you can avoid.

God wants you to succeed and prosper *(Jeremiah 29:11)* but He also wants to be involved. So, include Him today, Champion, and make sure that plan to build or develop something is not just a good idea but also a 'God idea'. The *Psalm* says we, *"labour in vain"* when we do not build with Him but the good news is that when we acknowledge Him in all our ways and build with Him then what we build is strong and remains long term.

What a waste to spend your life building something and, at the end, you find out it was all in vain or for nothing. Don't do it, Champ, but let God be both the architect and business partner of every blueprint that is in your heart. You will be glad you did.

Food for thought:
An excellent spirit will get you promoted in whatever crowd you may find yourself.

Champion's Challenge:
Stop and think. Are you including God in all you are building today?

Be an untangled soldier

No one engaged in warfare entangles himself with the affairs of this life, that he may please him who enlisted him as a soldier.

2 Timothy 2:4 (NKJV)

Living to please the One who enlisted us by His grace should be our greatest pursuit and desire. Let us remember that, as well as being God's kids, restored to son-ship by the obedience of His Son, we are also all a part of the Lord's army and we daily fight a very real fight of faith and the reality is, as I heard someone once say, there are no de-militarized zones.

There is a fight on right now for the soul of man, even as you sit and read this. God has called each and every one of us to be a part of an army that daily pushes back unrighteousness, establishes justice and delivers people from one kingdom, darkness, to another, light. The truth is, we will never be as active or effective as His soldiers when we are distracted and entangled by other stuff. This is so often the plan of the enemy: to de-mobilize you and your potential by entangling you with the *"affairs of this life"*.

Let's be honest, when it comes to the affairs of life, we all have cares and responsibilities we need to keep busy with but that is different to being entangled by them. Be careful, Champion, not to get entangled by things that will freeze and demobilize your potential as an enlisted soldier. The devil is very cunning, like a fox, and daily lays his nets out to try and entangle us. But our God is always one step ahead and, if we follow close to Him, He will always keep us from planned entanglement.

What if you are entangled today? Maybe by debts that need to be paid that weigh you down – ever disabling you, keeping you from marching as you desire to for the Lord? Well, I believe that God, in His mercy and grace, is ever ready to untangle us from that net and any other situations we can find ourselves entangled in. Call on Him today to untangle you, and, when He does, be careful not to get tangled up again. There is a war to be won and we are God's enlisted soldiers!

Champion's Prayer:

Father, help me to stay untangled from the things of this life that come to wrap me up. Set my life free and daily help me to keep it free so that I can be what You need me to be and go where You need me to go. Take from me today any entanglement, set my life free to serve You – Amen.

Don't get all tangled up again

Stand fast therefore in the liberty by which Christ has made us free, and do not be entangled again with a yoke of bondage.

Galatians 5:1 (NKJV)

We spoke yesterday concerning being soldiers for God, not entangled by the cares of life but free to be and do all that He needs us to. I want to continue the thought of being entangled as I feel it is a very relevant one for us all. The gift and invitation of the Gospel of Jesus is liberty, not captivity. Our Saviour's plans for us are plans of freedom, not bondage; yet our enemy, the devil, has only plans of entanglement for us and ever desires to entice us away from liberty and tie us up in the webs of his deceptions.

We need to remind ourselves that entanglement and limitation are not our portion or inheritance in Christ. We can be entangled by many things in life and need to walk wisely concerning the webs that daily beckon us.

- **Habits:** seemingly harmless habits can easily turn into life-controlling addictions that entangle you and steal your freedom. Manage habits correctly, Champion, and break bad habits while they are like cobwebs so you don't have to deal with them when they become like steel cables.

- **Fears and insecurities:** If not dealt with by knowing the Word and the identity and authority you have in Christ, these two can become very real webs that constantly entangle and restrict you from attempting the things that Jesus has freed you for.

- **The law:** Paul was specifically referring in these verses to the enticement and entanglement of the law and religion. He was instructing the Galatians that they had found and obtained total freedom through faith in the grace of God and warned them not to go back to the bondage and entanglement of the law.

These verses remind us again that, when we try to re-embrace the law, to make God like us, which is performance-based Christianity, we 'fall from grace' and become entangled again in a web of self-effort.

DON'T DO IT. Law will always entangle you again and again and leave you restricted whereas grace will consistently make you freer than you have ever been – free to love, free to live, free to give. *Galatians 5:2-4 (NKJV)*

**Remember, Champion, it was for freedom that Christ has set you free.
Stay free!**

Called out!

But you are a chosen generation, a royal priesthood, a holy nation, His own special people, that you may proclaim the praises of Him who called you out of darkness into His marvellous light;

1 Peter 2:9 (NKJV)

These verses remind us, again, of who we now are in Christ. It's good to remind ourselves who we are because, at the same moment, we are reminding ourselves who we are not any longer! Remember, we will always live out of what we think; we first think, then we feel, then we behave. This is a great process if our thinking is correct and based on God's Word and opinion of us but if our thinking is wrong or warped in any way this will always affect the behaviour or output of our day to day lives.

Let's look again into the mirror of God's opinion today and see our true identity: we are **chosen**, **royal**, **holy** and **His own special people**.

At the same time, these verses remind us that we have now also experienced a change of location – we have been called out of darkness and into His '*marvellous light*'!

Our lives are no longer darkness but light! We are no longer in the darkness that we once were so we should never live out our lives like we are still there. Our post code is now '*marvellous light*'. Don't let the enemy try and trick you to pilgrimage backwards to darker, former places but rather purpose to set your face ever forward, deeper into His brightness!

You were called out of darkness, Champion, so ever let darkness be a thing of your past. You are now a citizen of the light so let '*His marvellous light*' shine through your life again today.

Whether in the work place, community or home, let your 'not-so-little light' shine. Be that city on a hill! Shine bright for God today in a dark world; the darker it gets the brighter our lives should become. You are called to shine, so go ahead and shine knowing who you are!

Champion's Prayer:

Thank You, Jesus, that I am no longer a child of darkness but a child of light. You have delivered me from the power of darkness and planted my life into the kingdom of the Son of Your love. Today, let Your light shine through my life. I do not want to live to blend in but to stand out. Help me to remember that the former ways of darkness are no longer my ways; they are the ways of a place I once knew, not the place that I now call Home. Thank You, that You have made me a child of the light – Amen.

It's not what you know but who you know

Not everyone who says to Me, 'LORD, LORD,' shall enter the kingdom of heaven, but he who does the will of My Father in heaven. Many will say to Me in that day, 'LORD, LORD, have we not prophesied in Your name, cast out demons in Your name, and done many wonders in Your name?' And then I will declare to them, 'I never knew you; depart from Me, you who practice lawlessness!'

Matthew 7:21-23 (NKJV)

Wow, here's a nice sobering thought for our breakfast together this morning. It gives us a couple of good home truths that should certainly motivate us to check our priorities concerning the importance of who God is to us versus the importance of what we do for Him. When it comes to 'entering the kingdom of heaven', this verse teaches us that the most important thing is not what you have been doing, even if it felt really important and looked impressive, but who you have been knowing.

Remember we are called 'human beings' not 'human doings'. First of all we are called to 'BE'. What are we meant to be? Simple, friends of God.

It is then out of our knowing Him that we naturally live out the will of His Father in what we daily do, but notice the vital thing or first thing is always the knowing of Him. This can be really hard when you have been raised in a 'works based' world that focuses so much on doing. Such a world chooses to know us by our doing rather than our being. We have to dare to cross over and live in a kingdom where knowing and being are of greater value and importance.

Notice the cry of the people in these verses. Look at the language they use to try and convince Him of their rights, "Didn't we do this and didn't we do that?"

Jesus then turns and says, "Get out of here you workers of lawlessness." The real scary bit is when you read what they had been doing, because you see it was actually the works of ministry! What can we learn from this? Everything we do for Him must flow out of our knowing of Him otherwise it is of no worth to Him. Even if we deceive ourselves that it is of great worth or meaning, it is actually worthless.

So, today Champion, top of the list: know Jesus more! Move to second place all the stuff you do even if it is prophesying, casting out demons and working wonders and re-focus on the One who it is all about. He remains the beginning and the end and everything in the middle. Invest good time in knowing Him and that really will be time well spent. Remember this when it is time to go through the gates of heaven. It's not what you know or what you have done that will matter but who you have known and been known by.

Create capacity for God

Then he said, "Go, borrow vessels from everywhere, from all your neighbours – empty vessels; do not gather just a few. And when you have come in, you shall shut the door behind you and your sons; then pour it into all those vessels, and set aside the full ones." So she went from him and shut the door behind her and her sons, who brought the vessels to her; and she poured it out. Now it came to pass, when the vessels were full, that she said to her son, "Bring me another vessel." And he said to her, "There is not another vessel." So the oil ceased.

2 Kings 4:3-6 (NKJV)

Here we have yet another classic account of God supernaturally supplying increase into the life of someone responding in to Him in faith. If you get a chance, read this whole account. There are some great lessons in it. In brief, you see the prophet turn up in this widow's moment of great need and he then instructs her to use the apparent little in her life, the jar of oil, to cause the breakthrough she needed. He tells her to gather empty vessels. She did what he said and returned with as many as her reasoning would let her believe God would fill. She then began to pour the small jar of oil and each empty vessel was filled. She filled to the brim every empty vessel then the moment came that the oil stopped.

If she knew before the miracle what she knew after the miracle she certainly would have got a lot more vessels than she did. This account also shows us that the limitation was not an issue of what God was willing to give but rather one of provided capacity; when the capacity was no more, the outpouring stopped. Let us be inspired by this to always make sure we are creating capacity for God to fill – in our lives, our situations and, indeed, our churches. I don't want God to have to stop pouring out His good stuff. How about you? For this to happen we need to take responsibility to be ever creating capacity and more space for Him.

When we consider our lives, there are two ways of making more space for God to keep on pouring. Firstly, commit to being stretched. Like the tent in *Isaiah 54*, allow God to keep stretching you because, as He does, He increases your capacity, making you able to contain more of what He has for you. Secondly, commit to emptying some old stuff out. Imagine a glass is full of water and rocks; when the glass is full to the brim with water you can quite rightly say it is full but if you take out some of the rocks you create new space and give the glass new capacity.

As you walk with God, you regularly become aware of things that do not need to be in your life anymore. Have the courage, Champion, to empty out some old clothes in the wardrobe of your life to make room for some new ones that God has for you. Create some space for your God to fill.

Where do you keep your treasure?

Do not lay up for yourselves treasures on earth, where moth and rust destroy and where thieves break in and steal; but lay up for yourselves treasures in heaven, where neither moth nor rust destroys and where thieves do not break in and steal. For where your treasure is, there your heart will be also.

Matthew 6:19-21(NIV)

I believe, with my whole heart, that God wants to prosper you in this life *(Jeremiah 29:11)* but that He also wants the life you choose to live now to affect your eternity, your life after death. We should all live in such a way here that, when we eventually leave this earth and awaken in Heaven, we have great treasure waiting there also.

One important key to living a successful life is to always live in 'the light of eternity', the knowing that one day we will all leave this life we know and be in Heaven with God forever and that what we have stored there, with the lives we have lived here, is not subject to the destruction and decay of this life but will remain forever. This must be the greatest investment opportunity available; the chance to store treasure in an eternal place where no thief can steal or rust destroy.

We produce treasure in Heaven by the way we choose to live here. As we purpose to live for God and His kingdom, to love what He loves and build what He desires to build, we establish eternal inheritance that cannot be stolen or destroyed. Many people today are building great things for themselves in this life but many will one day find that everything they spent so long building did not last. Wise people build well in this life too but also remain conscious of the larger chapter of life called eternity and live in such a way to have treasure there as well.

For what profit is it to a man if he gains the whole world, and loses his own soul? Or what will a man give in exchange for his soul? For the Son of Man will come in the glory of His Father with His angels, and then He will reward each according to his works.

Matthew 16:26-27(NIV)

Let's all be inspired again today to live for more than just the profit we can know in this life, let us live for God and live in such a way that, when we arrive in eternity, we are not bankrupt or without treasure.

Have a great day and live life conscious of both God and eternity today, not in a way that makes you fearful, but in a way that motivates you to live a great and effective life **here** that produces a great harvest **there**.

You get so much more with Jesus

For if by the one man's offense death reigned through the one, much more those who receive abundance of grace and of the gift of righteousness will reign in life through the One, Jesus Christ.

Romans 5:17 (NKJV)

This is one of my all time favourite verses because, in it, we find both the goodness and the generosity of God towards us.

The good news of the message of redemption is that if it took one perfect man, Adam, to get us all in to trouble, or separation from God, then it takes just one perfect man, Jesus, to get us out of it and rejoined. Offence and death reigned through Adam and we all, by natural birth, became inherently partakers of it, becoming separated from God and His life. But now, righteousness has come to us as a gift and reigns in all of those who put their faith in Jesus. In Him we find new birth and reconciliation and stand justified in the sight of God the Father, having every sin – past, present and future – settled by His one-time blood sacrifice at the cross.

Some key words are worth underlining in these verses.

- *"much more"* – Notice how it says "much more". Grace and righteousness causes us to reign in life, much more than the sin of Adam held us in captivity to death.

- *"receive"* – It is always vital to remember it says we receive, not we achieve. Everything we get from God is received and not earned or begged for. We enter into all the things of God by faith and receive them as gifts, not achievements or wages paid for things we have done.

- *"abundance"* – Today, in Christ Jesus, you have and daily receive abundance of grace – God's undeserved, unearned, unmerited favour – for every situation that you may face. Our God is the God of abundance (*Ephesians 3:20*) and His grace is sufficient for you in whatever you may need.

- *"righteousness"* – Our righteousness, or right standing with God, is a **gift**! And by it, we are commissioned to now rule and reign in life!

Champion, today, again make the quality choice to turn away from trying to impress God by performance or earn things from Him to simply receiving, by faith, everything you need to rule and reign in this life from Him as a gift.

Jesus, by his sacrificial death on your behalf, has positioned you to rule and reign in life though Him so, GET UP AND REIGN!

The world starts with your world

And He said to them, "Go into all the world and preach the gospel to every creature. He who believes and is baptised will be saved; but he who does not believe will be condemned".

Mark 16:15-16 (NKJV)

When you read this commission – which we all have in common – it can seem very daunting, especially if you read it in one of the older translations of the Bible. I want to take a couple of days to break it down and make it more do-able for everyday folk.

Firstly, we need to remind ourselves that this is the Great Commission not the Great Suggestion. Jesus has commissioned us, His body, to be busy with the incredible honour of introducing others to Him and helping them to be His followers too. If this is important to Him, it should be important to us. But again, it should be something that is fuelled by desire from the heart not obligation from the mind.

So let's start at the very beginning: *"Go into all the world "*. How huge and seemingly un-doable is that? Let's re-look at it to make it something that we can all get busy with.

Before you pack and set sail for Africa or the remote regions of China, let's consider your individual world. After all, the disciples were told to go first to their city, Jerusalem, then to surrounding areas then, finally, to the ends of the earth *(Acts 1:8)*. We must all realise the first world we need to be passionate to represent Jesus in effectively is the one that is unique to us right now. Without going anywhere, you have a very real world that is unique to you, made up of your friends, neighbours, people you work or go to school with. The first people we need to go to with the good news of who Jesus is and what He has done is surely them because if you don't take responsibility for them, who will?

This personal world can actually be the most demanding one – let's face it, in many ways it is easier go to the ends of the earth and stand up for Jesus with people that don't know you! You can project anything or impersonate anyone. But with the people in our everyday world you have to live it out too because they know you and will be watching to see if you live it or just talk it, right? This does not need to be a negative reality but rather a strength for you. As you purpose to live out the new life God has given you in an authentic way, you will catch the attention of those who know you; the changed life you live out before them will prompt the questions that you want to be asked.

So don't read the Great Commission and think you have to rush out and buy an air ticket for a mission trip some place far off; rather, ask the Holy Spirit to show you the people in your Jerusalem, your immediate world, that need God and ask Him for the courage to reach out to them on a daily basis. When the life you daily live matches the words that come out of your mouth, that will turn some heads for sure.

GO INTO YOUR WORLD

Tell them your story

Then He said, "Go into the world. Go everywhere and announce the Message of God's good news to one and all. Whoever believes and is baptised is saved; whoever refuses to believe is damned."

Mark 16:15-16 (The Message)

L et's stay with the theme of the Great Commission, our call to evangelism. Again, these can be very scary words to both the newly saved or more timid of character. Evangelism should not be scary – it is simply you representing the most special person in your life to others around you.

So, yesterday we dealt with the *"Go into all the world"* bit and focused our attention initially on the personal world that is around us, that is unique to us – our Jerusalem. That's not to say, don't go into **all** the world but a reminder that your personally unique Jerusalem is a good place to start.

Next we hear the call to *"announce the Message of God's good news to one and all"*, or 'preach the Gospel to every creature'. Again you may say, "You know what, Andy? I am not a preacher and the thought of standing on a box shouting absolutely terrifies me!" That's okay. Let's redefine this one too to make it do-able for everyday folk and not just the 'superstar preachers' who are overloaded with confidence. How about we say, "Go into the world unique to you and communicate effectively, in your personal style, how good Jesus is and what a change He has made in your life". That seems more do-able, right?

That's all God is expecting of you: to represent Him in your world on a daily basis, to be unashamed of Him, telling people, in your own way, your story. When someone is dear to you, it is not an unnatural thing for them to find their way into every conversation you have. If you spend any amount of time with me, it won't be long before Gina and the kids come into the conversation. Why? Because I have an active and healthy relationship with them. In the same way, it should not be forced or strange that Jesus and His church pops into a whole bunch of the conversations you have on a day-to-day basis.

Evangelism, like worship and prayer and the other things we do as a Christian, was never meant to be reduced to being a project, something we force ourselves to do once a week but rather a lifestyle, something that is naturally a part of who we are. You have a story that is unique. It's that story the people in your world need to hear, not some made-up one or someone else's – **yours**.

It's a good story, a true one, so go tell it.

Keep it relational

Whoever is ashamed of Me and My words, the Son of Man will be ashamed of them when He comes in His glory and in the glory of the Father and of the holy angels.

Luke 9:26 (NIV)

We have been speaking about the Great Commission: God's desire for each of us to walk through the world, indeed our world, representing Him in a way that makes people want to run to Jesus and not from Him; ever willing to tell the story of what He has done for us at every and any opportunity.

Here's one of the main keys: keep it relational. He is a **who**, not a **what**! God is not wanting you to represent or stand up for a theory or a set of facts but rather a person – the person of Jesus. The Bible says that the story of Jesus (the Gospel) is good news to the hearer *(Romans 1:16)*. Let's always make sure we are giving people 'good news' and not some other old story. When you know Jesus for yourself, you know you have nothing to be ashamed of and everything to be proud of. Religion is, indeed, another story and if you start telling that one, with all its judgments and rules, you'd better believe you will get embarrassed. But not with Jesus – everything about Him is so attractive.

Today's text is a very strong one. I don't know about you, but I don't want Him to be ashamed of me so no way am I going to be ashamed of Him. There are too many Christians who treat Him like an ugly girlfriend or boyfriend; when they are in church they sing all the love songs to Him and act all adoring but then, after church, on the way home, when they bump into some friends who maybe don't know Him, they push Him in a bush quickly and pretend they were not just with Him!

If you were that boyfriend or girlfriend being shoved in a bush every time someone came around the corner, how would you feel? How long would you put up with that behaviour before asking the questions, "Are you embarrassed of me and why?"

Come on! Jesus is certainly no one to be embarrassed of. If He has done in your life what He has done in mine, then you know He deserves to be paraded, not hidden. Keep religion hidden away but let Jesus be seen, lift Him up as He really is and watch how, just as it was promised, people are drawn to Him. Remember, they will be drawn to Him in you because you are now His home.

Champion's Challenge:

Read again the gospels and remind yourself how awesome He is – He should never be your best-kept secret.

Life is a Garden

As long as the earth endures, seedtime and harvest, cold and heat, summer and winter, day and night will never cease."

Genesis 8:22 (NIV)

I want to inspire you today with this thought and remind you that the eternal principle called 'sowing and reaping' will affect every area of our daily life. When we choose to remember this, it can help us to cultivate harvests that we want and desire in our future. Life really is like a garden and when you treat it like one, being always mindful of what you are sowing, it can be a great place to be and call home. Let us remind ourselves of the timeless promise made to Noah after the flood on that first morning of what was indeed a whole new beginning. As we read it, let's remember that it is not a law but rather an eternal principle that is still very much active and in motion today and not a mere one-time-only promise made exclusively to a man named Noah.

It says, *"As long as the earth endures".* Tap your foot on the floor – if it is still there then this eternal principle, established for our benefit, is still very much in motion! The fertile ground of another day is waiting for you to join in with it, sowing and harvesting all manner of things. As with gravity, there is no choice and no days off from this principle and, as with gravity, you can try to ignore that it exists but it will just keep on producing because God ordained it: *"what a man sows, that will he reap"*!

Too many, sadly, experience the negative harvests produced by this principle because what they sow is not good seed; but we, the people of God, should understand the workings of this promise and daily use it to produce harvests that are worth having and fun to run through when fully grown. Seedtime and harvest affects every flower border and lawn of the garden of your life. If you want to bring some changes somewhere in your 'life-garden', then consider what you are sowing there. If you want carrots then don't plant cabbages, plant carrots – every seed bears fruit according to its own kind.

For example, what you sow into your relationships each and every day will determine what you will harvest from them. This is a sobering thought for anyone who has a dream of greatness in the relationships of their life. And remember, this is just one small part of the garden of your life so take time to think what you're sowing in each and every part of it.

Another great question is, "Do you really want the harvest of your present actions or attitudes?" Hopefully, most of your responses will be, "Yes!" but if not, then do something about the seed you're using today, because the seed you are sowing will determine the harvest one day you will eat!

Remember, life is a garden! What you sow is what you mow.

It really is an issue of whatever

Do not be deceived, God is not mocked; for whatever a man sows, that he will also reap.

Galatians 6:7 (NKJV)

Welcome to another day where you have the opportunity to again live and function in the God-established eternal principle of seedtime and harvest, knowing confidently that what you choose to sow you will reap.

For me, the key word in this verse is *"whatever"* because it declares that the principle includes whatever you sow in absolutely any and every area of your life. It is effective across every square inch of the landscape of your existence.

Think about this, the eternal principle of sowing and reaping is relevant today in:

- Your health and fitness

- Your finances and wealth

- Your relationships and, especially, your spiritual relationship with your Creator

These are just a few very significant areas you need to purpose to sow well in. With these areas and with all the others, we can be certain that what we put in always affects what we get out. Think about the area of worship in your life: if you put your energy and passion into worshipping God, it is amazing what you will harvest out of it while the person standing next to you choosing not to enter in to it can leave the exact same worship experience with apparently nothing. Why? One sowed, the other did not.

Look at that same verse from *The Message* translation:

Don't be misled: No one makes a fool of God. What a person plants, he will harvest. The person who plants selfishness, ignoring the needs of others – ignoring God! – harvests a crop of weeds. All he'll have to show for his life is weeds! But the one who plants in response to God, letting God's Spirit do the growth work in him, harvests a crop of real life, eternal life.

Galatians 6:7-8 (The Message)

Let us today again be motivated to make sure we are sowing wisely throughout the entirety of the garden of our life and that we are not mocking God and deceiving ourselves. And that we are happy with the seed we are using – that we are making sure that we are not going to end up with a harvest of bitter weeds but instead the finest wheat!

Live ready, not afraid

But mark this: There will be terrible times in the last days. People will be lovers of themselves, lovers of money, boastful, proud, abusive, disobedient to their parents, ungrateful, unholy, without love, unforgiving, slanderous, without self-control, brutal, not lovers of the good, treacherous, rash, conceited, lovers of pleasure rather than lovers of God.

2 Timothy 3:1-4 (NIV)

You will hear of wars and rumours of wars, but see to it that you are not alarmed. Such things must happen, but the end is still to come. Nation will rise against nation, and kingdom against kingdom. There will be famines and earthquakes in various places. All these are the beginning of birth pains.

Matthew 24:6-8 (NIV)

Sounds a bit like today, right? These verses are good for reminding us all where in history and, indeed, in God's plans we are presently located. When you read through the list of 'end times evidences' you would have to do it with your eyes closed to not see the day and time we are presently in. Also, when you have a good look around at what is happening in and around Israel, at the rise in Muslim and Islamic rights and even with the radical changes to climate, all these things send out a very real call to the dozing Christian: "WAKE UP".

These very real prophetic sign-posts, set into position many years ago, should not produce fear in the heart of the believer but rather motivation; they should motivate us to make the knowing of Jesus the greatest priority in our lives, to making His Good News known to all men before His return, to living as the kingdom people He has called us to be in our generation. Notice that Matthew writes, "When you see these things, don't be alarmed (afraid); they are the starting contractions to the coming of something great", or should we say **someone** great. He does not say, "Freak out, get scared, and give yourself a heart attack with fear and worry", but that we should realise, with soberness, the hour in which we are living.

I don't know about you but these verses awaken me to the destiny I have to live and the true purpose for why I am alive now.

Don't let present day life with all its distractions keep you from knowing the hour at hand. Don't let the comfort of modern life coax you into the restful sleep of apathetic living. Rather, awaken your heart and be alert, knowing that, as with a birthing mother when the contractions begin, the process has started; there is no going back, only an imminent arrival.

Live ready, Champion, for the return of the King. Don't be afraid, rather live ready!

Get rid of your 'ifs … buts and maybes'!

"From childhood," he answered. "It has often thrown him into fire or water to kill him. But if you can do anything, take pity on us and help us." "If you can?" said Jesus. "Everything is possible for him who believes." Immediately the boy's father exclaimed, "I do believe; help me overcome my unbelief!"

Mark 9:22-24 (NIV)

Jesus comes across this man who had a very desperate situation with his son who was being demonically tormented. He asks about the situation and the man fills him in with all the history of the problem, then says to Jesus, "If you can do anything, please do". Jesus had great compassion for this man and his son and helps them, but before He does, He focuses in on one of the key words the man had used in his request: that word was "*If*". When you read this account, this is the moment that you would have seen Jesus look over the top of His glasses, if He had worn them, and say slowly, "Sorry, did you say if?"

Jesus then shares an eternal truth with the desperate man – all things are possible to those who believe! The man then immediately responds with honesty and great sincerity saying, "I do believe but I know there is room for improvement. Please help me with that!"

Look at this same verse in *The Message* translation:

Jesus said, "If? There are no 'ifs' among believers. Anything can happen." No sooner were the words out of his mouth than the father cried, "Then I believe. Help me with my doubts!"

Mark 9:23-24 (The Message)

What a great statement. There are no '*ifs*' among believers. As we journey with the Lord we should be ever losing our '*ifs*' and discovering our 'I believes'. There is a massive problem if we have more 'ifs' and 'buts' now than when we started!

We often refer to ourselves as believers and, that being the case, it is fundamental that we remind ourselves what believers do: they believe! Here's the question for today: are you believing? Are you a believing believer? What I love about this account is that there is room for honesty. If you still struggle with 'ifs' and 'buts', why not do as this man did and ask the Lord to help you because there are no 'ifs' with Him? He will help you to realise this!

Champion's Prayer:

Jesus, please help me with my 'ifs' and 'buts'. Please turn my question marks into exclamation marks because I want to see the miracle things You have for me – Amen.

Be a believing believer!

Then they said to Him, "What shall we do, that we may work the works of God?" Jesus answered and said to them, "This is the work of God, that you believe in Him whom He sent."

John 6:28-29 (NKJV)

Allow me to challenge you further concerning being a **believing** believer. Remember, it is our belief in God and His promises which causes everything He has intended for us to manifest. The very epicentre of our believing is, of course, our believing in Jesus. As we daily choose to believe in Him and in all that He accomplished for us through His perfect finished work, we see the release of all we need to fulfil our lives and destinies.

The question was simple and sincere, *"What shall we do?"* The answer was simply profound: *". . . believe in Him whom He (God) sent."* Here we see the only real work that God requires from us is to believe in Jesus! This can so grind against our works-based, performance-driven, factory setting that says that everything we see produced is always in accordance to what **we** do or have done. Jesus reminds us here again that, as new creations in Him, we are not human **doings** but human **beings**. Our responsibility is to be the believers He has called us to be and, through our faith, see the incredible things He has promised to come into being and fulfilment.

As you read through the Gospels and witness Jesus doing incredible things for people on a daily basis – most of whom were not religious synagogue attendees – you see many times, before releasing the miracle, He would ask the same thing, "Do you believe I can?"

Believing in Him is **the** most powerful thing that we can do. It produces more than we could ever produce through our own ability and leaves us humbled in the presence of a great and mighty God who calls us His child.

Let's make the decision today to be busy with the work that God desires from us, which is to be found believing in the One He sent. He is our Saviour, Healer, Provider and so much more.

Food for thought:

As with Daniel, a person with an excellent spirit will get promoted and catch the attention of kings in whatever crowd they find themselves in.

Seven or seventy times seven?

Then Peter came to Jesus and asked, "Lord, how many times shall I forgive my brother when he sins against me? Up to seven times?" Jesus answered, "I tell you, not seven times, but seventy-seven times."

Matthew 18:21-22 (NIV)

When it comes to the subject of forgiveness and having to forgive people, it is something that we can all relate to – some from a platform of victory and some, maybe, out of an ongoing struggle. Forgiving people is not an optional extra but a vital part of this Gospel we say we believe. Always remember, Christ is the standard of our forgiveness issues. Freely, He has forgiven us of so much and now He expects us to freely forgive others.

In this conversation between Jesus and His disciple, we see the measurement of forgiveness that Jesus expects us to use. The disciple said, "*seven times*", Jesus says, "*seventy-seven times*." (Other translations even say "*seventy times seven*"). This is a massive ratio for us to see the difference between the power of human love (*philio*) and the potential of God's love (*agape*). Remember, we are now the containers of God's love and not just human love, which means that we can go further than we thought we could. Remember also, God is love and that means that if you acknowledge you have God in you, then you also have to acknowledge that you have a never-ending well of divine love in you too. It is out of this resource of love that we can always find what we need to love people beyond the human potential of a mere seven times.

Let's face it, when it comes to forgiving with human love, seven times is a lot. Most people get written off after the three count, right? Three strikes and you're out. God wants us to ever be breaking down the limiting barriers of human love with all its conditions and regulations and, instead, choosing to love and forgive people from a bigger love: God's agape love that is now resident in our lives.

As always, this involves choice. Will you choose to drop a bucket into God's bottomless well of love within you and pull up what you need to release and forgive that person you said you never would? Remember, forgiving someone does not make them or what they did right – it sets you free! God wants us to be free in every area of our lives and when we choose to forgive we do not just open the prison door for others; often we are letting ourselves out too. We can then be free to live, love and move on with life. Remember what we learned from *1 Corinthians 13*? One of the things that makes God's love different to human love is that it keeps no record of wrongs. He doesn't so nor should we.

Champion's challenge:

Is there anyone you need to forgive or forgive again? Then go ahead and get it done.

Let Him work on those knots

The end of all things is near. Therefore be clear minded and self-controlled so that you can pray. Above all, love each other deeply, because love covers over a multitude of sins.

1 Peter 4:7-8 (NIV)

We spoke yesterday about living a life that forgives people whether they are people in your past or your present. Forgiving people is a manifestation of the potential of God's love in you and it always sets you free. When we get to talking about forgiving people, it can get a bit uncomfortable for some. I guess it's a bit like going for a sports massage when you have knots in your back. Man, it hurts during the massage but a couple of days later you feel so much better.

I can remember when I had a sports massage on my shoulders and back. I had strained something and a friend called Paul, who is in the church, offered to help me out because he is a sports masseur. If you have never had a sports massage, all I can tell you is that it is not that health spa stuff! There's no gentle music or soft strokes. Instead, there's loads of pain but pain with the purpose of bringing repair to what is damaged.

As I lay there, biting the towel to muffle my cries, Paul said something interesting that got me thinking. He noticed my twitches of pain and said, "Sorry, I have to keep working on these same knots because if I don't, you won't feel better." He then said, "I have to get the blood flowing through them to get them to repair properly". Wow, what a great thought concerning the knots of unforgiveness some may be feeling. You have to let the blood get to them and through them if you want true freedom from the pain they cause. The all-forgiving blood of Jesus, allowed to flow through, will heal and repair every knot of unforgiveness that has ailed you.

Maybe God is wanting to massage some knots of unforgiveness in your life? If so, know that he is not doing it to cause you pain but to heal and mend you and to make you strong again.

Hey, Champion, if you have any knots, let God loose on them. Let the blood of Jesus flow. It may hurt a bit now but real soon you will feel so great. Indeed, weeping may endure for a night but rejoicing comes in the morning.

Hatred stirs up strife, but love covers all sins.

Proverbs 10:12 (NKJV)

Champion's Prayer:

Father, I invite You to get Your healing hands all over me. Where there are knots that are causing me to live in a lesser way than I could, please remove those knots with Your loving hands. Father, let forgiveness and life flow through everything that I am. I trust You Lord, that You never intend to cause me pain but bring me into healing and freedom — Amen.

What thoughts are you entertaining today?

For the weapons of our warfare are not carnal but mighty in God for pulling down strongholds, casting down arguments and every high thing that exalts itself against the knowledge of God, bringing every thought into captivity to the obedience of Christ

2 Corinthians 10:4-5 (NKJV)

Your thought life is such a powerful thing and, as I have heard it put so well before, the mind can really be a battlefield sometimes. We need to be ever taking authority in the realm of our thought life and making sure that we are not entertaining or inviting thoughts that can produce what we really don't want, or need, to stay for a while. Somebody once said that you can't stop the birds flying above your head but you can stop them from making a nest in your hair. There is some massive truth contained in that statement concerning thoughts and temptations and how we are to deal with them.

Every day, all of us are bombarded with different thoughts from many sources – ourselves, the devil, worldly advertising to name just a few. So many different sources daily throw thoughts at us to process and it is what we choose to do with these thoughts that causes us to walk on a road of defeat or of victory. You can either choose to birth sin or gain a breakthrough.

Paul advises us to develop the habit of taking every thought captive and then using Jesus to see if it should stay or go. If the thought does not fit the mind of Christ, given to you *(1 Corinthians 2:16)*, throw it away and don't let it land. Great plans can come from simple, single thoughts but so can great sins. Remember, every sin in your life started as a small thought. Come on, we have all gone through this simple equation *(James 1:14-15)* at one time or another.

- You thought it (temptation came).

- Not dealing with the thought (temptation) correctly caused it to turn into desire.

- Desire grew and burst out of its box and turned into action that then produced sin.

- Remember, the end of the road is death because sin, full blown, always produces death.

All of this could have been different if the initial thought was taken captive, held against God's Word to see if it was right and quickly dealt with, taken prisoner and cast out if it wasn't. What thoughts are you opening the doors of your life to today, Champion?

Food for thought:

Remember, when it comes to leading people or raising children you will never get away from the principle of 'monkey see, monkey do'. Let your life be your message, not just your words.

Paul's 'thought chart'

And the peace of God, which transcends all understanding, will guard your hearts and your minds in Christ Jesus. Finally, brothers, whatever is true, whatever is noble, whatever is right, whatever is pure, whatever is lovely, whatever is admirable—if anything is excellent or praiseworthy—think about such things.

Philippians 4:7-8 (NIV)

We spoke yesterday concerning NOT entertaining thoughts that won't profit your life or take you in the direction God has for you. Here, in *Philippians*, we see Paul give us a real good 'thought chart' to enable us to know which ones to throw away and which ones to keep.

Whenever you get a thought and are unsure where it is coming from or whether it should go or stay, as well as seeing if it fits well with the mind of Christ given you, hold it against this simple chart of Paul's and if it gets a tick of approval, let it stay and think about it some more. If it does not get a tick, then chuck it out because you do not want what that thought has the potential to give birth to and produce!

The New Kings James advises us to *"meditate"* on the thoughts which are good. That is a much better word than *"think"*. When you meditate, you muse. Forgive the analogy, but it is like a cow chewing the cud. It keeps chewing and chewing till every last bit of goodness is squeezed out. When you find a good and Godly thought, chew that baby dry!

When you think about God's Word, mentally chew it over like you have a toffee in your mind. Don't swallow it quickly like sherbet. I have found when you take a God thought, a verse or principle from His Word, and keep on mentally chewing it, it's amazing how much revelation and understanding continues to flow. Why? The Holy Spirit is helping you to understand that which you have chosen to think about.

Use Paul's chart but also remember you now have the mind of Christ so it is not too hard to know if a thought fits in or not. If not, deal with it before it starts breeding or infecting anything you don't want it to.

For "who has known the mind of the LORD that he may instruct Him?" But we have the mind of Christ.

1 Corinthians 2:16 (NKJV)

Don't forget your keys!

"I will give you the keys of the kingdom of heaven; whatever you bind on earth will be bound in heaven, and whatever you loose on earth will be loosed in heaven."

Matthew 16:19 (NIV)

What Jesus promised to Peter in these verses was also a promise for the Church and not just the Church that was around then but the one that is still alive and well today: us!

After Jesus rose from the dead, He delivered on the promise and gave the keys of the Kingdom to the Church and we, who believe, hold those keys and have the power to open things up and close things down on earth and in heaven today. They are keys that hold great purpose and they enable and empower us to close, bind, things on earth and in heaven and open, loose, things as well.

My challenge this morning is simple. Are you tolerating stuff that you don't need to tolerate simply because you won't pick up your keys and use them? If so, make today a new day, a day of victory. Pick up the keys today, my friend, and begin to use them effectively.

Jesus restored our right to rule and reign and have righteous dominion on the earth. God originally gave this right to Adam, but Adam sold out through his deception and disobedience. But through His obedience and sacrifice two thousand years ago, Jesus won the rights back for us by his victory at the cross and has delivered it to us by His Spirit. He has given back the keys of authority for us to use in our daily lives and not for them to just sit on the sideboard of your life. Go ahead, Champion, pick them up and start to use them!

The God-given keys that are now in our possession have the power to release things from heaven to the earth and into your life. Think about it, if I gave you my keys, you would have access to and full use of what was mine; among other things my house, my car and my office. Jesus has given you His keys to use. Listen to how *The Message* puts the verse we read.

"And that's not all. You will have complete and free access to God's kingdom, keys to open any and every door: no more barriers between heaven and earth, earth and heaven. A yes on earth is yes in heaven. A no on earth is no in heaven."

Matthew 16:19 (The Message)

Hey, Champion, don't leave home without your kingdom-keys and have a great day opening and shutting doors you need to with them.

Are you still living on benefits?

Praise the LORD, *O my soul; all my inmost being, praise his holy name. Praise the* LORD, *O my soul,* **and forget not all his benefits** – *who forgives all your sins and heals all your diseases,*

Psalm 103:1-4 (NIV)

We are living in a time when the statement 'benefit entitlement' is very commonly used and understood. The British government offers many ever-changing types of benefits and credits to people with varying income and family situations. Sadly, it is amazing that many people, especially older people, still miss out on so much because they don't know what benefits they are legally entitled to. Sadly, many Christians do the same thing and they live average lives or struggle when they should not because they don't have an understanding or no one has ever informed them of their kingdom of God benefit entitlements.

There was a tax office media campaign recently that simply said, "Do you know what benefits you are entitled to?" That is my question to you today.

Here is a legal document from Heaven concerning your benefit entitlements today and as the British government advise, do not forget them, you really can't afford too!

Benefit one: He forgives ALL your sins.

What an incredible eternal benefit this is. Notice it does not say **some** or **past** ones but *"all"*. Jesus died for all of your sins – past present and future. His one-time, perfect payment and sacrifice has qualified you for the benefits of justification and total forgiveness so that you can stand before your God today, holy and blameless, with your chin held high. Just as though you had never sinned. What a great benefit. Don't go forgetting that one today, Champion!

Benefit two: He heals all of your diseases.

Here is another great benefit. Again, notice the absence of the word **some**. Again, it uses the all inclusive word *"all"*. As well as making payment for your sins, He also made total payment for your healing so that you can arise out of every sickness and infirmity by faith in His promises.

Don't go forgetting that one either. Remember these benefits were not cheap and they cost a lot to make them available to you. The good news is that another man, Jesus, paid the taxes required to release these needed benefits to you and me. Thank You, Jesus!

Think about these two foundational benefits and we will look at some more tomorrow. Have a great day. When you understand the benefits that are yours in Christ, it is hard not to.

Food for thought:

He is the God of every season of your life. Don't just worship Him on the mountain tops (when everything is great) but also in the valleys and the wilderness times too. He is Lord in them all and with you in them all!

Don't be a victim of benefit fraud!

Bless the Lord, O my soul; And all that is within me, bless His holy name! Bless the Lord, O my soul, And forget not all His benefits: Who forgives all your iniquities, Who heals all your diseases, Who redeems your life from destruction, Who crowns you with loving kindness and tender mercies,

Psalm 103:1-4 (NKJV)

D on't let the con-man of your salvation, Satan, rip you off from receiving the benefits that are rightly yours in Christ. How does he do that? Through the daily use of an ever-effective and favourite tool he has called **ignorance**. Don't fall for it, rather daily discover and know for certain what God has qualified you to be entitled to. Ignorance is **not** bliss, it is a thief in the life of people who are entitled to so very much. Remember the benefits from yesterday? He forgives all your sins and heals all your diseases. Let's look at a couple more.

Benefit three: He redeems your life from destruction!

To redeem is to 're-purchase or buy back'. A good example of this would be someone returning to a pawn shop to pay for and be reunited with an item that they had left while borrowing cash in a time of need. When you redeem something, you bring back to yourself, by legal means, something that once belonged to you that you may have had to sell, had lost or even had stolen.

Remember, in the beginning, in *Genesis*, we were made by God to belong to God and were destined to be friends of God and not slaves. The story of *Genesis* then reveals that we were stolen from God through the foolishness of Adam. Humanity was sold out to another owner. We legally, because of Adam's sin and disobedience, became the property of the father of sin, Satan. The good news of the Gospel is that we have now been purchased back! The price for the redemption of humanity was set and it was the precious blood and life of God's only beloved Son.

What a hugely costly price! God loved us so much that He paid the price for our redemption and brought us back to Himself, redeeming our lives from destruction. Redemption is a benefit that you can't afford to forget about and that is why the Bible instructs us, *"let the redeemed of the Lord say so"*.

Let the redeemed of the Lord say so, Whom He has redeemed from the hand of the enemy,

Psalm 107:2 (NKJV)

Wow, what a great benefit! He both originally made you and then bought you back to Himself. Think about that. That makes you 'twice His' so don't be defrauded by any lesser gospel.

Don't forget your benefit claim

*Bless the LORD, O my soul, And forget not all His benefits: Who forgives all your iniquities, Who heals all your diseases, Who redeems your life from destruction, **Who crowns you with loving kindness and tender mercies**,*

Psalm 103:2-4 (NKJV)

We have been looking at the benefits that are legally ours in Christ. Make sure you are claiming these benefits that are rightfully yours on a daily basis. Another great benefit is that the King of Kings crowns you and I with two incredible things:

Loving kindness – not judgment, wrath and disappointment. These were all poured upon His Son at the cross as He hung there on our behalf. Remember, we are now qualified by Christ to live continually in the benefits of the divine exchange of the cross. He took what was rightfully ours and gave us what was rightfully His.

God made him who had no sin to be sin for us, so that in him we might become the righteousness of God.

2 Corinthians 5:21 (NKJV)

Tender mercies – continual, undeserved goodness and grace towards us from the hand of a gentle loving Father. The perfect work of the cross put the Father's crown of delight upon our heads as well as upon the head of His beloved Son. His heart is again turned towards you to only do you good.

Different Bible translations put it the following ways:

He crowns you with love and mercy—a paradise crown.

2 Corinthians 5:21 (The Message)

Who beautifies, dignifies, and crowns you with loving-kindness and tender mercy;

2 Corinthians 5:21 (Amplified Bible)

- He has made all things beautiful – *Ecclesiastes 3:11.*

- He has restored our dignity.

- He has crowned us with love, kindness and mercy.

Take time to think about that today and go into your day praising Him because He did not have to do this but rather He chose to. Why? Simple, He loved you!

Don't stop living on His benefits

Who satisfies your desires with good things so that your youth is renewed like the eagle's.

Psalm 103:5 (NKJV)

In Great Britain, the government are ever trying to come up with plans to stop people living on benefits. In contrast, God never wants you to stop living on the benefits He has given you. Let us consider again the benefits that are ours in Christ and remind ourselves of our benefits list so far:

- Forgives all your sins.

- Heals all your diseases.

- Redeems your life from destruction!

- Crowns you with loving kindness and tender mercies.

Benefit five: He satisfies your desires with good things.

Notice that it says He *"satisfies"*! When you purpose to seek God and His kingdom first, He satisfies your desires with good things. Why? When you are seeking first Him and His kingdom, most, if not all, of your desires will be in alignment with His will anyway, 'two hearts beating as one'.

> *Delight yourself in the LORD and he will give you the desires of your heart.*
>
> **Psalm 37:4 (NIV)**

He is a satisfier not a disappointer! His desire for your life is satisfaction not disappointment.

- He is interested in your desires and if the truth be told is the author of most of them.

- He knows both your deepest and your shallowest desires and has interest in every one.

As with any loving father, the desires of His kids mean a lot to Him. Not just the big ones but those seemingly little desires too. *Romans 1: 24* says concerning wicked people with evil desires that He *"gives them over to their evil desires"* but when it comes to a righteous person with good desires, He does not give them over to them, rather He gets involved and makes those desires manifest realities: dreams come true.

Bless you. Love God first and foremost then watch Him turn even the smallest desires into manifest blessings.

Our compass bearings – love God and love people

"Teacher, which is the great commandment in the law?" Jesus said to him, 'You shall love the LORD your God with all your heart, with all your soul, and with all your mind.' This is the first and great commandment. And the second is like it: 'You shall love your neighbour as yourself.' On these two commandments hang all the Law and the Prophets."

Matthew 22:36-40 (NKJV)

Here's a reminder of the true compass bearings for our lives this year; if we live by them we won't get lost and will never go far wrong. All of us have priorities that we live by, they help direct us and make sure our time is spent effectively. But all of us should have these two things right at the top of our list. The ones that come next may change or differ but these first two should be set in stone:

- Love God with everything you are, live to give Him the best of you, live to daily grow your relationship with Him because in this is found true wealth.

- Love people – not just the lovable, but all people. Love people as you love yourself; choose to live beyond yourself again today for the benefit of someone else.

The opening question was asked of Jesus in regard to the law. Even though the law has now been fulfilled in Christ, these compass bearings remain good. It is actually by understanding the power of grace rather than the obligation of law that we are empowered to do them to the greatest effect. Notice from these verses that God does not want "with some" He wants *"with all"*. He wants all that we are and not just a little bit. What right does He have to expect this? Well, He set the benchmark by giving us everything He was in Jesus.

Loving your neighbour today? Maybe it's a good moment to re-think who is your neighbour? Who does that statement include? Who should it include? Who do you need to show love to today? According to these verses, you can never love your neighbour effectively till you can love you. Make sure, today, you have healthy love for yourself; see yourself as God does. Often people find it easy to love others but not themselves. God does not want 'either or', He wants both. The final statement says 'everything hangs on these to priorities'. This is true, you see, because God is love, love is how He chooses to introduce and describe Himself. To Him, everything rises or falls according to love.

Love is patient, love is kind. It does not envy, it does not boast, it is not proud. It is not rude, it is not self-seeking, it is not easily angered, it keeps no record of wrongs. Love does not delight in evil but rejoices with the truth. It always protects, always trusts, always hopes, always perseveres. Love never fails.

1 Corinthians 13:4-8 (NIV)

Time to take the lampshades off!

"Here's another way to put it: you're here to be light, bringing out the God-colours in the world. God is not a secret to be kept. We're going public with this, as public as a city on a hill. If I make you light-bearers, you don't think I'm going to hide you under a bucket, do you? I'm putting you on a light stand. Now that I've put you there on a hilltop, on a light stand — shine!"

Matthew 5:14-16 (The Message)

As we walk through this God-given year with faith and expectancy, let us also purpose in our hearts that this will be the year where we shine our brightest for Jesus and for His saving message of love and truth. God has made us light-bearers. How? By coming to live inside of us, just as light, in other words, Jesus once came into the world and confounded the darkness in it. Now light has come into each and every one of our worlds, or lives, and is making a difference – that's salvation. *(John 3:19).* What an amazing thought; truly he caused light to shine out of darkness when He came and lived within each of us.

Now that we have His light in us the only decision that remains is: are we going to daily let it shine from us? Will we live uncovered lives so that His light can shine into the worlds of those we daily live and work alongside? Will we allow His light now in us to be like the shining of a lighthouse, leading those around us to the safe harbour of relationship with Him?

It's time to take the lampshades off and let the life of Jesus, now in us, shine greater and purer from our lives than in any year that we have lived yet. It's time to cast away any lampshades that we may have which in any way diffuse or dull His light coming from us lampshades of fear, especially fear of men and what they may think if we come out of the closet as a God lover.

Maybe it will be you losing your lampshade of fear that will result in them meeting Jesus and finding everlasting life? Maybe it is the lampshades of compromise or apathy that need to be thrown away? If so, let us dare to lose them so that our lives can be all He called them to be: those cities set on a hill. It's time to shine!

Champion's Prayer:

Father, help me today to get my lampshade off and shine for You my very brightest. Empower my life again by Your Spirit to be the living advertisement board You need it to be, a walking talking advertising board for You and Your kingdom, not for religion or self – Amen.

Twinkle, twinkle little star

Do everything without complaining or arguing, so that you may become blameless and pure, children of God without fault in a crooked and depraved generation, in which you shine like stars in the universe.
Philippians 2:14-15 (NIV)

Yesterday we spoke about being the light-bearers that God has called us to be, daring to lose every lampshade that may dull His light coming from our lives. We also spoke about coming out of the closet with the purpose of being a *"city on a hill"* for Him.

He has called us all to shine and stand out in a crooked and depraved generation, not blend in. We are living in days where wickedness is certainly on the increase and all around us we see people losing their fire-like love for God, often exchanging it for the love of other inviting pleasures and lesser things that seem good to their soul. These times were foretold and we must soberly understand where in history we are and be motivated to be what He has destined us to be: light-bearers.

"And many false prophets will appear and deceive many people. Because of the increase of wickedness, the love of most will grow cold, but he who stands firm to the end will be saved."
Matthew 24:11-13 (NIV)

Wickedness increasing in the world should actually define us and cause us to look like stars in a universe, not cause us to be lost in the haze of unrighteousness. Our verse today gives us a lovely picture of what God sees when He looks over the banister of eternity. Yes, He sees an ocean of wickedness on the earth but then He sees us, those with the light of Christ in them, shining like stars in a dark, night sky.

We, shining like stars and not blending in like hypocrites, cause the darkness to be disturbed. Just as darkness was confounded, confused and driven out by Christ, so it is today when we decide to live lives that shine for God. Don't become obsessed with present darkness that won't produce anything but rather consider the presence of His light in you and the effect that has on a sin-darkened world – then arise and shine for your light has come!

When the world gets darker we get brighter. Like that lighthouse in troubled seas, may our lives so shine that they lead others out of danger and into the safe harbour of knowing God.

Be a worshipper first of all

Now as the ark of the LORD came into the City of David, Michal, Saul's daughter, looked through a window and saw King David leaping and whirling before the LORD; and she despised him in her heart.

2 Samuel 6:16 (NKJV)

D avid was, indeed, a great king, leader and warrior but he was also a passionate worshipper. I believe the first great thing he was in life was a great worshipper. As a young man, he spent years sitting on a hillside as a shepherd and, in that time, he developed a passion inside him for worshipping God. He was wise and, even when he was king, he lived a life of worship because he knew where God had brought him from and what God had done for him and, indeed, was now doing through him. We also always need to remember where God has brought us from and what He has done for us and promised for us. When we do, that should be more than enough to ignite authentic worship to Him.

Some people, namely David's wife Michal, did not appreciate his passion for worship. Did that stop him? No way! He knew his worship was not for her or about her but it was about his God. I am so grateful that when he was confronted about his 'offensive' worship lifestyle he did not back down; far from it, he actually announced he would be getting a lot worse!

So David said to Michal, "It was before the LORD, who chose me instead of your father and all his house, to appoint me ruler over the people of the LORD, over Israel. Therefore I will play music before the LORD. And I will be even more undignified than this, and will be humble in my own sight."

2 Samuel 6:21-22 (NKJV)

Like David, the worshipping warrior, make sure you are not allowing people or stuff to cause you to tone down your worship. Rather, like David, have future plans to be even more undignified and passionate! Like David, make sure your worship ever flows from the knowledge and remembrance of, firstly, who He is and then all that He has done for you. Like David, above every other title that man can give to you, set your heart on being known as a passionate worshipper. If you get that right then every other position and title will naturally come to you by God's doing and appointment. Like David, worship God as the One who sees in you what others can't see.

David must have been continually amazed that, when others only ever saw a shepherd boy, God saw a king. Champion, give God your best worship again today and don't let anyone hold you back.

Do you stand with the worshippers?

Then, as He was now drawing near the descent of the Mount of Olives, the whole multitude of the disciples began to rejoice and praise God with a loud voice for all the mighty works they had seen, saying, "Blessed is the King who comes in the name of the LORD! Peace in heaven and glory in the highest!" And some of the Pharisees called to Him from the crowd, "Teacher, rebuke Your disciples." But He answered and said to them, "I tell you that if these should keep silent, the stones would immediately cry out."

Luke 19:37-40 (NKJV)

I suppose the challenge here is "What side of the road are you going to stand on when it comes to giving Jesus the worship He deserves?"

Jesus entered the great city of Jerusalem and, as He did, there were a bunch of everyday people on one side that praised Him passionately with loud, unashamed voices, while on the other side of the street there were a bunch of religious folk that chose not to join in but rather stand and judge what was happening. When it came to the moment of someone getting corrected for their wrong or unfitting behaviour, notice that it was the religious, 'please turn it down' posse that got it straight between the eyes, not the everyday worshippers.

Imagine, that with all their religious knowledge, they could not recognise or appreciate God in their very midst while, at the exact same moment, every day people who had had lives changed by Him could not hold back from giving Him what He was due. I pray I am always found with the people who are passionately worshipping and never with the ones complaining, judging and moaning about sound levels. How about you?

Finally, my other choice concerning worship is that I am never going to let an insignificant stone take my place. Jesus is destined to be worshipped and what He was saying here is, if we don't voice worship to God, then something else in creation will. My response to this is that I am not going to give away the awesome privilege of worshipping my King to any other person and especially not a rock!

Today, take a moment to celebrate His presence in your life. Today, He rides through the alleyways and roads of the Jerusalem of your life. He wanders down the *Via Dolarosa* of your soul. Make sure that, at every corner, your life is giving Him the praise He is due. Bless you, live extra large today.

Be an all-season worshipper

So David arose from the ground, washed and anointed himself, and changed his clothes; and he went into the house of the LORD and worshipped. Then he went to his own house; and when he requested, they set food before him, and he ate.

2 Samuel 12:20 (NKJV)

Worship is something we choose to do in every season of life. For most of us, when we were first saved we learned to worship when everything was going well but often we would stop when it looked like things were not going so well. It is when we grow up a bit more in God that we learn to be an 'all-season worshipper'. We read earlier this week about King David worshipping the Lord in a time of great celebration as they brought the ark of God's presence back into the city. That was truly a great time to 'get your praise on'. Today, we read an account of David worshipping, not from a high mountain top but from a very deep valley!

You have to fully understand what had just happened to see the power of his worship on this occasion. This is just moments after the child he had had by his affair with Bathsheba had died. He had spent a long time fasting and crying out to God to save the child he had produced in sin but the child died. His servants were scared to tell him of the child's death, fearing a bad reaction – but they were surprised by his response when they did. He did not go into a rage but rather got up, washed and went to God's house and worshipped. David was indeed an 'all-season worshipper'. Even though things did not go as he wanted, he still worshipped and that's a big challenge, isn't it? What do you do when things don't turn out like you think they should?

He worshipped because his trust was in the Lord. He fully trusted God even beyond what he knew or could reason. When you trust God, worship flows through every season; when things make sense and when they don't. When my mum passed away I couldn't understand why – it certainly was not the result I wanted. But one thing I did do was take David's example and when I left the hospice, I went to the House of the Lord and worshipped. Why? Because I trust Him and, like David, I know that it is in the place of worship that my heart and life are made strong again. Every one of us will go through the different seasons of life; purpose not to be a good-time worshipper only but resolve in your heart that, like David, you will worship Him on the mountain tops, in the valleys and even in the wilderness. Worship displays your trust in Him! Worship is the lifestyle we choose to live, not an event we may attend

Food for thought:

He is the God of every season of your life. Don't just worship Him on the mountain tops (when everything is great) but also in the valleys and the wilderness times too. He is Lord in them all and with you in them all!

God wants you to handle miracles

Late in the afternoon the Twelve came to him and said, "Send the crowd away so they can go to the surrounding villages and countryside and find food and lodging, because we are in a remote place here." He replied, "You give them something to eat." They answered, "We have only five loaves of bread and two fish — unless we go and buy food for all this crowd" (about five thousand men were there). But he said to his disciples, "Have them sit down in groups of about fifty each." The disciples did so, and everybody sat down. Taking the five loaves and the two fish and looking up to heaven, he gave thanks and broke them. Then he gave them to the disciples to set before the people. They all ate and were satisfied, and the disciples picked up twelve basketfuls of broken pieces that were left over.

Luke 9:12-17 (NIV)

Here is the classic account of Jesus taking five loaves and two fish then multiplying them miraculously to feed a multitude of people. We do not know exactly how many. We know that there were about five thousand men, now add wives and children – we can safely say it was a very big need. The disciples' plan was to break up this life-changing event and send the people out to get their own food. This was actually good crowd management but not what Jesus had in mind for the moment at hand. Jesus had a much more dynamic response to this situation.

His plan served two purposes

Firstly, it would take care of the physical needs of the people because Jesus was genuinely concerned for the welfare of His listeners' physical condition and not just their spiritual one, unlike many of the Pharisees. Secondly, He wanted to use this great opportunity to get His team to feel what miracles felt like in their hands! Jesus had felt miracles in His hands for many months as He demonstrated the power of God to change situations for people. Now He wanted to graduate His disciples to a higher level of experience. So this day, right in the middle of a demanding moment, Jesus says, "I am not doing it, I am going to pray – then it is down to you boys!" He prayed, handed them the supplies then sat back and watched. As the seemingly little bits of bread and fish left the hands of the disciples, they multiplied supernaturally to become exceedingly and abundantly more than what was needed for the moment. Where did this miracle happen? **In the disciples' hands!**

Listen, Champion, God wants to graduate us today from being spectators of miracles, which is good , to experiencing them in our hands and our lives, which is great! What if the disciples got scared and chose not to join in? They would have missed out on handling miracles for themselves. If we don't join in with Jesus when we have the opportunity, we will miss out on handling miracles too. All God needs is willing, courageous hands and a little bit of something to supernaturally increase. How about you? Are you going to let Him do it through your hands today? Remember, all things are possible to those who believe.

Live in your revealed identity

By faith Moses, when he was born, was hidden three months by his parents, because they saw he was a beautiful child; and they were not afraid of the king's command. By faith Moses, when he became of age, refused to be called the son of Pharaoh's daughter.

Hebrews 11:23-24 (NKJV)

The life of Moses makes for an interesting read. It's another one of those God-inspired life adventures. Moses is born to parents who are Levites, a part of Israel; as a baby, to save him from Pharaoh's child-murdering plans, his parents set him afloat in a basket on the Nile, strategically aiming him for the courts of Pharaoh. Pharaoh's daughter finds him and raises him as her own.

He grows up in the household and kingdom of Egypt thinking that this was his true identity, living by their ways and beliefs although, I believe, he always sensed all was not right and something deep inside of him never sat completely well with it, always feeling a little different. One day, someone reveals to him that he is actually not an Egyptian but a part of Israel, God's people. He discovers the nurse that cared for him was actually his real mother. Wow, what a day that must have been!

Now he has a choice to make: he has been raised as one person but that is not who he really is. He makes the choice to stand up as the person he really is and his life goes in a whole new direction.

When you read this account there are things that we can relate to. Each of us has been raised in a kingdom to which we thought we belonged; daily we joined in with all its ways and beliefs. Then, one day, we find out we actually belong to God and were separated by what Adam did at the dawn of time. When we realise this fact, we then have a choice, as Moses did. Do we keep on acting and living in accordance with the life we were raised in or do we step out and decide to be, from this point on, who we really are?

If we stand up and live according to our true identity, our lives too will take a new direction. Yes, it may even attract persecution and cause challenge but, at the end of the day, like Moses, you will know you are now being the person that you really are not the one you were raised to be.

God is your real Father and through Jesus you have been re-united. Be who you really are – like Moses, refuse to be called any longer what you are not.

Champion's Prayer:

Father, thank You that I now know who I really am and to whom I truly belong. Help me to shake off and walk away from every lesser identity and arise and stand in my true identity. Thank You that my family line is very short: there is You, then me. You are my father and I am Your child, Your kingdom is my true home – Amen.

Live in the measurements of God

For as high as the heavens are above the earth, so great is his love for those who fear him; as far as the east is from the west, so far has he removed our transgressions from us

Psalm 103:11-12 (NIV)

In this *Psalm*, we are given two God-ordained measurements that, when we get a revelation of them, have the potential to change our lives forever.

The first measurement deals with the incredible vastness of His love towards us, – *"as high as the heavens are above the earth"*. If you're able to, why not take a moment to stick your head out of the window and look up. Can you see the heavens? Can you work out that measurement from the heavens to earth? No. Well, in the same way, His love is far beyond what you will ever have the human ability to measure.

Look at the interesting terminology here in this verse, *"as far as the heavens are from the earth"*. I was walking today and thinking about how extreme that measurement is and I felt the Lord say to me, "That is the length of the journey Jesus travelled to save you." Wow, it's true. Think about that, for love's sake, Jesus laid aside His crown of majesty in the heavens to come save you and me on the earth. That's a long way and that's big love!

Let's look at the same thought put another way by Paul the Apostle.

For I am convinced that neither death nor life, neither angels nor demons, neither the present nor the future, nor any powers, neither height nor depth, nor anything else in all creation, will be able to separate us from the love of God that is in Christ Jesus our LORD.
Romans 8:38-39 (NIV)

God's love is not small, breakable or fallible. Reside again today in that love that can neither be broken or humanly measured as Paul did. Know deep in your heart that nothing has the ability to separate you from it. God's love is a stable love that you can build your life upon. He is not sitting in a field with a daisy, plucking off its petals, saying "I love you, I love you not". His mind is made up about you and His love was demonstrated in what and who He gave to get you. Don't spend your time evaluating it, rather, throw off every restraint and bathe in it.

Food for thought:

In challenging times, don't absorb fear but release faith.

Live in the measurements of God (cont'd)

For as high as the heavens are above the earth, so great is his love for those who fear him; as far as the east is from the west, so far has he removed our transgressions from us.

Psalm 103:11-12 (NIV)

We looked yesterday at the measurement of God's love towards us who fear Him. I don't know about you, but I was both very blessed and very impressed.

The same Psalm mentions a second measurement that has equal potential to redefine and revolutionise your walk with God and your day-to-day experience of this thing called Christianity. It is the measurement concerning the extent of God's forgiveness toward our sins and transgressions. How forgiven are we and what's the measurement for it?

According to God's Word, the measurement for the removal of our sins is *"as far as the east is from the west"*. Would you be able to measure that? No, nor would I because that's a long way. Let's face it, there is bound to be some bright spark right now that could give the exact measurement of the divide between the east and the west of planet earth but the reality is, He is actually speaking of a one-way moving direction which is, in fact, endless. Like when you fly around the globe, it's a direction not a measuring point.

Here is my other thought. What if God was not speaking of the measurements of a single planet like earth but rather the entire universe? Now that really is a big, old measurement. It makes sense to me because the measurement He used to describe the size of His love for us left the limiting boundaries of just planet earth, *"as high as the heavens are above the earth"* so why would the boundaries of His forgiveness of our sins not follow the same track? I suppose the choice is yours, whether to define what is meant by east and west as the earth or the universe. I will go ahead and choose the universe because, in that option, is the possibility of infinity!

The bottom line this morning is to realise and accept that Jesus did a fantastic job of settling the sin issue for you by providing His life as settlement for its full requirements and, in doing so, He removed sin far, far away. Righteousness reigns where there is no sin, so go ahead and, today, let righteousness reign in your life! Think about those two measurements and apply them to your life today and tomorrow and hey, why not the rest of your life?

Champion's Prayer:

Father, thank You for the measurement of Your love towards me and also of the distance my sins have been removed. Thank You that You love me and are for me. Thank You that You are not some abusive ogre, ever trying to catch me out, rather a father, ever willing me forwards to greater things. Help me to live in Your measurement and not the lesser ones that man offers – Amen.

First things first

For the pagans run after all these things, and your heavenly Father knows that you need them. But seek first his kingdom and his righteousness, and all these things will be given to you as well. Therefore do not worry about tomorrow, for tomorrow will worry about itself. Each day has enough trouble of its own.

Matthew 6:32-34 (NIV)

It is not a wrong thing to seek after certain things in life but you must always determine to make the greatest seeking in your life God's kingdom and His righteousness; to seek Him first. When you do, God promises that everything else you need will be added to your life by His hand.

The verses above start by giving us a warning of what we are not to be like: it says that we should not be like those who don't know God, *"pagans"*, who spend their lives, and often give their lives, to obtain what they think they need to be complete in life. Rather, realise that you are already complete in Him and when you dedicate your life to seeking and knowing the King and advancing His kingdom, you actually live every day from a starting point of completeness and success.

Notice also it says that God knows both what we need and what we want and, as you make Him the greatest thing you seek and pursue, He will go ahead and make sure that your life has everything it needs added to it. This gives us all the same common choice again today: will we spend our lives striving to get the stuff we think we need or will we make God our number one pursuit and watch Him keep His promise and freely add to us all He knows we need?

Then it finishes with the important thought concerning not worrying. The way to end worry is simply to trust in God; trust Him concerning the unknown life you are yet to live. Each of us can enter into the next day with confidence rather than fear when we have made these promises our reality – "God, as I seek You first in my life, I trust You to add to me all that I have need of, whether that be material, relational or spiritual."

Hey, Champion, don't kill yourself trying to get what God wants to freely give to you – just go ahead and seek Him first!

Champion's Prayer:

Father, today I declare that You are my greatest seek. I will seek first You and Your kingdom. Thank You that, as I do, You will add to me all the things that You know I need and want. Help me to always keep You at the top of the list when it comes to the things I am seeking. Thank You that I do not have to worry but simply live each day for You – Amen.

When you pray 'be yourself'

And when you come before God, don't turn that into a theatrical production either. All these people making a regular show out of their prayers, hoping for stardom! Do you think God sits in a box seat? "Here's what I want you to do: Find a quiet, secluded place so you won't be tempted to role-play before God. Just be there as simply and honestly as you can manage. The focus will shift from you to God, and you will begin to sense his grace." The world is full of so-called prayer warriors who are prayer-ignorant. They're full of formulas and programs and advice, peddling techniques for getting what you want from God. Don't fall for that nonsense. This is your Father you are dealing with, and he knows better than you what you need.

Matthew 6:5-15 (The Message)

Hey, Champion, let's talk about our personal prayer lives. Prayer can, of course, take many forms and have differing expressions. It's a big old subject. Today, I am not talking about your church prayer meetings or any other public-type prayer expressions, I am talking about your personal one, that one-on-one time you have with your heavenly Father. We should all have 'grand designs' concerning this and if we want to build an effective, healthy prayer life with God then it is good to remind ourselves of some real basic truths:

Prayer is communication

To me, the true success of growing in your walk with God lies in understanding the fact that it is not a religion rather a relationship; a living relationship with the creator of your life and lover of your soul, the One who knows you and has always known and loved you. As with the development of any other relationship in your life, the key to your relationship with God, experiencing desired health and growth, is dependent upon communication – talking and listening. Just as a married couple will never grow correctly together if they never communicate, so it is with the relationship that you have with God. It is vital that we are effectively communicating with Him and allowing Him to communicate back so that this relationship we have begun can ever be maturing and developing with greater confidence and intimacy.

God does not want you to impersonate someone else you saw pray well once! He wants you to be you and, believe me, He really can handle you being you. Remember, God is not giving you points for a great performance – this is not a talent show! Rather, He desires to connect and communicate with you, heart to heart. When you read through the gospels you see that Jesus had a problem with the performance, hypocrisy and pretence of the Pharisee, not the honest cries of everyday folk. Be honest; God can handle the truth and can't be shocked by you or how you may be feeling. Let Him know what you love and hate, what makes you happy and what causes you sadness. As with Jeremiah, He has known you from before you were born; He did not suddenly notice you when you got saved. When we understand this, we can throw away every dusty, wrong-fitting costume that religion and ignorance have convinced us to stupidly wear.

When you pray, 'find your groove'

And when you pray, do not be like the hypocrites, for they love to pray standing in the synagogues and on the street corners to be seen by men. I tell you the truth, they have received their reward in full. But when you pray, go into your room, close the door and pray to your Father, who is unseen. Then your Father, who sees what is done in secret, will reward you. And when you pray, do not keep on babbling like pagans, for they think they will be heard because of their many words. Do not be like them, for your Father knows what you need before you ask him.

Matthew 6:5-8 (NIV)

Our personal prayer life with our God should be exactly that: 'a personal thing'. So personal, in fact, that we realise and enjoy the fact that it will be different to other people's in certain ways and this is OK! God wants your 'one-on-one time' with Him to be unique to you and Him because then it will also have authenticity to it and not be some religious ceremony. He has made us all very different, which means the way we enjoy spending time with Him and communicating with Him is likely to differ from each other.

It's a bit like dancing

When it comes to dancing, every person has to find their own style or groove. There are certain general moves that you can imitate but it is when you add the 'you' factor to your dancing that it truly becomes unique, alive and original (that may look good for some and bad for others!). Prayer is like this – we may do certain things in common because they work well for all but there should also be a personal touch to it. This is what makes it unique and real.

Or like buying a new suit

When it comes to our prayer life, the truth is that it is like a man getting himself a new suit: he can go for an 'off the peg' one from a department store, where you get one that kind of fits all people who are about your size and shape, or you can go for 'tailor made' where your suit is made to fit you perfectly and looks good on you when you're wearing it. I believe that your prayer life finds its fullest potential when it is 'tailor made' rather than having one just like someone else's.

Prayer is the incredible privilege to discover and develop an intimate relationship with your God that is unique and authentic – go for it. Designing a prayer life that is 'tailor made' always fits and looks much better than an 'off the peg' one ever will and is far more enjoyable and natural to wear on a day-to-day basis. Yes, be inspired by other people's methods and habits but then take time to design your own prayer life. Answer some simple questions for yourself, like: when fits you best? Where do you find it easier to pray? Do you like a lot of worship? Do you read the Bible during it? These are a few of the many questions you can ask if you really desire to design a prayer life you love to live in. Be yourself and find your own groove. Remember, He wants authenticity not performance, reality rather than entertainment!

When you pray, 'get positioned right'

The effective, fervent prayer of a righteous man avails much.

James 5:16 (NKJV)

W e have been looking at developing effective, authentic prayer lives. We have defined prayer as simply communication and reminded ourselves that God wants us to be who we are and to avoid all religious performances.

Today, let us consider the position we are to use when we pray. You will be glad to know I am not referring to being on your knees, lying on the floor or any other physical position but rather your spiritual position. When you pray, you need to pray from the position of righteousness – being righteous. I'm not talking of the stance of self-righteousness that holds for us no confidence at all, rather the position of 'inherent righteousness' – that we have been made righteous by God. In Christ, we have received the right standing we need as a gift, not a wage or achievement. If we never deal with this simple, yet profound truth, we will never have confidence in our approach and God wants us to have bold confidence when we come to pray and communicate with Him.

> *Let us therefore come boldly to the throne of grace, that we may obtain mercy and find grace to help in time of need.*
>
> Hebrews 4:16 (NKJV)

Boldness or confidence can only be a reality when you know you stand before God, forgiven of all sin and justified – made innocent in His sight. We can all have this confidence when we consider and believe the facts that our righteousness is not the result of our performance (law-based) but rather a free gift from God (grace-based). Jesus initiated a divine exchange when He hung on the cross two thousand years ago. Everything we were – guilty, sinful, shamed – He took upon Himself and everything He was – innocent, righteous – He gave to us. Sound too good to be true? Read it for yourself:

> *For He made Him who knew no sin to be sin for us, that we might become the righteousness of God in Him.*
>
> 2 Corinthians 5:21 (NKJV)

So, stop trying to earn by imperfect performance that which has been given because of His perfect sacrifice. The righteousness that is needed to give us confidence to stand before God knowing we belong and are welcome comes only by placing faith in what Jesus accomplished on our behalf two thousand years ago. When we position ourselves in His righteousness, which is outside of our efforts, we stand in that which is not fallible or random but rather constant and, from this position, we have confidence to approach God in prayer boldly in time of need or anytime we want to, expectant of mercy and grace, not judgment!

When you pray – speak the language that pleases Him

But without faith it is impossible to please Him, for he who comes to God must believe that He is, and that He is a rewarder of those who diligently seek Him.

Hebrews 11:6 (NKJV)

It's true that we enter His gates with thanksgiving and His courts with praise but we attract and keep His attention with **faith**. God loves faith, He takes pleasure in His people approaching Him with confidence, knowing the righteousness that is theirs in Christ, daily placing child-like trust in Him. The Bible never encourages us to come to Him in prayer whining or moaning or letting Him know how big our problems are. God takes pleasure when we come to Him agreeing with His Word and promises about what will happen in the situations we are going through.

Dad, you said!

Every parent hears this statement on a regular basis from their children – you make a promise or agree to do something and then forget you made it. But your kids don't, right? No. When you least expect it, you suddenly here those famous words, "Dad, you said!" What's happening is they are holding you to your word because they know your integrity is at stake. To any parent, this can be so annoying but, guess what? God actually wants us to do this to Him. He does not mind or get offended when we quote His Word or promises back to Him. He actually invites us to because everything He will ever do is found in the boundaries of His given Word. When you pray in faith, you must pray in accordance to what He has already promised you in and through Christ.

For as the rain comes down, and the snow from heaven, and do not return there, but water the earth, and make it bring forth and bud, that it may give seed to the sower and bread to the eater, so shall My word be that goes forth from My mouth; It shall not return to Me void, but it shall accomplish what I please, and it shall prosper in the thing for which I sent it.
Isaiah 55:10-12 (NKJV)

His Word will not return without effect but will accomplish and prosper in our real life situations. God knows what you are going through; He is not after further information or facts from you. He wants you to believe in what He is able to do and to come into agreement with His promise for what you may be facing, **especially** when it does not make sense to you. Remember, *Hebrews 11* teaches us that faith is the substance and evidence of things not seen; it is, in itself, all the evidence we need to stand with confidence in each and everything we may face. God is pleased when we relate to Him with the language of faith. It both attracts His attention and keeps it.

Delighting in His Word will prosper you

Blessed is the man who does not walk in the counsel of the wicked or stand in the way of sinners or sit in the seat of mockers. But his delight is in the law of the LORD, and on his law he meditates day and night. He is like a tree planted by streams of water, which yields its fruit in season and whose leaf does not wither. Whatever he does prospers.

Psalm 1:1-3 (NIV)

A nother great *Psalm* that promises so much to the person who will commit to delight and meditate, not in the wisdom of the ungodly, but in the "*law of the Lord*". As we have established many times in this devotional, we are no longer under the law but under grace and positioned in Christ by our faith, in His grace, not our works. So how does this word or promise apply to us today?

In two ways. We may no longer be under the law contained within the Old Testament as it was fulfilled by Jesus perfectly but we should still daily remain under the teachings of its truth and wisdom, living to daily apply the incredible principles of God found within each of its pages. The Word, i.e. the Bible, will always do your life good and cause your life to flourish as you submit to it. Why? Because the Bible is a living book that is jammed full of God's thoughts and ways and, when you clearly understand the covenants, what's relevant and what's not to your life, and know how to apply the truth of His Word to your life, it will always cause an outbreak of life and blessing in every part you expose it too.

If we change the word "*law*" for "Word of God", it holds the same power of promise for us today. God's Word is good for your life when you daily delight in it and mediate on it – your life will consistently experience incredible blessing and flourishing and go from strength to strength.

Another thing to consider is Jesus Himself. The Bible refers to Him as the "*Word of God made flesh*".

The Word became flesh and made his dwelling among us. We have seen his glory, the glory of the One and Only, who came from the Father, full of grace and truth.

John 1:14 (NIV)

Because Jesus is the Word of God made flesh, as we behold Him daily, we are beholding the Word of God. As we daily gaze upon Jesus, delight in Him and meditate on Him, we are actually delighting and mediating on the Word of God as He instructed us to and that will cause your life to flourish and prosper so you will be like that promised tree that is planted by the river, ever bearing fruit even into old age.

Have a Dependence Day!

Then the serpent said to the woman, "You will not surely die. For God knows that in the day you eat of it your eyes will be opened, and you will be like God, knowing good and evil." So when the woman saw that the tree was good for food, that it was pleasant to the eyes, and a tree desirable to make one wise, she took of its fruit and ate. She also gave to her husband with her, and he ate.

Genesis 3:4-6 (NKJV)

Every fourth of July, America celebrates Independence Day: a federal holiday when the whole nation remembers and honours the moment in history when it separated itself from the rule and governing hand of the nation of Britain. It was back in 1776 when America declared their independence from British rule and became autonomous. This meant that they were now responsible for themselves having concluded they knew how to better govern their own lives and future.

In *Genesis 3*, we read of another 'independence day' only this one would actually sink all of humanity into a spin, leaving all of us in need of redemption by a loving God. Satan deceived Adam and Eve into believing that they needed something other than what they had under God's care. The truth was that they did not. The governing or oversight of God their Creator had bountifully provided everything they needed or could ever want. They daily resided in the garden of His grace, provision and protection.

Sadly, they believed the devil-inspired lie that they could be like God and could get something they were 'missing out on'. When they believed the lie and took the fruit they were tempted with, they disobeyed the Lord and, in doing so, chose independence or autonomy from His rule and government. They yielded to an, "I will do it my way" nature and thought they knew better. That is when it all started going so wrong for them and all of humanity that was represented in them. The good news, of course, is that, through the obedience of Jesus Christ, the rebellion of Adam and Eve has been repaired and we are no longer independent of His grace, protection and covering us and, let's face it, who would really want to be?

It is good to remind ourselves of the fact that we are no longer independent, self-governed mutineers but rather Kingdom people living again dependant on the daily goodness and promises of our heavenly Father. Live dependant on Him today.

Pledge allegiance to the Lamb

For our citizenship is in heaven, from which we also eagerly wait for the Saviour, the LORD *Jesus Christ, who will transform our lowly body that it may be conformed to His glorious body, according to the working by which He is able even to subdue all things to Himself.*

Philippians 3:20-21 (NKJV)

Through placing faith in Jesus Christ, we have become citizens of His kingdom, a kingdom without an end. It is to the King of that kingdom that we should daily give our service, submission and allegiance.

Here is a good question: "Who and what are you pledging your allegiance to today?"

Staying with the American theme from yesterday, another ceremony that Americans have had for many years is one of pledging allegiance to flag and country. This ceremony, which is now also carried out in the UK, happens when someone comes to America from another nation and purposes in his or her heart to make the new nation their homeland or place of residence.

After the process of application and immigration, a special ceremony takes place where you stand before the flag and, raising your right hand, pledge your allegiance to the nation of America. These days, Americans can hold dual nationality with another nation but when it was first instituted, you could not. You had to choose one nation or the other. You would stand and renounce your allegiance to the kingdom you came from, thereby disassociating yourself from it, and then pledge allegiance to the one you desired now to be a part of.

Spiritually, this is exactly what happened to us at salvation. We all came from another kingdom, the kingdom of darkness, into a new kingdom, the Kingdom of the Son of His love. We too are called to renounce the governing rule and influence of our former spiritual citizenship, darkness, to adopt and submit to the governing rule of the new one, light. It is when we do not do this with an absolute heart that we get into a lot of trouble with things like compromise.

The fact is, we are called to now be citizens of God's kingdom, pledging our lifelong allegiance to the King of that kingdom: Jesus, the Lamb of God.

As we do, we walk away from autonomous, self-governing rebellion and walk into a citizenship of total dependence upon God. We become as Adam was originally designed to be: reliant on our God for all we need. That may sound a scary place but it is actually the very safest place you could ever know.

What He started, He will finish!

Looking unto Jesus, the author and finisher of our faith, who for the joy that was set before Him endured the cross, despising the shame, and has sat down at the right hand of the throne of God.

Hebrews 12:2 (NKJV)

Throughout the Bible, Jesus is called many things, each describing another wonderful facet of both who He is and what He does. Here, we see a truly great one: He is the Author and Finisher of your faith.

We know that this verse speaks about the context of our salvation but think about it also in the context of that situation you may be experiencing right now in your life. God starts by giving you a promise concerning the thing you are going through or hoping for – that makes Him the author. But God is also the one who will see that promise through to its total fulfilment – that makes Him the finisher too.

Maybe you are in the middle bit right now – you have a God-breathed promise but you have not seen it yet come to pass and you say, "Andy, I just don't 'feel God'." Then make the quality decision to not live by your feelings but by the revealed truth of His word – He says He is the Author and Finisher which means He has not left you and will not quit on fulfilling that promise He authored until it is totally complete. This should cause both faith and assurance to rush into your soul and peace to return even in the very midst of the storm.

Let's look at this guarantee in another verse.

Being confident of this very thing, that He who has begun a good work in you will complete it until the day of Jesus Christ.

Philippians 1:6 (NKJV)

He starts the breakthrough in your situation with His promise and finishes it in accordance to His faithfulness; He is not quitting, so make sure you don't either! Just as He did not get off the cross till it was finished, so He won't quit on anything else He has authored by a promise.

Champion's Confession:

Thank You, Father, that You, who have begun a good work in me, will finish it. It is You who starts things by Your grace and brings them to fulfilment by Your faithfulness. Today, I submit to Your plans and, as I do, I will see things both started and finished by Your hand.

Walking on what He has promised

*Then as He entered a certain village, there met Him ten men who were lepers, who stood afar off.
And they lifted up their voices and said, "Jesus, Master, have mercy on us!" So when He saw them, He
said to them, "Go, show yourselves to the priests." And so it was that as they went, they were cleansed.*
Luke 17:12-14 (NKJV)

We live in a world that teaches us from an early age that **seeing** is believing but then we are born again into a kingdom that teaches us that actually it is our **believing** which causes us to see and experience things. Remember, you being completely saved and made perfectly fit for Heaven is the result of you believing before you see.

Here we see ten needy lepers approach Jesus and ask for a miracle. As always, Jesus was delighted to help them but notice He did not do it for them then and there but rather told them to go and show themselves to the priests: this was requirement of the law of Moses for them to be allowed back into society. The Bible says that as they went, they were cleansed. They had no evidence, they had not seen their skin change, yet all ten of them chose to live beyond what could be seen. They chose to trust the words that had been spoken to them by Jesus.

Think about it, what if they had argued with Him, "Oi! Before we go anywhere, we want to see some evidence."? Nothing would have happened. It was these men daring to walk away without seeing anything that activated what had been promised to them. They walked away standing on the promise of Jesus and that was all they had but also all they needed. We need to ever understand that the promises of Jesus, those words He speaks today to us, are all we need to walk away from our prayer times with confidence, even when, 'naturally', nothing looks different.

First we believe and then we see. What are you believing for today? Walk confident as the lepers did. Get a promise from God for your situation and walk away holding it. Mix faith with that promise and anything can happen at any moment. But you may say "I still need some evidence and something of substance".

Remember that *Hebrews 11:1* says that faith is both the substance and evidence for everything you are hoping and believing God for.

The planted will flourish

Those who are planted in the house of the LORD shall flourish in the courts of our God. They shall still bear fruit in old age; They shall be fresh and flourishing.

Psalm 92:13-14 (NKJV)

The local church is *"the House of the Lord"* and God still loves His Church. When you commit to let your life be planted in it, you set yourself up to get blessed and to flourish throughout your life. Being planted means you are not popping in to visit anymore but rather unpacking your spiritual suitcases and calling it home. In these verses, God uses gardening terminology to help us to see how He desires for us to relate to His house, the local church. Notice that the promise of a flourishing life belongs to those who plant themselves in and not those who casually visit.

Any gardener will tell you it is when a plant is unpotted and bedded into the soil of the flower bed that it can begin to draw on the nutrients that the soil has to offer it. If you casually rest a potted plant, still in its pot, on a flower bed it cannot benefit from all the goodness the soil has for it although, in regard to location, it is so very close. It is the same with how we relate to His house. We need to get planted in so that our roots can go down and spread out, to draw on the goodness of the ground.

Great promises for the "planted"

- You will have a life that shall continue to bear fruit and be 'highly productive', even into your old age.

- Your life will remain fresh, vibrant and flourishing while others around you fade away.

The local church is, and will always be, God's divine flower bed. Find a life-filled local church and plant yourself into it and you will see incredible growth in every area of your life. Plant your family into it and watch Godly vibrancy and flourishing break out in them also. Remember, a life-filled local church remains God's master plan for changing the world and it is the only thing He has committed to build on the earth *(Matthew 16:18)*.

Bless you. I pray you get planted in your local church and stay planted. Remember, it is a two way relationship; you need the church but the church also needs you. It needs you to bring what you are. Like a part of an engine or an individual muscle of an athlete's body, you can be a vital part to making God's house run and function to its best potential. So don't hold back. When you plant yourself in and stay planted with a servant attitude, church becomes an even more effective place and, as God promised, your life will flourish too!

Blessed are those who...?

Blessed are those whose strength is in you, who have set their hearts on pilgrimage. As they pass through the Valley of Baca, they make it a place of springs; the autumn rains also cover it with pools. They go from strength to strength, till each appears before God in Zion.

Psalm 84:5-7 (NIV)

I have been considering how pilgrimage affects so many areas of our lives; also, how it is not a bad thing but, more often than not, a God-designed thing for our lives.

Here are some thoughts for you: "What is it to pilgrimage?" you may ask. The word pilgrimage means 'to journey', so when God speaks of pilgrimage in this Psalm He is saying, "Blessed is the person who sets his heart on journeying" and that is so true, especially when it comes to our walk or journeying with God. Blessed, daily, is the person who sets his heart on journeying with the Lord. Other faiths in the world have a spiritual pilgrimage mentality but theirs are always to physical places and landmarks, like Mecca and Lourdes, but it is not to be that way for us. Our pilgrimage is to a person – the person of Jesus – ever towards a deeper relationship with Him.

Christianity is not meant to be something or somewhere you totally arrive at instantly. In one way, yes, in the fact that when we believe, we receive from God everything we are going to get, His *"fullness" (John 1:16)*. But in another way, no, because we are called to spend the rest of our days, *"till each appears before God in Zion"*, journeying into everything He has given us, to understanding and embracing all that He has done and given to us in Christ. God wants us to "Keep on movin'." We are not to be parked cars but ever-moving ones that walk, like Abraham, into all the promises and intentions God has for our lives.

So, our pilgrimage does not end when we reach a historical landmark because, if it did, how sad would that be? You would be left thinking, "What next?" No, God commits to walk with us each and every day on this pilgrimage that He has called us to and every day it gets better and better. It's when we set our hearts to journey with the Lord that we learn all that we need to and He is revealed to us so we know Him closer and more intimately as the miles of our days pass by.

Think about those two disciples that walked with the freshly risen Jesus on the road to Emmaus (*Luke 24*). For some reason Jesus had not allowed them to recognise Him but appeared as someone they did not know. It was as they walked with Him that He made the mysteries of the scriptures easily understood and then it was during the journey that He revealed Himself to them.

As we set our hearts to journeying with the Lord, He also helps us to daily understand His mysteries and daily reveals Himself to us, as He did to those two disciples and He causes our hearts to burn within us, as their hearts did in them.

Journeying with God

Blessed are those whose strength is in you, who have set their hearts on pilgrimage. As they pass through the Valley of Baca, they make it a place of springs; the autumn rains also cover it with pools. They go from strength to strength, till each appears before God in Zion.

Psalm 84:5-7 (NIV)

We spent time with this one yesterday and established that blessed, happy and empowered to prosper is the person that sets their heart on pilgrimage or journeying, especially those whose heart is set on a continual journeying with the Lord. Every journey, especially a life-long one (remember, we journey till we stand before Him in Zion) will experience different seasons: some fun, some not so much fun, some happy and some sad. Every real life journey has all of these moments and so many more.

This verse then makes a strange statement that caught my attention: *"As they pass through the Valley of Baca, they make it a place of springs"*. I wondered where Baca was and, after a short search, discovered that no one really knows where this valley was but most live by the interpretation rather than a physical place. Its most common interpretation is 'valley of weeping'. We all, at one time or another on our pilgrimage, will go through valleys or 'times of weeping' but God promises, as we journey and stay with Him through these seasons, He will cause them to be places of refreshing springs.

When you walk daily with Jesus, He causes life and joy to break out in the saddest or seemingly driest places. He causes rivers to flow in what are the desert times of our life. He does not call us to avoid or by-pass these valleys but walks with us through them – remember, He promised *"I will never leave you or forsake you"*. He is not a 'good-time God', only there for the good bits. Rather, He remains a good God in all the seasons we experience on this pilgrimage called life. Remember, David in *Psalm 23* said, *"though I walk through the valley"*. He included valleys in his great 'pilgrimage with God' *Psalm* because he knew we all go through them!

If you are in a valley today, remember, Champion, you are not alone – He is with you and will turn that place to into a place of springs. If you are not in a valley, remember it for the next time you find yourself going into or through one. It says that when those on pilgrimage pass through valleys, they make them places of springs. Remember, Christianity is not just about Jesus doing things in our lives but us doing things in other people's too. When we find someone in a valley of weeping, let's make sure that we allow Christ in us to make their presently tough experience a place of springs and life. He is the God that causes springs to flow in dry places with us, in us and through us!

We just get stronger and stronger

Blessed are those whose strength is in you, who have set their hearts on pilgrimage. As they pass through the Valley of Baca, they make it a place of springs; the autumn rains also cover it with pools. They go from strength to strength, till each appears before God in Zion.

Psalm 84:5-7 (NIV)

Today is another day of journeying with the Lord. I often wonder what it must have been like for the first disciples to physically journey with Him: the excitement and daily interaction must have been awesome. Then I remind myself that today, in the twenty first century, I have the privilege to journey with the very same Jesus that they did – He is alive! As they experienced supernatural things when they daily walked with Him, so can we; as they learnt to expect incredible things to happen in situations that looked challenging, so can we. He is the same Jesus, alive and able to be for us everything He was to them.

Psalm 84 teaches us that journeying with the Lord causes your life to go from strength to strength, not from strength to weakness. As we dare to daily journey with Him, He causes us to become strong where we are weak and fully developed in the areas of our life that we are not. Each stage of our pilgrimage causes our lives to be enhanced and empowered for the road and journey that still lies ahead. Remember what we learn about David's pilgrimage when it came to the moment he needed to take down a giant, Goliath? His life was prepared and ready, his life was more than strong enough. Why? Because the pilgrimage, or God-journey, of his life had brought him to, and through, the defeat of bears and lions; Goliath was the next logical victory and he was destined to win that encounter too.

It was his ongoing journey that made him strong for what God had for him next and so will yours as you daily commit to journey with the Lord. Through things that may seem big and scary, He builds you up for the victories that lie further ahead. As the disciples walked with Jesus over the three years of their discipleship, they went from strong to stronger in their ability, knowledge and confidence. We don't have three years: we have a lifetime! As you commit to walk with Him daily, as they did, your life will also go from strength to strength too.

Remember, this is a life-long journey so stay prepared and ready to keep getting stronger until that day when you appear before Him in Zion. Bless you, may today make you stronger as you walk with the very same living Jesus the disciples did.

Journeying produces appreciation

Blessed are those whose strength is in you, who have set their hearts on pilgrimage. As they pass through the Valley of Baca, they make it a place of springs; the autumn rains also cover it with pools. They go from strength to strength, till each appears before God in Zion.

Psalm 84:5-7 (NIV)

So blessing remains upon the one who journeys with God, not the one who thinks they have arrived, parked and refuses to move anymore! We all love the destination and the arriving bit. God loves the journey just as much, because in the journey He does a whole lot of stuff in us which is always good for our long-term life. He is looking at the book of your life, not your present chapter. Let's face it, when it comes to the promises of God and seeing them manifest in our lives we are all like a bunch of kids in the back of the car on the way to a summer holiday.

Independent of where we may be en route to the question that comes from the kids in the back is always the same. Come on, you know it; you have either heard it or were the one that said it when you were younger. Yeah, that's the one: "ARE WE THERE YET?" Kids do not appreciate journeys: they like instant arrivals! Meanwhile, the parent is actually enjoying the journey (except for the kids keeping on) and the journey is actually producing patience and appreciation in the life of the kids; when they finally get there they will love it. God has promised we will arrive, and arrive we will, but we, like the kids in a car, need to remember that God is not in a hurry. He knows that the journey can produce a whole lot of good and effective stuff in us that would never be produced if we had an instant arrival with our destinies. It is often on the journey that we gain valuable things like appreciation. When you have journeyed toward somewhere you really appreciate it when you get there. One common example would be if you save up for something: you appreciate it a lot more than if you put it on the credit card! Journeying towards something really does cause appreciation and value.

Another would be relationships: when you take time to journey towards each new season of relationship with someone, you appreciate the journey a whole lot more than if you try to get engaged, married and have a child in the first week. My journey with Gina over the years of our relationship has created an incredible appreciation for her in my heart; the time we have had together believing for future things and seeing them happen; the targets we set and hit; the hurdles we jumped together. It's a great journey with a lot of miles left.

Keep looking forward to the promised destinations in your life but also take time to enjoy the journey too – chances are you may not walk this way again.

Be a patient pilgrim

Blessed are those whose strength is in you, who have set their hearts on pilgrimage. As they pass through the Valley of Baca, they make it a place of springs; the autumn rains also cover it with pools. They go from strength to strength, till each appears before God in Zion.

Psalm 84:5-7 (NIV)

Hopefully, our time looking at these verses has inspired you concerning the pilgrimage of your life. As I said yesterday, we are often in a hurry when God is not; we cannot make a slow-cooking God live in our, too often microwave, way of doing things. Pilgrimage with God produces many things when God is the author of it. If you face a delay or opposition sent to slow you down by man or Satan, then kick that thing out the way and charge on through in Jesus' name but if it is just a part of the journey ordained by God, learn to smell the flowers and find the value in the whole road trip.

The journey creates appreciation; it will also create faith as you continually trust in God while still en route. When we talk of faith, we should always look around for its best friend, patience. I like faith more and would like to hang out with it on its own! The problem is that God most often sends them as a team because patience produces a lot too – and together they produce true greatness. Let's think about the power of patience this morning; the art of waiting for something.

- Patience is a fruit of the Spirit of God living in you – *Galatians 5:22-23 (NIV)*

- It is to be imitated alongside faith.

We do not want you to become lazy, but to imitate those who through faith and patience inherit what has been promised.

Hebrews 6:12 (NIV)

The Bible tells us to imitate people of faith and patience, not just faith, but those who can both trust God and wait for His perfect timing. When we choose to walk in faith and patience, we will inherit everything God has promised. Remember, God works in the delay and the things He has promised are always so worth waiting for. Keep away from shortcuts that produce look-alikes and hang out for the genuine thing which comes from the very hand of God.

Hey, to be honest with you, patience was never my favourite fruit – I would have loved for God to give it to me as an instant download! Trouble is, He would not. Why? Because He knows that patience does us good and when we have it and mix it with our faith incredible things start to happen.

You were born for such a time as this

For if you remain completely silent at this time, relief and deliverance will arise for the Jews from another place, but you and your father's house will perish. **Yet who knows whether you have come to the kingdom for such a time as this?**

Esther 4:1-4 (NKJV)

In this moment of the story of Esther, we see that everything had gone seemingly very wrong for the Jewish nation. A wicked national leader called Haman had risen to power and had come up with a scheme that could totally wipe out the Jews as a race if someone did not do something. One young lady could make all the difference and her name was Esther. She had supernaturally, by God's doing and favour, become queen. Mordecai, her cousin, now gave her a plan that involved her approaching the king to ask for a favour. This was a fifty-fifty plan because if she found favour in his sight then she could ask for anything up to half of his kingdom but if he was having a bad day or was not happy and gave her the royal thumbs down, she would be killed.

Mordecai ran the plan of approaching the king past her and she, naturally, was hesitant in her response. She said, "Maybe that is not what I want to do. Maybe there is another plan that does not put me at risk?" Mordecai's reply to her was, "Yes, God could use someone else but that won't help us now. Maybe you are God's well-positioned master plan for this moment. Maybe you were born for this moment."

Esther found courage and did what she needed to do; God was all over it and caused the whole situation to turn around. Good guys lived, bad guys died. A nation was saved because she did not back down from a moment she had been born for.

Hey, Champion, why not look at your situations differently? Just like in Esther's life, God does not make mistakes concerning where you live and when you were born. Maybe you are in a situation and you are looking for a hero or deliverer. Here's a thought – **maybe you are the hero and deliverer and were born for this moment.** Trust in the favour of God and go ahead and do what you know needs to be done. Who knows, maybe you were born into that situation for a time such as this, like Esther?

Champion's Prayer:

Father, thank You that my life is positioned for Your purposes. Today, show me what You need me to do and use me for what needs to be done – Amen.

Things are different when He turns up

When He had finished speaking, He said to Simon, "Put out into deep water, and let down the nets for a catch." Simon answered, "Master, we've worked hard all night and haven't caught anything. But because you say so, I will let down the nets." When they had done so, they caught such a large number of fish that their nets began to break.

Luke 5:4-6 (NIV)

The tired fishermen had been busy fishing all night and had caught nothing and they were experienced fishermen, not novices. They knew their trade and had done their best but had caught nothing! They were probably very tired, looking forward to finishing then cleaning the nets so they could go on home and get some rest.

Then, suddenly, after preaching, Jesus said to them, "Hey boys, have another go!" Remember, they were not yet His disciples, just hearers and onlookers. It was what would happen a little later that would change that. They could have responded a number of different ways, maybe in anger saying, "Are you having a laugh?" They could have responded sarcastically, saying, "We heard about you. You're a carpenter's son. Stick to chairs, pal, and leave fishing to us." Instead, they dared to be obedient to His Word and were certainly not disappointed. He turned a bad fishing trip into a great one that blessed many other fishermen as well that day.

Ok, think about it: same fishermen, same boats, same nets. Everything was the same except one thing, Jesus was now with them! It was that one new additive to the scenario that made all the difference. Jesus being with them caused what they did to prosper abundantly.

We may not be fishermen but, like them, Jesus is now with us in what we do and that means that we too can expect success where we have maybe experienced failure. Maybe you have tried things before in business or relationships that just never worked. Listen, if Jesus tells you to have another go, don't let your past experience stop you from letting down your nets again. Like the fishermen, you can think this does not make sense but do what they did and have a go anyway, then praise Him and believe in Him when you see a result that is so different. Everything in the situation you're facing may look the same but Jesus, now in it and with you, can make having another go work out really well.

HAVE ANOTHER GO AT SOMETHING!

Faith always takes you deeper

When he had finished speaking, he said to Simon, "Put out into deep water, and let down the nets for a catch."

Luke 5:4-6 (NIV)

Another thing I noticed about this fishing trip was that Jesus told the fishermen to, *"Put out into the deep water"*. He never said to them "Hang around the edges," but rather, "Go deeper". The catch of fish they never could have imagined existed in their wildest dreams lay deeper out in the ocean.

As you walk with God over time, He ever calls you out to deeper waters in your faith; places you have not been before and things you have never experienced. Why? He wants to **grow** your faith! Faith will never increase by the shoreline of your life. It is where we all begin but that is not where God leaves us to fish and that is not where we are destined to end this fishing trip called life.

God wants you to experience the 'big catches' in your life but the reality is they happen in deeper waters. When you leave the shore you leave what you have known to be safe and in doing that you focus your trust on God. As you leave your comfort zone and the still harbour of safety, you sail into the tide of the supernatural and it is in the currents of the deeper waters that God does the things that are beyond what you can imagine *(Ephesians 3:20).*

Remember, Peter was in 'deeper water' when he stepped out of the boat and walked on the promises of God *(Matthew 14:30)*. Great things happen deeper out!

Hey, Champion, don't live by the shore when it comes to God. When you hear Him bid you to go deeper, cast off your lines and take a deep breath of faith so you can sail towards what He has promised.

So, do you want to catch cockles and mussels by the shore, or tuna and swordfish in the deep? As for me and my house, we are going after the big ones. How about you?

Food for thought:

Faith is rarely reasonable. We have been called to be faithful (full of faith) not reasonable (merely able to reason).

His grace is sufficient

But he said to me, "My grace is sufficient for you, for my power is made perfect in weakness."
Therefore I will boast all the more gladly about my weaknesses, so that Christ's power may rest on me.
That is why, for Christ's sake, I delight in weaknesses, in insults, in hardships, in persecutions, in
difficulties. For when I am weak, then I am strong.

2 Corinthians 12:9-10 (NIV)

Our thought this morning is concerning the incredible sufficiency of God's grace towards us and the situations we may face. When you read through this chapter and see the context of it, you see it is when Paul is talking of a 'thorn in his side' sent from the enemy. There have been many opinions concerning what this thorn may have been, my personal one being that it was not sickness or infirmity rather another type of ongoing obstacle sent from the enemy to slow him down and lessen his impact but, as with others, it never succeeded.

As with Paul, we all have times when our own abilities are at a low and maybe what is needed to be achieved seems so much bigger than who we are or what we think we can do. This is when we need, as Paul did, to celebrate God's grace which is the unmerited, immeasurable and unearned power and potential of God that comes into the situation and turns it around causing great success. Notice that Paul speaks of boasting in his weakness or apparent inability so that the power of God, grace, would rest on him. Wow, that's a fresh way of looking at challenge and trial. Instead of moaning or pretending whilst in it, we choose to celebrate our inability or weakness so as to attract and release God's power, grace and potential.

Remember, God's grace is never nearly enough or just enough. It is always more than we need. It is God's grace that empowers us to be strong in times when we may naturally feel weak or even overwhelmed. We all so need His grace each and every day of our lives. It is when we operate daily in His grace that we too can own a life that delights *"in weaknesses, in insults, in hardships, in persecutions, in difficulties."* knowing that we too have all we need in Him.

Notice Paul says, *"When I am weak then I am strong"*. I often have heard that preached, "When I am weak, then He is strong," but it does not say that. Why? Because grace operates through us and not just outside of us; because God is in us and we are the postcode of His residence. His grace makes us strong to face any and every challenge and obstacle sent to stop us. It really is enough for us too. There remains only one doorway into this all-sufficient grace that Paul knew and that is faith. It is when you release your faith in the bigness and presence of your God and in the validity of His promises that you will see and receive His all-sufficient grace manifested in the midst of what you are going through.

To put it another way, 'God comes through'. Champion, faith is the trigger to releasing the grace of God, so why not pull the trigger again today?

Faith sings before it happens

Sing, barren woman, who has never had a baby. Fill the air with song, you who've never experienced
childbirth! You're ending up with far more children than all those childbearing women. God says so!

Isaiah 54:1 (The Message)

I magine if you could not have children and you went to the doctor for help and he looked at you over his glasses and gave you as advice, "Sing, woman, sing!" And then gave you a prescription to sing songs about how many kids you were going to have and how awesome they would be! You probably would not be that happy with him, correct? You may think that is kind of strange but that is the exact point of this verse. It is reminding us that people of faith do not just sing songs of thankfulness after things happen but can be heard singing songs of faith and thankfulness when they still seem impossible!

Remember, faith is the substance of things hoped for, not of things seen or experienced *(Hebrews 11)* which means that when we are believing God for something He has promised us, we do not need to wait until we handle it before owning it and singing about it. In fact, the prophet instructs us to sing from the position of apparent lack and barrenness. That's faith.

In *Exodus* we read about the incredible account of Moses parting the Red Sea with just his faith and an extended rod. The water supernaturally parts and they go through on dry land, their captors follow them and are consumed as the ocean closes over them, liberating the children of Israel from every oppressor. What an incredible sight that must have been. When they get to the other side, his sister, Miriam, got out her tambourine and started to play and sing songs of thankfulness to God for all He had done. And everyone gives a big well done to Miriam – but really, think about it: anyone can play the tambourine on the victorious finished side of the miracle. God is looking for some people who will play the tambourine of faith before the miracle happens and when it still looks impossible from a natural sense-based standpoint.

In *Zephaniah 3:14*, God gives the same faith based advice to Israel when they seem to be in a place of failure and are desperately needing victory. He says the exact same thing to them "SING!" Without faith it is impossible to please God, so sing Him a song that pleases Him today. Sing Him a song of faith, a song that agrees with the promises He has given you for the situation you are facing. Yes, sing it from the middle of that place of apparent barrenness. Why? Because He told you to and it's real good advice.

SING!

Carry a Spirit of Excellence

Then this Daniel distinguished himself above the governors and satraps, because an excellent spirit was in him; and the king gave thought to setting him over the whole realm. So the governors and satraps sought to find some charge against Daniel concerning the kingdom; but they could find no charge or fault, because he was faithful; nor was there any error or fault found in him.

Daniel 6:3-5 (NKJV)

I want to inspire you to consider a man in the Old Testament called Daniel because there are some great things we can learn from his life. He was a man who chose to live full on for God, he lived as a Champion in his generation and we can learn much from him. Daniel was a man who was living in a nation that was not originally his place of birth or upbringing. His nation had been taken over by Babylon. It may not have been his nation but he prospered in it and was promoted to the best places of leadership. Remember, God can promote and prosper His people anywhere if they will live for Him!

Daniel distinguished himself and stood out from the crowd above all the other leaders, even those who were locals. Why? Because he was a man of excellent spirit. He was a man who valued excellence and what he did, he always did well.

Excellence is a major God-key to promotion in your life. When you, like Daniel, choose to live an excellent life with an excellent spirit you will always rise to the top of the crowd, whatever crowd you find yourself in! It was his excellent spirit that caught the attention of the king. When we live putting value on excellence, we too will catch the attention of kings (important people). The king had been looking for someone to give great responsibility to. He had seen mere performers and gifted people but then he saw Daniel, a man who did things with excellence and gave him the job.

Why? Here are a few reasons:

Excellence always turns up on time; you can have great talent or gift but if it is not where it is meant to be on time, what use is it long term? Excellence does not leave till things are finished, which means you don't have to always manage other people's loose ends. Excellence does not cut corners, which means you do not have to follow behind a person, patching things up that were done averagely. There are many more but these will give you something to think about today.

Any employer worth his weight would look for excellence in someone he was going to promote. Guess what, so does Jesus our King and, as we commit, like Daniel, to live with a spirit of excellence, He will use us and send us to do things others only ever dream of.

Live out of what is in you!

Then this Daniel distinguished himself above the governors and satraps, because an excellent spirit was in him; and the king gave thought to setting him over the whole realm.

Daniel 6:3 (NKJV)

The Bible says *"an excellent spirit was in him"*. Remember, today, that an excellent Spirit is now in you too. Paul challenged the Corinthians not to act or live anymore like mere men but instead to remember that they were now God-filled temples. The Word tells us we are the temple, the dwelling place of the Holy Spirit, God's most excellent Spirit. *(1 Corinthians 3:2-4 and 16)*. God does not live in buildings made by men but in the hearts of His followers and that's you and me.

Look at the life of Jesus. He lived with and daily released a spirit of excellence in everything He did. Now that His Spirit, the same Spirit, is resident in our lives, we should acknowledge this residency to cause us to flow with excellence in everything we do to.

One thing that defines when an excellent spirit is in the house is that the small things are not overlooked. People who do not value excellence leave the little things or choose to only do the things they want to. A person of an excellent spirit sees the big picture and always takes care of the little things, not seen by man, as well as the large, that which gets applause. Make sure, today, you are taking responsibility for those small things in your world and remember it is always the little foxes that ruin the vineyard *(Song of Solomon 2:15)*.

Some common examples:

- Return the calls and emails you said you would.

- To the best of your ability, be on time for appointments and not late.

- Finish what you start. Don't be known as the one who always leaves first but as the one who always finishes well.

I teach that the enemy of excellence is, "That'll do." Like Daniel, don't settle for, "That'll do" in your life or in what you do. Always remember the principle of God that says "what you do with little, you do with much" *(Luke 16:10.)* Today, be great, be excellent with the things others think are little or insignificant because the King is watching and you will catch His attention if you do and He will entrust you with the great.

Let's show the world how excellent our God is by releasing His excellence through the way we choose to live, especially in the bits when no one is watching.

Living an excellent life will stir others up

Then this Daniel distinguished himself above the governors and satraps, because an excellent spirit was in him; and the king gave thought to setting him over the whole realm. So the governors and satraps sought to find some charge against Daniel concerning the kingdom; but they could find no charge or fault, because he was faithful; nor was there any error or fault found in him. Then these men said, "We shall not find any charge against this Daniel unless we find it against him concerning the law of his God."

Daniel 6:3-5 (NKJV)

When you choose, as Daniel, to live with a spirit of excellence, it will always cause a reaction in others. Some will be motivated and challenged to up their game and live at a higher level but, as we see with Daniel, others will be annoyed because it challenges them and they don't want to deal with challenge or change. We see in this morning's text that Daniel, living an excellent life, challenged the other leaders and instead of seeing Daniel as a great 'pace setter', they turned nasty and tried to set him up to bring him down. Why did they not find it easy setting him up? Because he was faithful. When they brought his life under the microscope they could not find infection because excellence went through to the bones of who he was. His faithful lifestyle made sure that there were no corners that could let him down. Wow, that inspires me. How about you? It says there was no *"error or fault found in him."*!

When you read on in the story, you see that they had to resort to setting him up according to his prayer life because there simply was no other ammunition they could use. That is because he was a man committed to excellence which meant all the corners were straight and the little things taken care of. Living from an excellent spirit sets you up to be blameless and people have to resort to lies and set-ups to catch you out as well. This is how God would have us to live. They eventually set him up according to his prayer life because they knew that he prayed three times a day with excellence. That's amazing because they set him up in accordance to something that was his guaranteed faithfulness. They could set him up in this because they knew he would not miss his prayer time.

It all ends good though because, even though they set him up, God had his back covered and what was meant to bring him down ended up getting him lifted higher. That's what happens when you live a God-filled, excellent life. Everything your enemy throws at you will only get you promoted.

I hope you're challenged by Daniel's life. Today, live in such a way that you motivate some to 'up their game' and aggravate others because any response is better than no response. Finally, always remember that there is a big difference between going after perfection and going after excellence. Perfection so often tries to do what it can't with what it has not got while excellence is committed to being the best you can be with what you are and presently have. Live an excellent life!

Where do you go when you are thirsty?

On the last and greatest day of the festival, Jesus stood and said in a loud voice, "Let anyone who is thirsty come to me and drink. Whoever believes in me, as Scripture has said, rivers of living water will flow from within them."

John 7:37-38 (NIV)

Here we see Jesus stand up in the middle of a very busy place and ask a very straight question, "Anyone thirsty?" It was the greatest day of a festival, so chances were that a whole bunch of people were thirsty but Jesus was not referring to a natural thirst – He was not offering chilled *Pepsi* to those who had been out in the sun too long! He was speaking of the deeper thirst each of us have within, that internal thirst which, in the same way as a natural thirst, drives people to all manner of places looking for quenching and satisfaction.

As it was then, so it still is today. People are walking around with a thirst that they do not know how to satisfy. We all did it; running around from place to place, everything from relationships to new fashionable things and places to be. Yet all these other places and things only ever satisfy for a moment and then the thirst always returns leaving the feeling of dissatisfaction once again. That's because only the living water which comes from God can truly quench the innermost thirsting of a person. We were designed to drink living water, that spiritual water that comes from the spring of God's own Spirit into the reservoir of our spiritual bellies – our innermost being – then, flowing out, it waters, refreshes and revives every part of who we are.

When God's river starts flowing within us and we begin to drink from it, every other thirst in our lives is satisfied and we no longer have to wander around seeking satisfaction from the other vendors we used to visit because we had no other choice. One taste of God's living water and the other stuff simply doesn't cut it anymore. It's like when you drink a real Coke; you can't go back to the cheap stuff you buy from discount stores – you know the stuff, ten bottles for a pound!

Hey, Champion, stop your hunting and settling for lesser refreshment and drink from the living water of God. As you do, it will well up inside of you, bringing the satisfaction you have been thirsting for.

DRINK!

What would you do for your mates?

Some men came, bringing to Him a paralytic, carried by four of them. Since they could not get him to Jesus because of the crowd, they made an opening in the roof above Jesus and, after digging through it, lowered the mat the paralyzed man was lying on. When Jesus saw their faith, He said to the paralytic, "Son, your sins are forgiven."

Mark 2:3-5 (NKJV)

This is a great account of Jesus healing a man and forgiving his sins. It is also a great account of the power of true friendship. These four friends had heard what Jesus was doing for people with impossible situations and made up their minds that they were going to get their friend where he needed to be.

I experienced this type of friendship on a recent mission trip. The missions team I was part of was travelling back from the Philippines where we had been for two weeks. On the day of our return, the volcano in Iceland decided to erupt and the air space over the UK was closed. We made it as far as Rome and had no way of returning to the UK. Being away so long already meant that I really needed to be back for my family and for the church. I was sharing a hotel with many, many people in the same situation yet mine suddenly became very different because of the friends I have in my life who love me.

One phone call triggered a 48-hour rescue mission from two of my friends. They took it on themselves to drive from Portsmouth to Rome (1250 miles), pick me and the team up and drive us back again. The people in the hotel were amazed that people we called friends would do this for us and the story of what they did for me has spread like wildfire, inspiring people to think, "What would you do for your friends?"

They did me a great favour but consider this man on a stretcher, who also had friends who would dare to rip a roof off to get their friend to Jesus. Like my friends, they knew the man's need and where he needed to be and made it personal. Like these men, we all have friends who need a touch from Jesus – let's be the type of friends who will put ourselves out to get people where they need to be, especially when it comes to bringing people to where they can meet Jesus and have their life changed by Him.

Champion's challenge:

What would the friends in your life do for you? What would you be willing to do for them? Are there friends in your life who need you to make the effort to get them close to Jesus, even if it means ripping a roof off? And are you willing to do that for them?

Whole-hearted or half-hearted?

Keep and guard your heart with all vigilance and above all that you guard, for out of it flow the springs of life.

Proverbs 4:23 (Amplified Bible)

Here's some real good advice concerning both your natural heart and your spiritual one. Naturally, life flows from your heart and your full potential is in the health and wellbeing of it. Face it, you can be an award winning body builder but if your heart stops, your other muscles, even though big, do not mean much at all. Life always flows from the wellbeing of your heart. The Bible often refers to your heart but it is not speaking of a natural blood pump but that unseen central place of who you are, that place that you decide, purpose and live out from on a daily basis. It is this heart that the writer of Proverbs specifically instructs us to be guarding.

The Hebrew word used for 'guard' means more than to just protect. It also means 'to watch over or observe'. This is very good advice because the condition, or wellbeing, of your heart will ultimately determine the wellbeing of your whole life and destiny. The heart of you has the potential to experience, contain and release many things. Here are a few mentioned by the prophets:

- *Isaiah 35:4* – God's people can be fearful-hearted.

- *Isaiah 46:12* – God's people can be stubborn-hearted.

- *Jeremiah 51:17* – We have the potential to be dull-hearted.

- *Ezekiel 3:7* – Says that we can be hard-hearted.

These are just a couple of examples of things that you need to monitor the activity of in your heart as none of them will take you where you need to go.

Another one I want to consider is the need to avoid being half-hearted. We all have the potential to do things half-heartedly or whole-heartedly. The choice of which one we work out of remains with us. Whenever we are half-hearted, it means that the outcome will never be as dynamic, fast or effective as if we were whole-hearted. When someone is half-hearted concerning a task, it means that they take a lot longer than they should or, worse, someone else has to step in and complete it for them which is never right.

When it comes to living for God, we should resolve that we will never be half-hearted in any way, rather whole-hearted concerning both Him and His purposes. A half-hearted Church will never change this world but a whole-hearted one will! A half-hearted Church will fade away into the pages of history but a whole-hearted Church will influence, change and even redefine the culture it finds itself in. Let us guard our hearts from half-heartedness and determine to give our God the full potential of a whole heart, dedicated and set apart.

Let's be whole-heartedly God's

*He answered: "'Love the L*ORD *your God with all your heart and with all your soul and with all your strength and with all your mind'; and, 'Love your neighbour as yourself'."*

Luke 10:27 (NIV)

T he key to experiencing everything that God has for you is to purpose to live whole-heartedly for Him. In these verses, we hear Jesus answer the question of some religious leaders which was, "What is the most important thing to do?" Jesus did not have to think long but answered directly, "Love God with ALL, ALL, ALL". Notice it does not say with some or a bit of but all! We need to realise afresh that God does not want a bit or even half of your heart: He wants the lot. He does not want to be sectionalised or compartmentalised with other stuff but desires that we should be whole-hearted concerning Him and His kingdom. Is He being unreasonable? I don't think so because it is He who both made us and redeemed us. It is He that gave His all for us and, because of that, He has the right to expect us to give our all to Him.

Whole-hearted pursuit will always find Him
When we set our hearts to pursue God, we must always do so whole-heartedly. Why? Because the promise that He will be always be found is not made to the half-hearted but to those who commit to seek Him with all of their hearts.

You will seek me and find me when you seek me with all your heart.
Jeremiah 29:13 (KJV)

Whole-hearted worshippers
When we worship Him, it should always be whole-hearted worship and never just settling for a sing-along or a lifeless, easy moment of worship. We should, instead, be like King David as he returned to Jerusalem with the Ark of the Covenant and passionately throw ourselves into it, lock, stock and barrel. Be whole-hearted in this expression of love. Whole-hearted and half-hearted have a different effect but also a very different sound. When a church worships God half-heartedly it can be a 'nice moment' but when a church worships God with whole-heartedness, man, that is a sound that lifts the roof and makes Heaven smile. It also causes devils to run.

Sing, O Daughter of Zion; shout aloud, O Israel! Be glad and rejoice with all your heart, O Daughter of Jerusalem!
Zephaniah 3:14 (NIV)

Champion's Challenge:
Purpose to be whole-hearted in every aspect of your walk with God.

Unleashing a church's full potential

Now the multitude of those who believed were of one heart and one soul; neither did anyone say that any of the things he possessed was his own, but they had all things in common. And with great power the apostles gave witness to the resurrection of the LORD Jesus. And great grace was upon them all.

Acts 4:32-33 (NKJV)

We have spoken these last few days about being whole-hearted people, especially when it comes to our walk and devotion to God and His kingdom. We have considered our pursuit and worship of Him and now let us today consider being people who are whole-hearted concerning building what He wants built here on earth – the Church.

The local, spirit-filled Church is God's masterplan for the world. May we be as passionate and whole-hearted about it as He is. In the above verses from *Acts* we see a people who were of one heart and one soul concerning the Church and its true potential. It was these people that initially impacted the world with such incredible, long lasting effects. Why? They were one in their whole-heartedness for God and notice how it says *"great grace was upon them all."* I want some of that *"great grace"*. How about you?

If we want to see great grace, we need to unite around that which God is passionate about. Remember, He only committed to build one thing on the earth: the Church. I think of the great account of Nehemiah rebuilding the city walls for God in Jerusalem and the amazing account of how he and those with him did it in just fifty two days. That's the power of being a whole-hearted people. You can build and rebuild incredible things for God in a small amount of time.

When a church is whole-hearted concerning building things for God, it is an unstoppable force that can achieve whatever is in their hearts to do. May that be us. We live in a time when the luxuries of mediocrity and apathy are no longer available. All around us, a sin-sick world plummets ever lower and ever more lost and confused. Laws that limit our freedom are subtly being passed and people stand confused concerning the simple truths of who God is and what He can do for them.

It's time for us to take the lampshade off, to rise and be the Church God has called us to be: unified, passionate and whole-hearted. Let us serve. Let us give and then let us do it again to see His kingdom come and people's lives changed as ours once were. Imagine what we can achieve and build in our cities if we unleash the potential of a whole-hearted church?

Don't have an identity crisis!

Therefore, from now on, we regard no one according to the flesh. Even though we have known Christ according to the flesh, yet now we know Him thus no longer. Therefore, if anyone is in Christ, he is a new creation; old things have passed away; behold, all things have become new.

2 Corinthians 5:16-17 (NKJV)

These are some of my all time favourite verses because, within them, we find the truth of our God-given, new identity. It is vital that we both know and then choose to live out who we now are in Christ. If we don't know who we really are, we will continue to daily live out of the old factory setting of who we were before Christ changed us and that is such a waste of a great redemption. Everything changed when we believed in Jesus. An old man, you, died and a new man was born (again) through faith in Christ.

Knowing this, that our old man was crucified with Him, that the body of sin might be done away with, that we should no longer be slaves of sin.

Romans 6:6 (NKJV)

I like how the NIV version translates *2 Corinthians 5:17, 'the old has gone, the new has come.'* This means we all daily have a massive, personally defining choice to make. Do we live in what was, which has now actually passed away in God's opinion or do we step up to the mark of who God says we are now and live out from that platform? Let's step up to the mark of the new! The only time the expression 'passed away' is ever used is at a funeral, around a grave side or at a crematorium. We need to both perceive and resolve that the person we were before is truly dead; dead and buried through baptism into Jesus. The person that you are now is a new creature; a new person and a brand new creation. We all need to look in the mirror and remind the person we see of this until it becomes a revelation to us.

When our identity is correct and we see ourselves correctly, our behaviour will come into alignment. If you see yourself as a dirty, old sinner you will very naturally live out the life of one. But, equally, if you agree with God and see yourself now as washed, forgiven and clean, the very righteousness of God in Christ, then your life will begin to manifest the life of that reality.

It's time to let the real you stand up and shine, Champion. Things changed when you placed your faith in Jesus. You died, were buried and have risen to newness of life – so live new, live unchained, live like you always wanted to!

What counts now is what is new!

May I never boast except in the cross of our LORD Jesus Christ, through which the world has been crucified to me, and I to the world. Neither circumcision nor un-circumcision means anything; what counts is a new creation. Peace and mercy to all who follow this rule, even to the Israel of God.

Galatians 6:14-16 (NIV)

Let us again consider the importance of seeing yourself as a new creation. According to these verses it is the only thing that really matters now anyway. Arguments concerning circumcision and such religious traditions mean nothing, which I am sure you will be glad to know – especially the men! What matters and counts is the revelation that, through Christ, you are not who you used to be! It is only our identification by faith with His death, burial and resurrection that gives us legal license to live as new creations, brand new people.

A timeless comparison would be that of the caterpillar and the butterfly. This insect, destined for transformation, starts its existence as a caterpillar crawling on the earth. Then a strange death and rebirth takes place and the caterpillar transforms into a beautiful butterfly. This creature is something so very different to what it once was. It emerges out of its cocoon and begins to fly freely. It is nothing like its former self. It looks completely different and acts in a new way too, doing things that were formerly impossible.

We were all like caterpillars, crawling around on the ground, then, through Christ, we die to that life and receive new life, His life, and we are transformed into beautiful butterflies. What a terrible waste it would be for the butterfly to continue to act like a caterpillar. What a waste of new life and potential. It is exactly the same when we, as redeemed children of God, refuse to see ourselves as new creations in Christ. What a sad thing it would be to see a beautiful butterfly rolling around in the filthy mud instead of flying above such things. That is what we look like when we refuse to recognise our transformation.

Today, know who you really are, Champion. Know that Jesus has given you new life and fly, don't crawl, because that's what you used to do when you had no choice. You are now transformed. Fly!

Champion's Prayer:

Thank You, Father, that today I am indeed a butterfly not a caterpillar, transformed by Your power and love. Help me to remember throughout this day that I am not who or what I used to be – Amen.

By faith!

Now faith is the substance of things hoped for, the evidence of things not seen. For by it the elders obtained a good testimony. By faith we understand that the worlds were framed by the word of God, so that the things which are seen were not made of things which are visible.

Hebrews 11:1-3 (NKJV)

What a great way to start this new week – the opening statement from the classic faith chapter, *Hebrews 11*.

As Christians, we should recognise that faith is a vital, everyday, non-negotiable part of our lives; we are called by God to be people of faith. By using faith, the elders, those who lived before us, obtained a great testimony or life story, and, by daily choosing to walk this faith walk with God, so shall we. Remember that it is faith that pleases God! (*Hebrews 11:6*)

Faith is simple, it's making the choice to believe and trust God and to believe that He is both willing and able to fulfil the promises He has made concerning your life. God is not a liar! He has given us so many great and precious promises because He has every intention of honouring them. As with Abraham, we need to make the choice to engage daily with God and His promises. How? By faith; simply believing that He who promises is faithful.

The Word says that by faith we can understand the mystery of creation and how the world was formed – and, let's face it, to actually understand creation you have to make the choice to believe that it was formed according to how God says it was. Simply believe He is telling you the truth. Faith is needed not only to understand our origins but also to understand the other, seemingly impossible situations in your life. In those seemingly impossible situations, you need to apply the exact same rule which is to hear what God says about it and then choose to believe, even when there is no visible evidence. Faith is the substance and the very evidence of the things God promises.

Begin to release your faith again today and hunt out the promises in God's Word that are fitting for the situation you are in and, even without adequate physical evidence, make the decision to believe the promise of God. Make His promise all the evidence you need.

You were saved by faith, to live by faith and it is faith that puts the 'zing' into Christianity. It delivers your walk with God from being a lifeless ceremony to being a fun-packed, ever-unfolding adventure where you look forward to the next day and the next mountain you are destined to conquer. How? BY FAITH!

A life lived by faith

Now faith is being sure of what we hope for and certain of what we do not see. This is what the ancients were commended for. By faith we understand that the universe was formed at God's command, so that what is seen was not made out of what was visible.

Hebrews 11:1-3 (NIV)

We too will be *"commended"* by God as we daily choose, as Abraham did, to walk by faith through this life of purpose and destiny that God has given us to rule and reign in. By faith, we understand that if you want to fully comprehend anything about God, you have to view it through the lens of *"faith"*: simply believing things are and will be because He said so. His eternal Word and promises to us are the only **substance** and **evidence** that we need to be moving ever forward into what we are believing for, even if there is no physical evidence. Remember that faith is acting on the promises without needing further evidence to do so; it is believing before you see and no longer living in the carnal world of 'seeing is believing'. Think for a moment of how many other things we do each and every day without first having evidence.

- Do you check every chair before you sit on it? No, because you believe the claims of the manufacturer that it will hold and support you.

- Do you check your brakes one by one every time you take the car out on the road? No, because you trust the mechanics, you trust that they have made your car roadworthy and functionally safe.

We all do so many things daily by faith **without any physical evidence**, so why is it people only get nervous when we speak about placing the same faith in God? Is the Creator of heaven and earth not more trustworthy and reliable than the chair maker or mechanic?

Trust Him today because He is more than able to both support you and keep you from harm. Let today be another day where you trust His promises for your life without the need for initial physical evidence. Remember, He makes things that are seen out of things that are not currently visible, He knows no limitation and He is for you.

Champion's Challenge:

Live beyond what makes sense today. Think of something that God is promising you that does not make sense to your 'natural' senses and begin to thank Him for it.

Use your sixth sense

The fundamental fact of existence is that this trust in God, this faith, is the firm foundation under everything that makes life worth living. It's our handle on what we can't see. The act of faith is what distinguished our ancestors, set them above the crowd. By faith, we see the world called into existence by God's word, what we see created by what we don't see.

Hebrews 11:1-3 (The Message)

I love this translation because it underlines that this trust we have in God is the firm foundation that we build our lives upon and what makes life worth living.

Why? Because faith turns a boring, normal life, limited by worldly restraints, into an eternal adventure that is freed from the limitations of that which is perceived by the five senses alone. Faith is that sixth sense that causes you to live in an unlimited dimension of experience. Today, you are living out your ever-unfolding story of faith. It is a story that not only has a beginning and an end but also a middle bit and the middle bit is presently being written by those faith choices you're making today. Remember, your journey with God started by faith.

Knowing that a man is not justified by the works of the law but by faith in Jesus Christ, even we have believed in Christ Jesus, that we might be justified by faith in Christ and not by the works of the law; for by the works of the law no flesh shall be justified.

Galatians 2:16 (NKJV)

It ends in faith. No one has seen heaven yet. We know in our hearts by revelation that when we die we go to be with Him. Why? Because He promised we would and we simply believed.

Do not let your hearts be troubled. Trust in God; trust also in me. In my Father's house are many rooms; if it were not so, I would have told you. I am going there to prepare a place for you. And if I go and prepare a place for you, I will come back and take you to be with me that you also may be where I am.

John 14:1-3 (NIV)

So we start by faith and we end in faith but what about the middle bit, that bit we are now in? The answer is, of course, "we are to daily walk by that same faith" (*2 Corinthians 5:7*). So today, take some bold steps, steps not based on the five senses alone but that sixth one, your faith!

Have you got letters before your name?

By faith Noah, when warned about things not yet seen, in holy fear built an ark to save his family. By his faith he condemned the world and became heir of the righteousness that comes by faith. By faith Abraham, when called to go to a place he would later receive as his inheritance, obeyed and went, even though he did not know where he was going.

Hebrews 11:7-8 (NIV)

Welcome to another day in the unfolding story of faith which is your life. Living a life of Godly destiny is not about just having letters after your name like 'BA' or 'PhD' but, according to the heroes of faith listed in the *Hebrews 11* Hall of Fame, it is all about having certain letters **before** your name. "What letters are they?" you may ask. Have a read through *Hebrews 11* and you will see them for yourself. Before the name of any hero mentioned come these letters: "BY FAITH".

It was their decision to trust and believe God that got each and every one of these biblical heroes into the *Hebrews'* Hall of Fame. Each of them experienced incredible things because they dared to believe and trust the Word of God in every situation they faced. Today, realise afresh that we are dealing with both the same God and the same promises. Today, in the twenty first century, we can engage with God and daily encounter the manifestation of His potential by daring to use our faith as those heroes of faith chose to use theirs.

"But they had great faith." you may say. So do you! Think about it: you have already believed for the biggest thing you ever needed to. At the start of your faith journey, you believed God and released your faith for the total forgiveness of all of your sins and the total redemption of your eternal soul. What can be greater than that? The same faith that you used to get eternally forgiven and saved can now be used to shake the world you live in. You only have one direction for your faith walk, Champion: **forwards**!

But my righteous one will live by faith. And if he shrinks back, I will not be pleased with him.
Hebrews 10:38 (NIV)

We are not those who shrink back to unbelief but push forward to greater and bigger things. Have a great day and why not go ahead and believe for something totally impossible?

Faith in God makes all things possible

Jesus looked at them and said, "With man this is impossible, but with God all things are possible."
Matthew 19:26 (NIV)

W e have been spending some quality time in the pages of the legendary faith chapter of *Hebrews 11* and reminding ourselves that our daily life is a faith walk, an adventure story in the making.

When you make the decision to step out of the mere ceremony of Christianity and into a **real time** life experience of walking with the Lord, you leave behind things that are branded impossible. Why? Because the focus of our faith is an eternal God who existed before anything else did and lives outside of the restrictions of such things as time and space. We so often judge everything we believe to be true or possible by a planet that we live on called Earth. God holds universes in the span of His hand. When we choose to engage with God Almighty by faith, we step into a realm of life where anything can happen and is possible. Remember, we serve and belong to the same God who is in the Bible, the God who:

- Parts oceans when His people need to get across.

- Causes walls to fall when His people dare to walk around them a few times.

- Stops the sun so that His people can win the fight they are presently in.

- Causes axe heads to float.

- Turns water into wine to make the party better, not worse.

- Raises people from the dead.

These are a mere handful. Read the book and you will find a whole lot more! The guys and girls in *Hebrews 11* saw God do incredible things because they engaged daily with Him by faith and, you know what, so can we.

And what more shall I say? I do not have time to tell about Gideon, Barak, Samson, Jephthah, David, Samuel and the prophets, who through faith conquered kingdoms, administered justice, and gained what was promised; who shut the mouths of lions, quenched the fury of the flames, and escaped the edge of the sword.
Hebrews 11:32-34 (NIV)

Remember, the God who did all that and more is **your** God. The trigger they had is the same one you now hold: FAITH! Only believe. All things are possible to those who believe!

Faith will turn a dead end into a highway

By faith the people passed through the Red Sea as on dry land; but when the Egyptians tried to do so, they were drowned.

Hebrews 11:29 (NIV)

Like a jukebox that gets stuck with a favourite record, I too am still stuck in *Hebrews 11* and the more I read it, the more inspired and fired up I am about placing faith in God. Let's stay there a little longer together.

When we choose to daily live by faith, we give God the opportunity to make a way forward for us in the times when we may seem stuck or where there looks like no possible way forward.

Picture this: the children of Israel had left Egypt under the leadership of Moses, a man who certainly walked a faith walk with God. Their captors, the Egyptians, had changed their minds concerning the freedom they had recently given the Israelites and were coming hard behind them to bring them back into slavery. The Israelites came to the edge of a large body of water called the Red Sea. They could not go left or right, nor could they go back. It looked like they had hit a real dead end with no further options available.

But then God responded to the faith of Moses and performed the impossible. Moses extended his rod over the ocean in accordance to God's instruction and the sea parted before them, giving them a brand new option and pathway to freedom. By faith – believing God – they passed through the centre of an ocean that was being parted in the middle by seemingly nothing because there was no physical evidence as to what was holding the water apart. And when the last Israelite had stepped out and the last Egyptian had stepped in, the waters closed, liberating the children of God from their captors once and for all. As the classic song says, "God will make a way where there seems to be no way, He works in ways I cannot see, He will make a way for me."

When you walk by faith, He will make a way for you too and when you feel you have reached a crisis point or a seemingly dead end, extend the rod of your faith, acting on the Word and promises of God, and watch what happens. Faith creates a route that often no man could have ever imagined was possible.

Food for thought:

If you want a successful life, always choose what will bring long term satisfaction over what offers short term gratification.

Don't absorb fear – release faith!

There was a famine in the land, besides the first famine that was in the days of Abraham. And Isaac went to Abimelech king of the Philistines, in Gerar. Then the LORD appeared to him and said: "Do not go down to Egypt; live in the land of which I shall tell you. Dwell in this land, and I will be with you and bless you; for to you and your descendants I give all these lands, and I will perform the oath which I swore to Abraham your father."

Genesis 26:1-3 (NKJV)

We are living in a time when it seems there has never been worse news pouring out of every media outlet. Daily, we hear of things like recession, the credit crunch, global epidemics and terrorism. We need to make sure that we are processing and handling correctly this information the media is giving out daily. Don't get me wrong, there is nothing wrong with getting information but often it is much more than information that the media is trying to give out. Often, without even knowing it, they are releasing fear and breeding panic by their continual, sensational statements. If you don't know God or have your faith in Him then yes, maybe you should panic; but if you're trusting in God, then don't worry! There have been plenty of tough times before. In the Bible, we read of many famines that came and went and of people who trusted in the promises of God through them.

Isaac was in a place of double famine and God told him **not** to pack up and move away but to take His promise of prosperity and sow into the place of apparent famine during a time when others wouldn't. He had a choice to either absorb the fear of the Philistine newsreaders and live in panic and lack or believe the Promise Maker and live with a different spirit in those troubled times.

Then Isaac sowed in that land, and reaped in the same year a hundredfold; and the LORD blessed him. The man began to prosper, and continued prospering until he became very prosperous.

Genesis 26:12-13 (NKJV)

Champion, God's promises still work in tough times! Listen to the media to get information but make the decision that you are not going to absorb the fear they are dispensing daily. Instead, release your faith to see God move for your good. I am thankful for good news programs but also and thank God that they are often wrong, especially concerning those who have placed their faith in God.

Begin to speak back to your TV when you hear a statement spoken that could produce fear. Why not answer the newsreader and say something like, "That will not come near my life or family, in Jesus' name"? Don't absorb the fear, release faith!

Selfless faith will change the world

I could go on and on, but I've run out of time. There are so many more — Gideon, Barak, Samson, Jephthah, David, Samuel, the prophets .... through acts of faith, they toppled kingdoms, made justice work, took the promises for themselves. They were protected from lions, fires, and sword thrusts, turned disadvantage to advantage, won battles, routed alien armies.

Hebrews 11:32-38 (The Message)

Wow, faith is very powerful stuff, isn't it! It was used by the people in Hebrews to:

- Topple kingdoms and make justice work.
- Protect themselves from incredible dangers and turn disadvantage to advantage.
- Rout and force out foreign, enemy of God, armies.

It is good for us all to grasp the fact that faith is about more than just you! God calls us to graduate out of the style of faith which is just about us, to a level of faith life that is also all about the wellbeing of others, people and things beyond us and our own wellbeing.

Faith will change your life, but selfless faith will change the world.

These men and women that we read about in *Hebrews 11* actually changed things in their nation and, indeed, the world by their faith; this really inspires me. We too can use our God-given faith to hold things back and release justice, to win battles for God's kingdom and force out 'alien armies', to turn disadvantage to advantage. The key is to simply make the decision to live beyond yourself, to see that the purpose of true faith is not all about us and our comfort but rather having an impact in the cities where we live and the world that God loves.

I don't know about you, but I do not want my spiritual obituary to read, "Andy was a man of faith who knew how to get a bigger house and a new car." Rather, something so much bigger, maybe something like, "Andy was a man whose faith impacted the world by regularly toppling and forcing out the plans and schemes of the devil and evil men and he could also stop lions' mouths too!"

Be inspired – let us use our faith for great and mighty things that affect the world beyond the boundaries of our own lives and comfort.

Champion's Challenge:

Add to your prayer list a couple of things that have nothing to do with you or people you are close to, pray for something for someone you don't know and for something your city or town needs.

Accompanying actions

You foolish person, do you want evidence that faith without deeds is useless? Was not our father Abraham considered righteous for what he did when he offered his son Isaac on the altar? You see that his faith and his actions were working together, and his faith was made complete by what he did.

James 2:20-22 (NIV)

If you want your faith to work like Abraham's did, if you want your faith to move mountains, then there are three things you need to have in alignment.

Firstly, **believe in your heart**. You need to get the promise of God for the situation in your heart so deep that it's a part of who you are. Next, **it needs to be found on your lips**. There needs to be a harmony and sameness between the belief you say is in your heart and the confession that is coming out of your mouth. Remember, mountains are moved when we speak to them and do not doubt but believe in our heart. And there is a third thing that needs to be in alignment, if mountains are to move for us. **We need deeds that accompany what we say we believe**.

By deeds I am referring to the life we live, the things we do and choose not to do on a daily basis. What we believe should affect how we live – if not, then we need to ask, "Do we really believe what we say we do?" Here we see that Abraham's actions were working together with his faith and actually making them complete! He didn't just have his heart and mouth aligned but he also had accompanying actions. He lived in accordance to what he said he believed. Notice he had these three things working together and, because he did, incredible things were released to him and through him. The Bible says that Abraham's promises are now ours in Christ, so we too can see – when we let these three things walk together in our lives – incredible things released to and through us.

When what we say we believe (parts one and two) is different to the way we live or the things we do (part three) then we are suffering from a dose of hypocrisy. Come on, let's face it, we have all had and still have an element of hypocrisy in us. It's as we determine to believe, speak and have matching actions that we drive every trace of hypocrisy out. Sometimes it's good to stop and listen to what you say you believe then take a moment to check that the actions of your life accompany the words coming out of your mouth.

Remember, when Abraham left Haran he believed what God had said in his heart. He changed his confession from referring to himself as Abram to Abraham but then he involved his actions: he left and walked towards what was promised. That's when stuff began to happen. Believe then speak and walk in agreement to what you believe – it's then you will see some mountains move!

Prisoners of hope

As for you, because of the blood of my covenant with you, I will free your prisoners from the waterless pit. Return to your fortress, you prisoners of hope; even now I announce that I will restore twice as much to you.

Zechariah 9:11-12 (NIV)

What a great text to start your day with! Whenever I read *Zechariah*, I stand amazed at the accuracy of the prophetic throughout his book concerning Jesus. He speaks so clearly of Jesus' coming and His purposes for coming, even to the specifics of Him entering Jerusalem on a donkey as its King and Saviour (verse 9), an event that would happen many, many years later. He also speaks of the finished work of the cross and things accomplished because Jesus' blood would be shed in covenant sacrifice for us.

Look at the results revealed in these verses: we are redeemed and delivered from waterless, dry and barren places. They also reveal that we become prisoners – not prisoners of anything negative but rather a people 'sentenced' to be prisoners of hope. To hope is to have a confident expectancy of good things happening to you. Then they finish off with a promise of two-fold restoration.

Today, this is fulfilled – Jesus has shed His blood, we are indeed prisoners of hope; no longer prisoners of guilt or sin but hope! When you woke up this morning, did you dream of the yet unseen, that which God has promised you? If not, start to. Just as Abraham, against hope (natural hope), had hope (Godly hope) we too need to be full of Godly hope, especially when we find ourselves in those moments that naturally look or sound hopeless.

I suppose it all comes down to who or what your hopes are in. Many people today are hopeless, prisoners of worry, suffering from sick hearts because what they had put their hope and trust in has been shaken or not produced what it promised to. The Bible says that hope deferred makes the heart sick *(Proverbs 13:12)*. God has not caused us to be the sick-hearted but those who see their wildest, God-given dreams come true on a regular basis.

Hey, if God has promised it, it will come to pass if you don't lose heart. Today, see yourself as a prisoner of hope – let the hopes you have in God hold you captive, not captive in a negative way but rather safe and secure, like a strong tower that cannot be breached. What an awesome thought! Why not do what the verse says: return to your fortress of hope, God and His word, and get ready to see God restore to you twice as much? It just keeps on getting better, doesn't it?

Giants don't go away – you have to slay them!

David said to Saul, "Let no one lose heart on account of this Philistine [giant]; your servant will go and fight him."

1 Samuel 17:32 (NIV)

Our thought this morning is taken from the classic account of David and Goliath. This is one of those stories that every kid who went to Sunday school learnt about, right? In this part of the story David, who was a shepherd boy, not yet a king, has turned up on the battlefield to bring food supplies from his father to his brothers. He turns up and finds a stand-off between the children of Israel and the Philistines. More specifically, a giant of a man named Goliath is standing mocking both Israel and God and inviting the best man that Israel has to come out and fight him. When you read the account, you see that he had been doing this for over a month with the same threats and the same invitation, "Come out and fight me – whoever wins gets everything". No one wanted to fight him; in fact, when he came out they all hid – including King Saul who I believe was the man who should have sorted him out.

Then along comes David, a shepherd boy who, in the opinion of others, had no experience to deal with this rather large, ongoing problem. They did not know he had trained when no one was watching, taking on lions and bears. David is more than willing to remove this obstacle or road block of a person, simply because he knew what he had in God.

We are going to talk a bit about slaying giants this week. We may not have to deal with a physical giant but we all have to deal with non-physical ones, sometimes on a weekly basis. God wants you to have victory over every giant that comes against you in your life and will enable you to take them out, as He did with David.

Facts you need to accept about your giant:

They are not going anywhere, no one is coming to take them away, you have to deal with them, Champion! They will stay where they are, mocking you and not letting you past till you slay them. Notice, also, that Israel knew the name of this giant. When you know the name of your giant, this is evidence itself that you have let it stay around too long. And finally, when you desire to live in the destiny God has for you face the fact that you will always be slaying giants of one sort of another – they can be anything from fears, habits, insecurities or different challenging situations.

Rise up, Champion, it's time to face the facts about the giant that is standing in your way today. He is going nowhere, so you need to look him in the eyes, rise up and run at him knowing who you are in Christ. Go ahead and slay him, then you can get yourself ready for the next one!

Victory is yours in Christ

Then David spoke to the men who stood by him, saying, "What shall be done for the man who kills this Philistine and takes away the reproach from Israel? For who is this uncircumcised Philistine, that he should defy the armies of the living God?"

1 Samuel 17:26 (NIV)

Champion, your giants can actually be moments of opportunity; get optimistic! As we saw yesterday, David turns up and finds a giant of a man called Goliath threatening and mocking the armies of Israel and, more insultingly, their God who was also his God. They may not have taken this personally but David did – he made it his problem but also his opportunity. I think David was a bit of an opportunist; he asks the other men, "OK, what is the prize in this fight? What does the winner get?" When we back up just one verse, we see that there were indeed some great opportunities for the person who dealt with the giant problem that Israel had.

And it shall be that the man who kills him the king will enrich with great riches, will give him his daughter, and give his father's house exemption from taxes in Israel.

1 Samuel 17:25 (NIV)

What were these riches?

- Great riches from the king (not just riches, **great** riches).

- A princess to marry: that would lift you instantly in your social circle; you would become a prince overnight!

- Tax-free living for your dad and his household (I personally like the sound of this one!).

David must have thought, "Wow, what a great deal, all that for giving that giant a slap he won't forget? It's a deal!" Again, remember, unlike Saul, David was not afraid and was in a position to think about possible opportunities because he knew that God was with him; and if *"God is for you who can be against you" (Romans 8:31)*, right?

Unlike the rest of the armies of Israel, who were frozen by fear, David was in a 'covenant-based calm' that enabled him to see that this was not about great opposition but great opportunity.

Think for a minute, Champion. What benefits will there be for you when you deal with your next giant? Be like David, see what others who are frozen by 'covenant-forgetting fear' cannot, get up and run at that giant that is in the way of you and some real great future benefits! God has anointed you to 'slap the living daylights' out of your giant, so what are you waiting for?

What fuelled David's charge can fuel yours!

So it was, when the Philistine arose and came and drew near to meet David, that David hurried and ran toward the army to meet the Philistine. Then David put his hand in his bag and took out a stone; and he slung it and struck the Philistine in his forehead, so that the stone sank into his forehead, and he fell on his face to the earth.

1 Samuel 17:48-49 (NKJV)

This is the bit of the story that we all love, right? The moment when David takes off, running at his giant! Notice how it says he *"hurried"* to meet the giant. He did not skip nicely, or walk slowly with fear-filled pigeon steps – he ran with great confidence. Let's look at what he knew – it was what he knew that fuelled his run and, when you know it too, it will fuel yours.

He knew that the covenant he had with his God was bigger and more powerful than the threats coming out of Goliath's mouth. The years he had spent on a hillside tending sheep had given him ample opportunity to bask in the bigness of God and get a revelation concerning the powerful covenant he had with Him.

He knew that God was enabling him in life once again and it was all he needed to win. He remembered the times when God had empowered him when he needed to defeat lions and bears. He knew that the same God that gave him the goods for that would give him the goods for this current problem. Finally, he knew that whatever God had for him next in life was on the other side of Goliath and he would have to go through him because there was no way around him.

David knew that what the king had promised as a reward was the other side of this Goliath but I think he under-estimated how much was actually on the other side of this victory. It was after David defeated Goliath that his life went to a new level in God and he stepped into what God had for him next. It was not long after this fight that he became king of Israel! What God has for you next – that next level – is the other side of the giant you need to slay today. Get hungry for what God has for you next, Champion, and realize it's just the other side of your present giant. That will fuel your charge!

Remember these things as you take off running at the giant that stands in your way today. You have a covenant – in fact, you have a better covenant with God than David (yours was established in Christ). God guided the stone David threw; with you He is in the hand that's throwing it! He is empowering you for your present victories as He did your past ones. Finally, what God has next for your life is the other side of slaying this present giant, so get it done.

RUN!

When fighting giants, wear what works for you

Then Saul dressed David in his own tunic. He put a coat of armour on him and a bronze helmet on his head. David fastened on his sword over the tunic and tried walking around, because he was not used to them. "I cannot go in these," he said to Saul, "because I am not used to them." So he took them off. Then he took his staff in his hand, chose five smooth stones from the stream, put them in the pouch of his shepherd's bag and, with his sling in his hand, approached the Philistine.

1 Samuel 17:38-40 (NIV)

So David goes and tells Saul he will sort this Goliath out. After convincing Saul he had a fighting chance, Saul offers David the suit of armour he would wear when he was going into a fight (bearing in mind this was Saul's fight). David tried it on and, because of their different body structures, it just hung on him, weighed him down and probably looked really stupid. He probably had major problems holding the sword that belonged to Saul for long as well because he was not used to it. Then we see him do the wise thing: he turns to Saul and says, "You know, thanks but this really isn't working. Let me wear what I am used to". He changed back into the shepherd boy outfit and picked up the weapons that were unique to him. These felt comfortable and he knew how to use them well.

The key lesson here, Champion, is don't wear another man's armour for your fight! When you purpose to be a giant slayer, you need to make sure you are not imitating or impersonating someone else at the cost of you not being true to who you really are. What weapons are unique to you? David did not feel comfortable with a sword but was an expert with a shepherd's sling and a few stones. How about you? What are the weapons you know how to use? Intercession, worship, praise? Use the weapons and wear the outfit that is unique and authentic to you, not another.

In addition, when David stepped onto the battlefield the giant may have been shocked by how David looked and the weapons he was carrying but at least he did not mistake David for Saul or see him dressed up as something he wasn't. David's confidence and authenticity to who he was in God caused him to win the day and it will cause you to win also. Yes, be inspired by others but don't wear their clothes for your battle – what works for them may not work for you, and vice versa!

Champion's Prayer:

Father, today I thank You that You have given me all I need to run at my giants and defeat them. Thank You that Your life and power in me is greater than it is in them. Help me to use the gifts You have given me to bring a great victory for Your glory – Amen.

The Lord has need of it

"Go into the village opposite you, where as you enter you will find a colt tied, on which no one has ever sat. Loose it and bring it here. And if anyone asks you, 'Why are you loosing it?' thus you shall say to him, 'Because the LORD has need of it.'" So those who were sent went their way and found it just as He had said to them. But as they were loosing the colt, the owners of it said to them, "Why are you loosing the colt?" And they said, "The LORD has need of him."

Luke 19:30-34 (NKJV)

I love this account of the disciples going to collect a donkey for Jesus. I have spoken before of the donkey but never about the man who owned it.

The disciples were told to go and collect something that Jesus needed to use to do what He wanted to do next. This thing, namely a donkey, belonged to someone else and we see this person suddenly appear when the disciples are helping themselves to his property. When they are asked, "What are you doing?" they respond with, *"the Lord has need of it"*. Hearing this, the owner let them take the donkey and waved them on their way.

This must have been a pre-arranged deal between Jesus and the man. Maybe, at some time previously, the man had experienced Jesus change his life in one way or another and said, "Look, I don't have much, I have a donkey if ever you need it – just let me know". Jesus needed a vehicle to go somewhere and remembered this man's kind offer and simply cashed in what had been promised. I also believe that when He finished with it He gave it back (but I reckon after having the Son of God sitting on it, it was a lot faster than before, eh?).

Jesus needed to use something that belonged to someone and the heart of this man inspires me. He simply, without any fuss, made what was in his world available to Jesus to use when it was needed. I want to be like that – how about you? When Jesus needs something that I have, I want to always have a heart that says, "No problem Jesus, it's all yours".

Jesus needed a donkey for that project – maybe today He doesn't need a donkey but something else? Maybe a talent or a skill that you possess in your life? Maybe a home you own to accommodate one of His team as they travel through? Maybe your money or wealth because He has a project He needs funded or a building He wants to get built? It all comes down to having a heart sold out for Him and His kingdom but it's also about whether you see yourself as an owner of your things or a steward of the things He has blessed you with.

I want to be like the man in this account saying to God that whenever He has need of something in my world, it's His to use. Remember, when He gives it back, it will work better than it did before.

Spend your life on what is essential, not just important

And now abide faith, hope, love, these three; but the greatest of these is love.

1 Corinthians 13:13 (NKJV)

Here is a very short yet very profound little statement and, over the last few years, this verse has really got into my heart and my life and turned it upside down in a very positive way. My prayer is that it will do the same to you.

So often we can all be involved in so many things that seem so important but we need to make sure we are busy with the things that are essential. What makes something essential and not just important is this: **"Does it matter to God?"**

In this verse, we hear the Apostle Paul underline for the Church what is essential from the viewpoint of God concerning our lives and what we spend them doing. Look at how he introduces these three essential life co-ordinates, *"And now abide . . .".* He does not mention law because that had now been dealt with by the perfect work of Jesus. Neither does he mention a whole bunch of other church 'stuff' that we often may deem important. No, just these three things: Faith, Hope and Love. I like the way it is put in the following translation:

So these three things continue forever: *faith, hope, and love. And the greatest of these is love.*

1 Corinthians 13:13 (NCV)

I don't know about you but I really want to spend the currency of my days on things that will continue forever and not just last a moment and, by forever, that does not just mean this life we know now but all of eternity. You see, the things we do that involve or are the product of faith, hope, and love will remain while other things that seemed important at the time will, like straw, be burnt away and never mentioned in eternity.

I don't want to stand in Heaven one day and watch as a whole bunch of stuff I spent my life building disappears in a moment because it was actually just 'important', not essential. I hope this thought stirs you, Champion, like it is stirring me. It causes me to look at what I am doing and ask myself this, "Am I busying myself with things involving faith, hope and love?" If not, it's time to get busy with them again because, without them, I am not giving God anything to be excited about.

Hey, let's talk some more about this tomorrow.

Spending our lives on what is essential, not just important

And now abide faith, hope, love, these three; but the greatest of these is love.
1 Corinthians 13:13 (NKJV)

L et's continue to talk about this short, yet very profound, verse which reminds us all again to be mindful concerning 'what remains'; that which is essential to God. The first of these three God-pleasing co-ordinates is *faith*. It is vital to remember that everything we are and have in God is the product of our faith being placed in the Son and the promises of His Word. Faith is not an extreme teaching but rather the very thing that pleases and impresses God and activates, or detonates, His promises and intentions.

And without faith it is impossible to please God, because anyone who comes to him must believe that he exists and that he rewards those who earnestly seek him.
Hebrews 11:6 (NIV)

It is what we do or build using our faith that truly pleases God and I suppose the million dollar question is, "How much of what you are doing or building involves faith, Champion?" We should never come to a place where we have everything covered or worked out merely by our own ability or understanding because that does not give God any space to show how faithful and incredible He is in the situation, dream or project. There should always be a percentage to what we are doing and building which is labelled, 'Only God can do this bit, if He does not turn up, we are stuffed'. We should actually design this into what we are doing and we should make lots of room for the 'God needs to come through' bit in what we set out to achieve. As we do, we roll out a red carpet welcoming Him to be involved.

It is when we dare to live and daily walk by faith *(2 Corinthians 5:7)* that we both please God and activate His power to perform that which He has promised. All that remains is faith, hope and love. Are you still believing God for something impossible? If not, why did you stop? Why not start again today?

In every area, or slice of the pizza of your life, make sure you're leaving a section for God to move because, when you do, He will! Faith makes room for God to join in and when God joins in, the outcome is always bigger and better than you ever imagined it could have been in your wildest dreams.

Spending our lives on what is essential, not just important (cont'd)

And now abide faith, hope, love, these three; but the greatest of these is love.

1 Corinthians 13:13 (NKJV)

Good morning. Breakfast is served!

Yesterday we looked at the first of three things that are essential in our Christian walk: faith. Paul said that it is these three things faith, hope and love that *"remain"* when all else is gone. When we one day stand in Heaven, it will be what we have produced with these three ingredients that will remain with us forever and when we stop and think about this, it should cause us to lay aside other things that are just merely important to embrace that which is eternally essential.

The second ingredient that we are to embrace as we live lives that please God and dare to build incredible things is *"hope"*. Hope is a very powerful force. When we became believers, we received hope; hope that changes us, hope that keeps us marching on through the toughest of times with heads held high. Hope gives us a reason to live passionately and with purpose and causes us not to quit. It is God-given hope that even causes us not to fear death or the grave. Jesus provides that infallible hope and that is, indeed, the steadfast *"anchor of [our] soul"*.

This hope we have as an anchor of the soul, both sure and steadfast, and which enters the Presence behind the veil

Hebrews 6:19 (NKJV)

Our lives should also release hope to others, not despair. When people encounter the atmosphere of your life today, they should leave feeling so much more hopeful, not hopeless. Why? Because of Christ in you, the hope of Glory! What, or should I say who, is **in** you should come **through** you to affect and inspire the lives of those who encounter you on a daily basis. Naturally speaking, we are living in times where the media daily dispenses huge portions of despair and hopelessness into the hearts of multitudes but we are God's antidote to their hopelessness and despair when we speak of our God and His promises. It is then that hope should rise in people's hearts as it has in ours and hopelessness should be dissolved. I believe with my whole heart that the local Church is still the hope of every village, town and city in our land, not the building but the Christ filled hopeful people within it.

Champion's Challenge:

Purpose to speak words that give hope today, to yourself and to those around you.

The greatest one is love!

And now abide faith, hope, love, these three; but the greatest of these is love.

1 Corinthians 13:13 (NKJV)

This week we have been hanging around this verse, daring to use it as a guide and measuring stick to check that we are actually spending our lives on that which is essential to God, not just important to us. We have looked at two of the three Godly co-ordinates which are faith and hope, so let's now consider the third one, which Paul underlines as the greatest of the three, and this is, of course, *"love"*.

Agape is the original Greek word used here for love and it means the 'God kind of love'. We need to understand that the love that is spoken of in this passage is exactly that, 'the God kind of love' and not the limited, fickle, easy come, easy go stuff the world so commonly uses. Let's rewind a bit in *1 Corinthians 13* to remind ourselves what 'God kind of love' looks and feels like.

Love is patient, love is kind. It does not envy, it does not boast, it is not proud. It is not rude, it is not self-seeking, it is not easily angered, it keeps no record of wrongs. Love does not delight in evil but rejoices with the truth. It always protects, always trusts, always hopes, always perseveres.

1 Corinthians 13:5-7 (KJV)

The love we see defined here is so different to the love that is marketed so freely in this world we live in. The love we have experienced in this world often does not protect, hope or care for the other person's needs, but rather it takes, demands and is all about self-satisfaction and self-preservation and gratification. It is only when God's 'Agape love' touches our hearts that we are changed forever and it is when we then live to release this 'God kind of love' that other people's worlds are impacted too. God's love, unleashed, can change the world! Let His Agape love both touch you and flow from you again today.

Love defines us – A hard truth is that we can be so busy doing seemingly good things but if faith, hope and, especially, love are not the motivation, what we do does not mean that much to God. Truth to tell, He counts deeds done without love to be equivalent to **nothing**. According to Paul's teachings, it is that which we do that flows from love for God and love for people that abides, remains and actually defines us.

*And though I have the gift of prophecy, and understand all mysteries and all knowledge, and though I have all faith, so that I could remove mountains, **but have not love, I am nothing**. And though I bestow all my goods to feed the poor, and though I give my body to be burned, **but have not love, it profits me nothing**.*

1 Corinthians 13:2-3 (KJV)

Join the love train!

And now abide faith, hope, love, these three; but the greatest of these is love.

1 Corinthians 13:13 (NKJV)

Anybody remember the song *Love Train* by the O'Jays? The chorus had these words in it: "People around the world, join hands, join the love train." I wonder if the songwriter was familiar with *1 Corinthians* because that is the simple call of *1 Corinthians 13*, to join God's love train. The whole chapter is worth another read because it teaches us what true love looks and behaves like. In that letter, Paul is teaching the Church to put high importance and value on what matters to God which is faith, hope and especially love.

God's love is a love that knows no measurement and is not selective, unlike the love the world so often offers. Often, when we have loved, we measured out who deserves what and when. God's love is poured out, unmeasured, upon all. God's love does not choose or select according to who is deserving or worthy of it but rather it includes and embraces all. The truth is, we all have people we find it easy to love and we all have people who we struggle loving, right? The love that God has given us and calls us to does not just love those who are easy to love but those who are difficult and even undeserving of it. Wow, what a challenge that is! Remember, in His teaching, Jesus said anyone can love the lovable but I have called you to love those that others don't or won't love.

Anyone can invite the one everyone wants to dinner but how about inviting the one no one wants? This is where rubber hits the road in our Christianity. Will we dare to live out the 'God kind of love' that has been shed abroad in our hearts through Christ or will we keep it like a secret to ourselves?

It is not when we love those who we find easy to love that we impress God but when we courageously choose to make the effort to love the least, the overlooked and the seemingly unlovable; those we may naturally struggle with. It is then that we are truly passengers on His incredible love train and cause a measurement which has meaning and relevance in heaven.

Then the righteous will answer him, 'Lord, when did we see you hungry and feed you, or thirsty and give you something to drink? When did we see you a stranger and invite you in, or needing clothes and clothe you? When did we see you sick or in prison and go to visit you?' The King will reply, 'I tell you the truth, whatever you did for one of the least of these brothers of mine, you did for me.'

Matthew 25:37-40 (KJV)

Let the spotlight remain on the star

He is the image of the invisible God, the firstborn over all creation. For by Him all things were created that are in heaven and that are on earth, visible and invisible, whether thrones or dominions or principalities or powers. All things were created through Him and for Him. And He is before all things, and in Him all things consist. And He is the head of the body, the church, who is the beginning, the firstborn from the dead, that in all things He may have the pre-eminence.

Colossians 1:15-18 (NKJV)

I love to read the book of *Colossians* because, from start to finish, you see Paul place the spotlight on the one true superstar, Jesus. Throughout its chapters, Paul continually brings the focus of the spotlight back to the Saviour King. In our lives, let us make sure that we also are continually putting the spotlight of pre-eminence where it belongs, on Jesus. The spotlights of our attention and passions, our delights and desires, need to be on Jesus.

Throughout this epistle, Paul says, *"He is . . . He is . . . He is . . ."*. Christ was indeed his only boast – may he ever be ours too. Paul also continually celebrates what Jesus has accomplished – let us take time today to do the same in our lives. Throughout Colossians we are reminded that:

- He, Jesus, is the image of the invisible God – everything you want to know about God the Father you can know by beholding Jesus the Son. You do not need to wonder any longer! Jesus was and is the perfect reflection of everything His Father is.

- He is the firstborn of all creation. He was and will always be God's blueprint for the new creation. As He carried the Father's likeness, we now carry His because we are produced in the very likeness of Him. He was the divine Seed sown and we are the harvest that carries the same likeness and DNA of that original seed.

- He causes all things to 'consist'. He created all things and holds all things together – universes, thrones and dominions but also our lives, futures, dreams and destinies. He is the divine glue that causes all things to hold together and work so well – don't go removing the glue!

Let's continue to look at this tomorrow but, today, make sure the spotlight is on the Superstar. He is the one who deserves all honour, worship and applause. Let us join with Paul in applauding and giving the first place to the one who deserves it – Jesus.

Let the spotlight remain on the star (cont'd)

He is the image of the invisible God, the firstborn over all creation. For by Him all things were created that are in heaven and that are on earth, visible and invisible, whether thrones or dominions or principalities or powers. All things were created through Him and for Him. And He is before all things, and in Him all things consist. And He is the head of the body, the church, who is the beginning, the firstborn from the dead, that in all things He may have the pre-eminence.

Colossians 1:15-18 (NKJV)

As we said yesterday, like the Apostle Paul did, let us ever keep the spotlight of fame upon the one who deserves it. Let's continue this morning to look at why. Because He is the head of the Church, not us. We are the body and it is good for us to remember this. He will always be the head and, by faith alone, we are joined to Him and find our life and existence in Him, just as in the natural world the same life that is in the head of a body is in the body itself. When you realise this, you can enjoy His life flowing in you and through you every day. Because you are, by faith, connected to Christ who is the head of the Church, The New Testament teaches that you can know His mind and thoughts for every situation you may face. What a powerful reality that is.

Because He is the firstborn from the dead. Champion, because He has risen from the dead, you have no need to fear death. He beat the grave and it has no legal right to hold you now. When our lives are finally 'spent' (hopefully, spent well) and we close our eyes to this life, we will rise to be with the Father for all eternity, just as He did.

Finally, the statement that I want to really take time to underline is this: *"in all things He may have the pre-eminence."* Pre-eminence is 'first or greatest place'. Jesus deserves the first place and the best place in all we do and are.

As we go again into our busy lives with all its demands and challenges, we can also walk in incredible blessing as we ever live to give Him the first place the best place. Other 'things' you need and want will flow to you and hunt you down if you allow Him to have the place of pre-eminence in every section of your life – not just today but always!

Champion's Prayer:

Lord Jesus, the spotlight belongs to You. Forgive me for the times I have put it on myself or on other things, You are the one who deserves the best and the first of all I am. Today, be seated on the throne of my life because You deserve that place. Jesus, I give You the place of pre-eminence in this life. Rule and reign through it – Amen.

Realisation is not enough to change a situation!

But when he came to himself, he said, 'How many of my father's hired servants have bread enough and to spare, and I perish with hunger! I will arise and go to my father, and will say to him, "Father, I have sinned against heaven and before you."

Luke 15:17-18 (NKJV)

These verses are from the account of the wayward son found in *Luke 15* where Jesus teaches a threefold parable concerning the recovery of lost things. It is a great story of a young man who made some real stupid mistakes but then has the sense and courage to turn it all around. The NIV uses different wording. It says, *"when he came to his senses,"* and that is something that we all do every now and then, right? We can all lose the way sometimes in one way or another but then a faithful God taps us on the shoulder with His finger of goodness and mercy and lets us see that what we have is not what we really want and we often have a realisation, or encounter with truth or reality. What is important is what we do next with that realisation.

A realisation on its own will not achieve the changes that we need. We need to add other things to it like the wayward son did.

The next thing we read is that he determined in his heart *"I will arise and go to my father"* and it was at this point that the situation actually began to change for the better. Things only improved when he made a resolution and not just when he had a realisation.

Whenever you have a realisation about something, make sure you quickly add a resolution to it or things will most likely never change. Like the wayward son, all of us ever need to be having realisations caused by the prompting of God's Spirit, then we need to be resolving what we will do about those realisations and have the courage to take the first step towards what needs to happen to produce that desired change. As you do, it is then that your realisations will become realities. If the son had settled for realisations alone, he would have died broke, eating pig food when he could have been eating fattened calf at a homecoming dinner!

Goals are dreams with a date or moment of movement attached to them. If you just dream, little happens, but if you dare to attach deadlines and dates to them, they begin to live and create in your world!

Food for thought:

Good intentions really do not profit anyone, but lived-out ones do! Live out your good intentions today, Champion.

Live to do all things well

"And they were astonished beyond measure, saying, 'He has done all things well. He makes both the deaf to hear and the mute to speak'."

Mark 7:37 (NKJV)

What a great testimony that is of our Lord Jesus that He has 'does all things well'. That is the sort of God He is; He does not do good in one area and average in another, but, rather, He does all things well. With everything He does He has one standard and that is to do it well. Let us remember we now have that same Jesus living in us and our lives are temples of His residency. Having His life and influence now in us, I believe, should cause the same attitude in life to what we do. We also should begin to desire more to do 'all things well'.

It is a great thing to just do some things well but God wants to empower us to do more than that. God's best is not that we have a great church and a below average marriage but rather that we do all things well. For example, God not only wants for us to do well in business but that our health would be good also and not poor due to lack of much needed exercise and terrible eating habits. God does not watch over one segment of our life but He watches the whole orange and His desire is not that we do well or experience success in one or two segments only but that, by His help, we do well in all the segments so that the whole orange is successful. He wants every section of what makes us who we are in a place of prosperity, health and well-being.

Consider your life as an orange, made up of many segments. Take a bird's eye, or God's eye, view of all the sections of your life and ask some honest questions about each of the segments, such as, "What areas am I doing well in?" and, "What sections do I need to let God help me to bring into a better place for my health or well-being?"

Have a great day and never stop pressing in for more of God: you will never run Him dry.

Food for Thought:

Faith will change your life but selfless faith can change the world.

Avoid the snare of fear

"Fear of man will prove to be a snare, but whoever trusts in the LORD is kept safe."
Proverbs 29:25 (NIV)

Fear of man is something that can affect us all at one time or another if we allow it to. The bottom line is we shouldn't!

When we know that God has positioned us and called us to do or be something, we just need to stand up and be what He has called us to be. The fear of man is like a snare and it really does have the potential to catch you, trap you and stop you being what you have been designed to be. Hey, Champion, be aware of it and keep free from it. When God gives a dream or a vision, often you can know it is God because, within you, you hear that old voice saying stuff like, "What will people think?" The true answer should simply be, "Who gives a rip?!" If God has given something to you, what does anyone's opinion matter anyway?

Remember what God said to Joshua when he appointed him to carry on from Moses and to take the children of Israel into their inheritance? He said, "*Do not look at their faces.*" What does that mean? It means: do not let them affect you or your confidence by the way they are looking at you or the comments they may be making.

Look at the verse now from *The Message* translation:

"The fear of human opinion disables; trusting in God protects you from that."
Proverbs 29:25 (The Message)

The cure for avoiding being disabled by the fear of man or, in other words, human opinions, is to trust in the Lord; He promises that He will keep you from every snare. Don't be caught in a snare today. If God has given you a dream or asked you to do something and you know it, then don't look at the faces of those who don't understand to help you determine whether you should do it or not. Look up into the eyes of your Heavenly Father and then, as it has once been termed, 'feel the fear and do it anyway'! When an animal is caught in a snare, it stops running free and cannot enjoy the freedom it was designed to know. It is the same with us. If we let people's opinions stop us from doing what God says we can do then we are acting like rabbits who have one leg caught, prevented from going where we want to go.

Don't get caught but run free again today! Fly like an eagle in the opinions and thoughts of your God who is for you.

FEAR NOT!

Take a step beyond information

But be doers of the word, and not hearers only, deceiving yourselves. For if anyone is a hearer of the word and not a doer, he is like a man observing his natural face in a mirror; for he observes himself, goes away, and immediately forgets what kind of man he was.

James 1:22-25 (NKJV)

Why is it that there seem to be two types of Christians walking the earth? Those who pray and read the Bible and seem to get next to nothing happen and those who pray and read the same Bible and it seems they get everything they pray for? Does God have favourites? If so, the question is how **you** do become one?

Of course, God does not have favourites. To me, the key to this dilemma is found with one simple, yet profound, key word and that word is **application**.

What James was saying to them, and is still saying to us, is that it is not enough to 'be a hearer' because all you do when you hear is gain information and knowledge. What we need to do is take another step further and commit to being 'doers'. These are people who, after reading, 'gain understanding' then choose to apply what they have discovered in their everyday life. To put it another way, they 'put some flesh on it and live it out'.

Example

I could be an expert concerning car seat belts. I could spend my life studying everything about them finding out everything there is to know about how they are made, how they work and even draw diagrams of the first ever mechanism used for a seat belt. Great! I would have 'heard well' and become highly informed. But the bottom line is, if I do not put it on when I drive and 'apply what I have learned' then, if I was to crash, I would fly through the windscreen, informed!

Every medicine or medical cream in your medicine cabinet says that it has to be applied before the benefit of the contents become a reality to your condition. In the same way, the Word of God works in the life of the believer. Not when it is read only, but when it is read and then applied!

With what eternal truth do you need to take a step beyond 'mere information' with today? Let us all purpose to **apply** God's eternally relevant wisdom and answers to every area of our lives. As we do, we will experience the benefits of them.

Champion's Challenge:

Choose one thing that you are going to apply today, not just believe. Let the Holy Spirit show you something that you are not currently applying then go ahead and do it today.

Don't forget what you look like

Don't fool yourself into thinking that you are a listener when you are anything but, letting the Word go in one ear and out the other. Act on what you hear! Those who hear and don't act are like those who glance in the mirror, walk away, and two minutes later have no idea who they are, what they look like.

James 1:22-25 (The Message)

It is always good to remember that the Word of God does not just reveal God and what He is capable of but it also reveals you and lets you know your true potential and capability. When we open the Bible, we look into a divine mirror that gives us a true reflection, or mirror image, of who we truly are in Christ.

What James is encouraging us to do is twofold.

Firstly, take time to look in the mirror to discover and affirm who you really are. Find your identity in God's opinion and turn away from looking into other temporal, man-made mirrors that promise to tell you your 'true identity' when they don't really know you. Find out who you are by gazing into your Maker's handbook.

Then, don't forget what you see. James said that when you get the true picture of who you really are and what you are capable of in Christ, don't walk away and forget the image you beheld but let it become your directing internal image and, from that moment, know yourself by it.

It is when we dare to read, remember, apply and 'live out' what we see in God's Word concerning our lives, that our lives are continually transformed into the likeness of Christ and, as with Gideon, the original full potential dream of God for our being manifests. The challenge today is to know what you look like and live in accordance and harmony with your divine reflection and not some cheap man-made one.

Champion's Prayer:

Father, today I see myself through Your opinion, not my own or that of others. Everything Your Word says about me is true. Today, I choose to make Your Word the true mirror in my life that reflects the image of who I really am. Help me not to walk away and forget but to live out of the image I have seen – Amen.

You can't do what's been done!

Surely He has borne our griefs and carried our sorrows; yet we esteemed Him stricken, smitten by God, and afflicted. But He was wounded for our transgressions, He was bruised for our iniquities; the chastisement for our peace was upon Him, and by His stripes we are healed.

Isaiah 53:4-6 (NKJV)

O nce, while on a mission trip, I witnessed a horrific, religion-related sight that I never would have imagined I would ever see in the twenty first century. During an Easter weekend, I was travelling with my missions team to the mountain region of northern Luzon in the Philippines. We passed through so many villages but in one particular village our truck was held up because of an Easter procession that was taking place. As we looked out of the window, we could not believe what we saw. Many grown men were whipping themselves with rope until their backs were bleeding – without exaggeration, blood was splattering everywhere because of the passion they were doing it with. Other men were carrying crosses and I was informed that later that afternoon they would allow themselves to be nailed to them as everybody watched. The sight was so brutal to behold.

What were they doing? Sadly, it what religion had told them to. Instead of hearing the good news of a gospel based on the finished work of Christ, they had heard, or been sold, a religious one that put the total emphasis on them getting God to like or tolerate them totally based on their performance.

The sad thing was, these men were so sincere but yet so sincerely wrong. If Jesus had physically been with us, imagine how upset and angered He would have been. I believe He would have jumped out of the truck and said something to them that was so simple yet so profound, "Stop it, you are wasting your time. You do not need to do that because I did all that for you two thousand years ago so you would not have to! You can't do what has been done already."

Another sad reality is that, if they really want to replace what Jesus did to make God like them, they would need to not stop at the nailing but go all the way – killing themselves – because His life, totally spent, was the actual payment that purchased our right-standing with God.

Seeing this sight made me so angry with religion, with its other gospel that makes people's lives worse not better. It also made me think, "How often do we do things to make God love us?" The truth for us is that, because of what Jesus bore on Himself two thousand years ago on our behalf, HE ALREADY DOES!

Like the man who spent the whole day emptying his shed, looking for his pencil only to find it behind his ear, we must realise what we already have and what has already been completed for us. Purpose again, today, to live in His finished sacrifice.

Remain open-hearted toward need

By this we know love, because He laid down His life for us. And we also ought to lay down our lives for the brethren. But whoever has this world's goods, and sees his brother in need, and shuts up his heart from him, how does the love of God abide in him?

1 John 3:16-18 (NKJV)

I can remember the first time I went on a mission to the Philippines this verse impacted me in such a profound way and, indeed, I am always reminded of it each and every time that I go on a mission. While travelling throughout the more rural areas of the Philippines, you constantly come across need; people needing things and needing help. You then have a choice: do you shut your heart so that you do not feel their need – and then you do not have to take responsibility for it – or do you keep your heart open and allow the pain and suffering of others to affect you, to affect you in a way that you end up doing something, even if it seems incredibly small, to help them?

I believe God wants His people to have healthy, open hearts concerning the needs of others. Notice how many times Jesus Himself was 'moved by compassion' throughout the gospels. In this verse, it specifically speaks of the needs of our brothers. I believe that it is referring to those who are people of God and a part of the same global family as us. What an awesome thought. When you said yes to Jesus, you became a part of a worldwide family. Even if we don't see it like that, God does and I believe He wants us to care for each member of that family as we would for each member of our natural one. Wow, what a challenge this is, especially when there is seemingly no end to the people in need of help out there!

It is, again, an issue of love – the verse says that 'he who shuts his heart to the needs of his brother is void of God's love in his life'. That's a very hard statement but a good one, good enough to awaken us all to be more open-hearted. Obviously, you can't do everything; I always leave the mission field wishing I could have done more but I always do what I can. And hey, if we all do that, we will, together, get a lot done.

Finally, it's not just about the mission field far away, is it? Around us all, daily, there is no shortage of people in very real need. Let us make sure our hearts are open to them and their very real needs. If you can do something to bless others in need, do it – as you do, you manifest the love of God that is in you.

Champion's challenge:

Let God show you someone in need today then step forward and make the difference. It may be with words, help or even money but dare to do it. You will feel God smile.

Caution, God at work

And I am convinced and sure of this very thing, that He Who began a good work in you will continue until the day of Jesus Christ [right up to the time of His return], developing [that good work] and perfecting and bringing it to full completion in you.

Philippians 1:6 (Amplified Bible)

The Apostle Paul was convinced, and you need to be also, that God is at work in you today and will continue working until He finishes what He started. Get convinced about that because He is not fickle and He always finishes and completes what He starts.

Have you ever driven down the road and seen road workers working on or in a hole in the road? Often, they have some fencing up to protect them from oncoming vehicles and, normally, there is a sign that says, 'Caution, men at work'.

Well, Champion, know today there is a fence of protection around your life and a big sign that says, 'Rejoice, God at work!' He has promised to keep working on us right up to the day of our collection and all we need to do is stay yielded to Him. Keep letting Him have the access He needs to what He needs in the hole He may be working on. Yielded and submitted is all He needs you to be for Him to work with you. He is aiming at full completion and nothing less. God is not into momentary patching up, He is into making all things new. Why not daily thank Him for the ongoing transformation of your life that is the result of His Word and His Spirit at work within you, both when you feel it and when you don't?

Two thoughts for you:

- Don't be harder on yourself than He is! Live to be a disciple but don't be too hard on yourself. Remember, you are a work in progress. Take a breath and enjoy the journey. Let's face it, you are probably not where you want to be but you are so much further on from where you started! He knows what needs to be worked on next so the best thing you can do is rejoice and yield.

- Don't be too hard on others! Remember, they are God's workmanship and, like you, they too are a work in progress. He is busy on them just as He is busy on you. When you think this way, it causes you to walk with grace. Let's dare to treat others with the same grace, mercy and patience that God treats us with 'daily'.

Have a great day and remember: REJOICE, GOD IS AT WORK – even when you can't feel it!

What do you smell like?

But thanks be to God, who always leads us in triumphal procession in Christ and through us spreads everywhere the fragrance of the knowledge of Him. For we are to God the aroma of Christ among those who are being saved and those who are perishing. To the one we are the smell of death; to the other, the fragrance of life. And who is equal to such a task?

2 Corinthians 2:14-16 (NIV)

A better way of saying *"smell"* would be to use the word 'fragrance' or 'aroma'. Paul's challenge to us is this: What aroma or fragrance is coming from our lives as we live them out daily?

God's plan is that our lives would spread everywhere *"the fragrance of Him"*. Is that what your life smells like today? When people get a whiff of your life, do they smell the scent of grace and the aroma of someone who knows and has been hanging out with Jesus? This is a good challenge for each of us to consider and, as with many things, there is a natural and a spiritual reality to smells and people. We can compare them both to make a point.

All of us have experienced or been exposed to, at one time or another, a person passing us with a nice scent – maybe an expensive perfume or aftershave. It's also very likely you have experienced the smell of someone passing near to you with bad body odour. Have you ever sat in the same room or enclosed place with someone who removes their shoes and they have really unpleasantly, cheesy smelling feet? Yep, we have all probably experienced both.

Naturally, our lives have the potential to release a smell, or a fragrance, that is either pleasing or not-so-pleasing to the senses of others and, spiritually, this is a reality too. What does your Christianity smell of today?

Smells are very interesting things, they can attract people or repel them depending on what type of smell they are. When people encounter you, do they smell the sweet perfume of knowing Jesus or the musty odour of religion, with all its various scents of law and legalism or worse, the pungent stench of hypocrisy?

May our lives, today, release, wherever we go, that sweet aroma of Christ in us. May that smell attract people to follow Him and not repel them from Him.

Bless you. Today be smelly in the right way!

What do you smell like? (cont'd)

But thanks be to God, who always leads us in triumphal procession in Christ and through us spreads everywhere the fragrance of the knowledge of Him. For we are to God the aroma of Christ among those who are being saved and those who are perishing. To the one we are the smell of death; to the other, the fragrance of life. And who is equal to such a task?

2 Corinthians 2:14-16 (NIV)

We should not have to struggle to daily release the sweet scent of Christ from our lives but simply remember that it is the natural essence of His life, resident now within us.

Again, look at the natural body as an example. The reality is that whatever is in you, or put into you, can play a large part concerning the odour that comes from you. Just recently, I took Gina out to eat and I ate a very large chunk of garlic without realising it was raw. By the end of the night, it was manifesting its odour nicely and continually from every pore in my skin and, by the next morning, it had contaminated every inch of who I was. The effect was unpleasant, especially for my family who, sadly, had to experience my breath and expressive pores.

The fragrance of your life should be Christ-like in its scent simply because of two things. Firstly, because Jesus now lives in you. You are not a hotel He visits but rather His home or place of residence. He does not pop in and pop out when He feels like it, rather He never leaves, according to His promise. Christ in you is the hope of Glory but also the very source of the pleasing fragrance that comes from your life. And secondly, because you realise and accept that your life is now His home and, as you do, you daily yield and submit everything you are to Him. The fragrance of His life then comes from every part and through every pore of who you are.

Also, while we talk about the principle of 'what goes in affects what comes out', it is important that you be daily feeding your life the stuff that you want your life to be smelling of. For example, if you keep feeding your life the Law of Moses then it will be the Law of Moses that you smell of to others. Feed your life daily the truth and grace that comes through Jesus and you will love the way your life starts smelling, and so will others.

Bless you and consider, again, the One who has now become the very contents of your life. Let His life and incredible scent flow out of you again today.

Food for thought:

The gospel was never meant to be a sedative that makes you rest, rather a stimulant that empowers you to live for a cause.

Your smell affects others

For we are to God the aroma of Christ among those who are being saved and those who are perishing.
2 Corinthians 2:15-16 (NIV)

T he fragrance that comes from your life affects three people, according to Corinthians. Let's look at the first of these three this morning.

First of all, God smells you

"... we are to God the aroma of Christ ..." How awesome is that? When God leans over and sniffs us living out our everyday lives, He smells the incredible fragrance of the beauty and righteousness of His Son, Jesus. You may say, "But you do not know what I did this week." My response is that you need to know that, according to God's Word, your life is now hidden, or positioned, in Christ and, when God smells you, He smells the fragrance of His son Jesus and of His finished perfect work of redemption that now surrounds you.

A great comparison is found in *Genesis 27:27*. This is the account of when Isaac blesses his son Jacob instead of Esau. Isaac was blind by this time and knew his sons by their touch and distinctive smells. Jacob, acting on the plan of his mother, wore the smell of his brother to get his father's blessing and it was because of that smell that Isaac was convinced he was with Esau, not Jacob, and blessed him. (Read the account, it's a good read.)

And he came near and kissed him; and he smelled the smell of his clothing, and blessed him and said: "Surely, the smell of my son Is like the smell of a field which the LORD has blessed".
Genesis 27:27 (NKJV)

The smell that is upon your life is the smell of the Son He loves and the field, the life of His Son whom He has blessed. How awesome is that! When you approach God, you smell like Jesus. Also, you need to know that, unlike Jacob, this is not a con but rather an intention of God because it is He who positioned you in Christ. Don't feel like a fraud, like Jacob did, because you're not. Your scent is the result of His intent and it is He that coated you in the Son of His delight.

Because of this, you can again, today, approach the Father knowing that His approval of you is established and settled in Jesus. You can, as it invites us in *Hebrews 4:16*, approach Him with boldness of faith knowing the Lord your God loves the smell of you.

Your smell affects others (cont'd)

But thanks be to God, who always leads us in triumphal procession in Christ and through us spreads everywhere the fragrance of the knowledge of him. For we are to God the aroma of Christ among those who are being saved and those who are perishing. To the one we are the smell of death; to the other, the fragrance of life. And who is equal to such a task?

2 Corinthians 2:14-16 (NIV)

L et's have one final look at these great verses to motivate ourselves concerning the fragrance, or aroma, being given off of our lives. Yesterday, we looked at the effect our lives have on the nose of God. This morning, let us finish by looking at the scent we carry in the nostrils of people we share our daily worlds with.

Two groups of people are mentioned in the above verses and two distinctive smells. If we let them follow their natural order, I think we may be able to see that God intended both smells to exist and both play their part.

Those who are being saved

Corinthians says that we are the smell of death among this group. Death? One way of looking at it could be that our lives should smell of the death we have experienced in Christ. When people – church folk – get to experience our aroma, they should smell the scent of the death we have died in Christ upon us. It is that divine death that separated us from everything we used to be, so liberating and enabling us to be the brand new creations we now are. They should also smell the death of such things as selfishness, pride and other scents that were once common to us and also realise that there is a new-creation smell to us now.

Those who are perishing

Our aroma among the unsaved should be one of extreme life. When unsaved people get a whiff of us, they should be overwhelmed by the scent of resurrection and new life that comes from every pore of who we are. Remember that through new birth – death, burial and resurrection – we have been made alive together with Him and so our lives should smell of life, not like the musty corridors of religion. Let's face it; the smell of life is so much better than the smell of death. Life is more likely to attract followers than death, right?

What would you follow? As we again step forward to possess our day, let us be conscious of the aroma our life is giving out to the world God has called us to change.

God bless you, Smelly!

Death of the hypocrite

"Woe to you, teachers of the law and Pharisees, you hypocrites! You clean the outside of the cup and dish, but inside they are full of greed and self-indulgence. Blind Pharisee! First clean the inside of the cup and dish, and then the outside also will be clean."

Matthew 23:25-26 (NIV)

In these verses, we can clearly see that Jesus really had a problem with certain Pharisees that were living like hypocrites. People who were saying they believed one thing but their lives announced, daily, that they actually believed another. They would tell people to do things yet they did not have any intention of doing them themselves. They would continually concentrate on how things looked externally but took no regard for the true condition of things internally.

If we are brutally honest, there can still be the potential of a hypocrite in us all. Don't get me wrong, the old you before you knew Christ is very dead, yet old ways of thinking and reacting can still have the potential to resurface every now and then. Have you ever heard yourself giving advice to others when inside you knew that you were not applying it to your own life anymore? I know I have. Have you ever put a nice show on so that people would think one thing about you when in reality things were very different?

As we daily walk with Jesus, our lives should become ever more authentic. By that I mean that what we say we believe matches more and more with what we daily live out.

I know I have not arrived, how about you? Yet, I am committed to the journey to make sure the death of the hypocrite is an ongoing reality in my life. May I ever be taking the medicine, i.e. the advice and wisdom, I am prescribing to others. The Holy Ghost is so good at helping us with this if we are wanting Him to.

The new creation in Christ is not a hypocrite but the real deal, a person of integrity who has one life that matches on the inside and outside of it. That is our true identity today so let's go ahead and live it out.

Food for thought:

Remember, your life is playing in 'real time' so don't waste a moment. There is no rewind button, live full on today enjoying every single scene.

What's the purpose of your life?

For when David had served God's purpose in his own generation, he fell asleep; he was buried with his fathers and his body decayed. But the one whom God raised from the dead did not see decay.

Acts 13:36-37 (NIV)

There can be no greater testimony to a life well lived than this statement found in the book of *Acts*. Our days really are like currency, precious coins kept in the purse of our existence. Our days, as with natural wealth, can be numbered in amount, though no man knows the amount each of us have left but God. The reality is when the coins, or days, of our life are spent, they are spent – and there are no refunds. This sobering thought should not cause fear but rather motivate us to live with cause and passion. What is important is not to dread them being spent but make sure we are investing each one of them very wisely. When they are spent, it is what was purchased and accomplished with them that determines their true worth and success. Let this motivate us all to spend them well.

Believers should not fear death because Christ has beaten it and taken the sting out of it. Instead, death should inspire and motivate us to live our lives well and purposefully. Many people spend their lives existing for purposes that have no benefit to anyone outside of themselves and that carry no eternal significance or reward. In this life, they may seem to have so much but, in the life to come, they could well find themselves bankrupt.

For what will it profit a man if he gains the whole world, and loses his own soul?

Mark 8:36 (KJV)

As followers of Jesus, we have chosen something far better than living for mere riches; we have chosen to spend the currency of our days as David did, for the purposes of our God. As we daily do this we ever release the kingdom of God, changing people's lives for the better and at the same time we get to live a life that is truly worth living.

Live on purpose – don't drift around like a boat on the ocean without an anchor but walk with bold steps of divine purpose today. Live for Jesus and the advancement of His kingdom on the earth and you set yourself up for what comes next.

Living for the purposes of Jesus

For this purpose the Son of God was manifested, that He might destroy the works of the devil.
1 John 3:8b (NKJV)

We have been speaking about living your life with purpose and what greater purpose is there than to live for God?

The Bible reveals that we are now in Christ Jesus through faith. This being true, we need to carry daily the same common purposes in our life as He does in His. Think about it: we are in Christ, He is the head we are the body so what He thinks, we should think; whatever He is passionate about and sees purpose in, we should have passion for and find purpose in. Why? Because we are now positioned in Him and are a part of Him.

In today's verse we see one of the major purposes of Jesus is to *"destroy the works of the devil"*. We could call this purpose 'devil demolition'. Jesus loves to daily tear down anything and everything that the devil has spent good time building up and we should find great fulfilment and satisfaction in doing the same.

- **In people's lives** – let us be living daily to set other people free, being an agent of liberty.

- **In our cities** – living daily to see the downfall of Satan's kingdom and the advancement of the kingdom of our God. Be an ambassador of His grace.

- **In our world** – living to take a stand for the truth of the Gospel. Standing tall for the One you love, be a display-board of His truth and goodness to a desperately seeking world.

We read yesterday that King David served his generation. We too are not called to serve any past generation but we **are** called to the one we are in now. This is the one we can see changed as we daily live to serve the purposes of God in it. As we commit to do this, we also affect the next generation by giving them a great example and standard to follow as David did for us. Live with purpose.

LIVE FOR GOD!

What are God's purposes for this week?

For when David had served God's purpose in his own generation, he fell asleep; he was buried with his fathers and his body decayed. But the one whom God raised from the dead did not see decay.

Acts 13:36-37

The Bible reveals all of the purposes of God for those who are looking for them. Among those purposes there are His continual ongoing ones; for instance, He ever wants to destroy the works of the devil, He always loves to restore people to relationship with Himself and mend broken lives.

God has great purposes today for your life and, in the rest of this week ahead, He wants to do great things both in you and through you. **In** your life today? Let him have His way and let the Holy Spirit minister to you the purposes and direction of the Father for your life. Have ears to hear. **Through** your life today? Submit your life to God as an ever-ready tool in His hand, and let Him send you somewhere. Allow Him to put you in the right place at the right time.

It says that, after serving God's purposes, David died and was buried with his fathers and his body decayed. Because of the victory of Jesus, we shall die physically but never decay spiritually because eternity is now in us and we in it. We shall all close our eyes to this life one day but, in a blink, we shall open them to everlasting life with God. Jesus has spoilt the grave and defeated death for all who believe and just as Christ did not see decay, neither shall we. The Bible says we shall receive a new body and we shall dwell together with Him forever.

Today, be inspired again to live in the light and knowledge of eternity. You entered into it when you believed in Jesus and were born again. Have assurance that your life shall never end, Champion.

In this opening chapter of eternity called 'the here and now', live for God, serve His purposes. Be conscious that, as the actor Russell Crowe said in the film *Gladiator*, "What a man does in life, echoes in eternity". May the echo of our lives be of the same quality as King David's, that we too served the Lord and His purposes in our generation!

Champion's Prayer:

Father, help me to know Your purposes in the places I live and work. Let me be conscious of what You are doing and desiring and then get involved. Let my hands and feet be Your hands and feet. Fulfil Your purposes through me and, as David's life did, may my life serve Your purposes in my generation – Amen.

Be careful what and who you're coupled to

Do not be yoked together with unbelievers. For what do righteousness and wickedness have in common? Or what fellowship can light have with darkness? What harmony is there between Christ and Belial? What does a believer have in common with an unbeliever?

2 Corinthians 6:14-15 (NIV)

Here we see a warning concerning certain associations in our lives. It is not a call to remove yourself from the world or the people in your world who don't yet know Jesus; rather, it is a warning concerning who you link your life to in partnership and covenant-type relationships.

Our lives are just like train carriages and we have the choice who we couple or join them to. As with a train carriage, you need to have wisdom concerning the coupling of relationships because the reality can so often be: where they go, so do you, especially if they have more steam or drive than you do! This, of course, is great news if the trains and carriages, or the relationships, you have coupled yourself to are heading for Godly, pleasant places but not so good if they are heading for certain derailment or a very serious crash.

Make sure the people and relationships your life is joined to are going in God's direction. This will certainly produce a great harmony in the journey of your life. Imagine, if two train carriages wanted to go in very different directions, this would cause a continual strain and stress between the two carriages. So it is when one life in a relationship wants to live God's way and the other does not. Why bring that strain into your world when you do not need to? Rather, couple your life together with people who want to go in the same direction (after God).

This is not a warning or call to separate yourself from unsaved people – far from it. If you did, what hope would they have of finding and experiencing Christ? But it is a warning concerning those closer, daily-walk relationships we all have including such relationships as future marriages, business partnerships and those closer-to-heart friendships; those where the person's words can affect your decisions and choices.

Be careful who you join your life to. Always ask the question, "Do you want to go where they are going?"

(Note: This thought is by no means meant to make anyone who is currently in a marriage where one is saved and the other not feel condemned in any way; may God's grace bring that unsaved party to full salvation. But it is a strong warning to those who are choosing future partners to make sure you have God in common).

Beware of fool's wisdom

Have nothing to do with godless myths and old wives' tales; rather, train yourself to be godly. For physical training is of some value, but godliness has value for all things, holding promise for both the present life and the life to come.

1 Timothy 4:7-8 (NIV)

I remember once preaching this verse in our church and as I did I used some props to make my point. Whilst reading it, I walked under a ladder, broke a mirror, spilt salt and did not throw any over my shoulder, as well as a couple of other apparently dangerous acts. The looks on people's faces were priceless. I then opened the Bible and said, "Someone show me one of those old wives tales in here!" and, of course, I had no takers.

Paul encouraged Timothy to have nothing to do with stupid superstitions and fables but rather to get fit in God's life-changing Word. This is also good advice for us as we set our desires to live like Champions. When was the last time you walked under a ladder or broke a mirror? Guess what, nothing happens! But when you take some truth out of God's Word and dare to apply that to your life, anything can happen – and it probably will!

So, the advice of Paul to Timothy is also very good for us today, "Don't waste your time becoming an expert of every old wives' tale present in the world but rather get into God's Word and become and expert of its contents." As you do, you step into God's gym.

His Word truly is the breakfast of Champions and it, and it alone, has the potential to make us fit for every challenge life may have in store for us and, according to this verse, it even makes us fit for eternity.

Finally, it encourages us that giving your body a good workout does some good for your life but getting fit with God's Word makes you strong indeed!

Food for thought:

We may enter His gates with thanksgiving and His courts with praise but we get and keep His attention with Faith.

Changing your philosophy

See to it that no one takes you captive through hollow and deceptive philosophy, which depends on human tradition and the basic principles of this world rather than on Christ.

Colossians 2:8 (NIV)

I was reminded the other day that the word or title *"Christian"* is mentioned only 3 times in the Bible, whereas the title *"Disciple"* is mentioned 239 times. Maybe we should see ourselves and live to be His disciples rather than just Christians?

Salvation, that is the moment you respond and give your life to Jesus, is a great step but only one step in a larger journey. That journey is you being a follower, or disciple, of Jesus and that journey continues till we stand before Him in heaven. Don't get me wrong, that first step is a powerful one – it gets you totally forgiven, made righteous and made alive in Him. But we should walk forward from this initial step. Using a kitchen worktop as an example, one of the things that determines if someone is walking with a commitment to discipleship is whether or not they are letting God work within the 'chipboard' of their life or just letting Him merely own the worktop and dust it every now and then.

When you are committed to 'being a disciple', you are hungry for God to deal with the very belief system of your life, that inner part of you that you daily live out from on a regular basis. We all have a belief system that has been formed by the things we have been exposed to over the length of the life we have lived. The wisdom you have so far been exposed to will be a major ingredient in what your belief and value system looks and sounds like. So, the problem is: what if some or all of the wisdom you were exposed to was not true? How do you know if it was true? The answer is very narrow-minded but needs to be: you hold it against the wisdom of God's word to see if there is a collision of wisdoms. If there is, you choose God's wisdom over any other you may have known – then you are a disciple!

We are all philosophers; you do not go to school or college to get a philosophy – you already have one; it is simply your system of beliefs and values. Philosophy is a real simple word when you see what it actually means. It is made up of two words – *philo* and *sophia*. Philo means 'to love', sophia means 'wisdom'. So philosophy essentially is 'the love of wisdom'.

Again, the question is: what wisdom are you loving? We all have a choice regarding where we source wisdom from. We can source it from the places we knew before God or we can source it now from God Himself. Our text today gives us a clear picture that there are different sources offering you wisdom, or knowledge, and the choice of where we source it from remains with us, *"human tradition and the basic principles of this world"* or Christ? Discipleship is daily making the choice to make God the source of the wisdom you choose to embrace and love in every section of your life. You are a philosopher; the question is: what is the wisdom you are loving and where did you get it from?

Get pure wisdom!

Wisdom is the principal thing; therefore get wisdom. And in all your getting, get understanding. Exalt her, and she will promote you; she will bring you honour, when you embrace her. She will place on your head an ornament of grace; a crown of glory she will deliver to you.

Proverbs 4:7-9 (NKJV)

This Proverb encourages us to "*get wisdom*"! Again, the question is where do we, or should we, get it from? There is certainly no shortage of apparent wisdom being made available in our twenty first century lives. Everyone and their brother seems to think they have 'pure truth and genuine knowledge', everything from evolution to humanism, there is no shortage of 'stores to get some wisdom'.

The problem is that all the other wisdom outside of God's is not pure wisdom – a lot of the other wisdom that is being made available is not evil but simply not as good for you as God's. *Colossians 2* actually gives us a strong warning about where we shop for wisdom to form our philosophies from outside of God. Listen to the opening of the verse from three different translations, all of them initially warning with words like beware:

See to it that no one takes you captive through hollow and deceptive philosophy

Colossians 2:8 (NIV)

Beware lest anyone cheat you through philosophy and empty deceit

Colossians 2:8 (NKJV)

Beware lest any man spoil you through philosophy and vain deceit

Colossians 2:8 (KJV)

So a wrong philosophy, wisdom given you to love and form your belief and value systems according to, has the potential to take you captive, cheat and spoil you! Be careful where you go shopping, Champion. You also need to keep your philosophy pure. A world that does not love or acknowledge our God is ever wanting you to make a cocktail concerning the wisdom you are loving. For example, they offer cocktails that take a bit of humanism, a bit of paganism, add a shot of Christianity and then give it a flashy name to make you want it. It may be a funky-looking concoction but it won't taste good to your life, in fact it's poison to your soul.

Keep it pure, Champion. Let God now be the brickyard for the wisdom blocks you need to build that new life you have been promised. Not all the wisdom that is available in the world outside of God is evil – a lot of it is just not as good as God's. So why get it from somewhere inferior when you have the opportunity and invitation to get what is genuine from the One who makes the real thing? I know this sounds somewhat narrow-minded but, let's face it, it has to be so. There is too much 'wisdom mixing' going on within Christianity today and it's time for us to look again to the Word of God and say, "This alone contains the wisdom I need for each and every situation I may face." Get God's wisdom!

Genuine or copy

When the woman saw that the fruit of the tree was good for food and pleasing to the eye, and also desirable for gaining wisdom, she took some and ate it. She also gave some to her husband, who was with her, and he ate it.

Genesis 3:6 (NIV)

W e have been talking about wisdom these last few days, specifically about where you get it from, bearing in mind the wisdom you choose to embrace and love will be the philosophy you will end up living out of.

Just like the autopilot on an aeroplane, your philosophy, or belief system, is the autopilot of your life and you will always fly in accordance to it. You can force the controls of a plane with a pre-programmed destination so that it goes another way for a while but, sooner or later, when you let go, it will go back to its original route – it is the same with us living from our beliefs. That's why God wants us to be disciples so that He can correct our wrong beliefs where He needs to so that our lives can go in the correct direction and keep on going in that right direction.

Remember, it is wrong-believing that produces wrong-living. God does not want to spend the length of your life collecting rotten fruit – He wants to deal with the wrong root belief that is causing it, He wants to adjust your philosophy where needed. The question is, will you let Him?

In this morning's text, we see Adam and Eve were originally in possession of pure wisdom, that which flowed directly from God and then they were sold another by Satan. They were told that there was another, better wisdom they could have. They were deceived and accepted that lie as truth and, in doing so, they embraced another wisdom and formed a new philosophy then began to live out of that. We, of course, know that they actually gave away on that day the best for the least, the genuine for counterfeit. We believe that in redemption everything that was lost through Adam was restored through Christ. That means everything! This means that we, as God's children, are now able again to daily approach God for our wisdom and, when we do, He gives it in abundance without reproach *(James 1:5)*. Just as Adam and Eve turned away from God's wisdom for another, now we need to daily turn away from another wisdom back to God's. His is the genuine article because it was in existence there first!

By wisdom a house is built, and through understanding it is established;

Proverbs 24:3

Champion's Prayer:

Father, today I ask You for abundance of wisdom, according to **James 1:5**. Thank You that You give it to me for every area of my life it is needed, abundantly, without reproach. Thank You, I receive it now – Amen.

Stay in your God-given righteousness

"No weapon formed against you shall prosper, and every tongue which rises against you in judgment You shall condemn. This is the heritage of the servants of the LORD, and their righteousness is from Me," says the LORD.
Isaiah 54:17 (NKJV)

Because you are positioned in Christ and belong to God you can know, Champion, that God speaks this promise over your life today and over your tomorrows too. The sad reality is that people may fashion weapons against you but the good news is that they shall not prosper. Those weapons may be plans or schemes but the promise of the Lord is that, as you stay in your God-given righteousness and keep loving Him, none of these things will harm you or remain; no arrow made for you or aimed at you will hurt you.

This verse speaks not just of plans and schemes fashioned to harm you but also of tongues that rise against you in judgment. Again, as you walk in your God-given righteousness, He will condemn lies spoken about you and defuse lies sent to harm your good name. The key is to daily know the position of righteousness you have in Him and make the daily decision to stand in it. As you do, things meant to harm you will fail to prosper and you will walk in God's blessing, not their intended harm.

According to God, this is our heritage. Look at the life of Daniel – nothing sent to harm him remained. He was set up to become lion food but the people who wrongly accused him an set him up ended up being what the lions ate for dinner that night! Stay in truth and righteousness and God will turn things around for your good.

Think also of Mordecai, Esther's relative. He was being set up by an evil ruler called Haman, set up for things he never did. Haman actually had gallows built to have Mordecai hung but, at the end of the story, Haman ended up hanging from the gallows he had fashioned for God's man Mordecai.

They may fashion things for your harm but, when God steps in, we do not get hurt by things fashioned against us but rather witness God turn things around, always for our good and benefit.

Just walk in truth and righteousness and, with confidence, leave everything that is going on and being said behind the scenes to Him – that's called faith.

SAY AFTER ME, NO WEAPON FASHIONED AGAINST ME TODAY WILL PROSPER. GOD HAS GOT MY BACK!

Get yourself some faith 'bolt-ons'

But also for this very reason, giving all diligence, add to your faith virtue, to virtue knowledge, to knowledge self-control, to self-control perseverance, to perseverance godliness, to godliness brotherly kindness, and to brotherly kindness love. For if these things are yours and abound, you will be neither barren nor unfruitful in the knowledge of our LORD Jesus Christ.

2 Peter 1:5-8 (NKJV)

Faith is truly an incredible thing and produces everything we need in our lives from our initial salvation to seeing all manner of mountains moved throughout the journey of our lives. Faith alone would be a powerful thing but Peter says that, if you are ready to experience some serious fruitfulness in your life, there are some 'bolt-ons' you can add to it. I got the term 'bolt-ons' when I recently went to purchase a mobile phone and the salesperson offered me certain 'bolt-ons' or added extras for being a good customer. These 'bolt-ons' were things that would improve my phone and make it work more efficiently for me. People have said that you cannot add anything to faith and this is right when it comes to making things happen in your life but, when it comes to your life being developed into all God intended for it to be, Peter said that, as well as patience and wisdom, there are actually seven more things you can add, or 'bolt-on', to your faith that will empower it.

He states that if you dare to bolt these seven things onto your faith and let them abound, you will keep yourself from being barren or unfruitful. I don't know about you, but I want to live a fruitful life for God. I don't want to live some barren, shrivelled thing that is like the withered fig tree Jesus encountered which was only good for cursing. I want a life that is blossoming and producing good healthy produce.

What do you need to do? Simply download and daily apply these 'bolt-ons'. Notice how each one fits systematically onto the other and how Peter teaches us to add the next one to the one we established or bolted on before.

Let's look at these seven things again from *The Message*:

- Good character
- Spiritual understanding
- Alert discipline
- Passionate patience
- Reverent wonder
- Warm friendliness
- Generous love

So, we learn today that there are some things that will mix, or 'bolt-on' to our faith and actually improve the potential of our lives. Be bolting these seven things on to your faith today.

His plans are bigger than yours!

"For I know the plans I have for you," declares the LORD, *"plans to prosper you and not to harm you, plans to give you hope and a future. Then you will call upon me and come and pray to me, and I will listen to you. You will seek me and find me when you seek me with all your heart. I will be found by you," declares the* LORD, *"and will bring you back from captivity."*

Jeremiah 29:11-14 (NIV)

Here is one of my all time favourite verses.

God reveals to this everyday man living an everyday life, "Hey, I got plans for you, and not just any old plans – great ones." Know today, Champion, that God has plans for you too. We are living on the other side of the cross where God has restored us to Himself through perfect redemption. His plans for us would never be less then Jeremiah's, only ever more. These verses challenge me to think destiny and I hope they challenge you that way this morning too.

We may all have our own plans for our lives, which may seem great, but they are nothing when held against His plans for our lives. When we discover His plans and purpose to live them out, we will find ourselves, as Jeremiah did, living in God-given destiny, daily experiencing the true purposes for which we were born.

His plans are better than yours!

Let's face it, none of us are idiots and our plans are always pretty good but His are always far beyond what we can imagine *(Ephesians 3:20)*. Remember again today, they are plans to:

- **Prosper you!** That's not just a financial promise. His plans today are to prosper every area of your life: your family, health, friendships and everything else that makes you who you are. As you dare to say yes to His plans, prosperity will break out throughout your life.

- **Not to harm you!** God is not out to harm you today but to do you good. As any doting father, God is out to do His kids good today. Don't anticipate harm from His hand but blessing.

- **Give you hope and a future!** In a world where hopelessness is ever-growing, He gives you hope. All across the world, people's hopes are failing them but yours won't! Your future is in His hands, don't fear what man may threaten to do to you; trust in God and what His plans for you are. Christ has become our cornerstone. When we build on Him, we cannot and will not be shaken.

Jeremiah had to choose, "My plans or His plans?" – the same choice is ours. Come on, let's face it, it has to be His plans, yours are not big enough!

Agree with what He is declaring over you

"For I know the plans I have for you," declares the Lord, *"plans to prosper you and not to harm you, plans to give you hope and a future. Then you will call upon me and come and pray to me, and I will listen to you. You will seek me and find me when you seek me with all your heart. I will be found by you," declares the* Lord, *"and will bring you back from captivity."*

Jeremiah 29:11-14 (NIV)

We looked yesterday at these great promises concerning Godly destiny and established that it was not just a promise to a single man named Jeremiah but the Lord also declares this over you and me today in the 21st Century! I love how it does not say 'mumble' or 'whisper' but rather He "*declares*". God declares over you today plans of prosperity, hope and a future as you commit to walk in His ways. All He is looking for from us is agreement: He will provide everything needed to make what He says will happen in your life, He just needs you to agree with His plans so they can be activated.

Remember, He is a God who designed choice; He will never violate your choice but He will inspire and provoke you with promises of bigger, more incredible tomorrows.

He did this with Abraham. When God stepped into Abraham's life, he was not down and out or broke. Abram, as he was then, was living, as far as we can see, a pretty good life. God had a great life for him but Abram had to want it and be willing to choose it over his own plans. In *Genesis 12* we see God turn up and reveal His plans to Abram, plans to take him from merely good to amazingly great.

What God promised him suddenly made his own previously big plans for his life suddenly look very small! But, as you read on, you notice that nothing happened until Abraham left what he had planned and stepped into and embraced what God had planned.

In the same way, the plans of God for our lives kick in when we dare to let go or step out of ours, the ones that are opposite to His. Remember, Abraham was 75 years old when he made this choice. You are **never** too old or have spent too much of your life for the promises and plans of God to come into play! In addition, when you're living in the plans of God for your life, as with Abraham, it's never just about you. God also promised that the people of the earth would be blessed through him. In the same way, God's plans for you are always bigger than just you! God has others in mind and wants to bless your life far beyond you. He will cause your life, ministry or business to save, restore and refresh many of people apart from you, many that you maybe don't even know.

Lastly, God says, *"I know the plans I have for you"*. The good news is, He is not wanting to keep them a secret, He wants you to know those plans too. There are no trick questions or puzzles with God, He wants you to know them and then live towards them.

God loves to use the unlikely

"For I know the plans I have for you," declares the LORD, "plans to prosper you and not to harm you, plans to give you hope and a future. Then you will call upon me and come and pray to me, and I will listen to you. You will seek me and find me when you seek me with all your heart. I will be found by you," declares the LORD, "and will bring you back from captivity."

Jeremiah 29:11-14 (NIV)

GOD ALWAYS CHOOSES TO USE UNLIKELY PEOPLE TO DO INCREDIBLE THINGS!

When we meet Jeremiah in chapter one, we do not see a superstar but someone who looks like an 'everyday fella'. God does this by design because He is not looking for superstars, He is looking for people who are faithful and will trust Him beyond their personally perceived capabilities. God is not like a judge from a television talent show. He does not select according to what we currently may look like or how we currently perform. Rather, He chooses according to what He sees in us and what He knows we can do. When God first approaches him, as recorded in *Chapter one*, He says, *"Before I formed you in the womb I knew you, before you were born I set you apart; I appointed you as a prophet to the nations."* Jeremiah then responds *"Ah, Sovereign LORD," I said, "I do not know how to speak; I am only a child."*

God knew his true potential and capabilities before Jeremiah did and that is so true with us. It is when we meet the Lord, listen to Him and discover what we are actually capable of that then, as Jeremiah, we become amazed by what God has pre-packed into our lives and equipped us to do. God loves to use normal, unlikely people because then the glory goes to Him. He does not want people running around thinking they did it by their own ability. That's why, throughout the Bible, you see God approach everyday people, with everyday hang-ups and ask them to do things that are totally impossible; guess what, He still does that today.

Think of King David's beginnings. When God sent Samuel to find the next King for Israel, He sent him to Jesse and said, "I will show you who it is to be". One by one, Jesse brought out all his strong, and apparently full-of-potential, sons. All except one, David, who was tending the sheep. The prophet Samuel went to each son, each strong son with natural ability, but to each one God said, "No!" Then Jesse finally brought out the disregarded David and, to the shock of everyone, God said "Yes" and had the prophet select him. The great truth we see here is that God does not see or select as man does. When others saw a shepherd boy, God saw the potential of a king within the shepherd boy!

Read it for yourself *(1 Samuel 16:7)*. You need to hear what God is saying about what He sees in you.

See yourself through His eyes

"For I know the plans I have for you," declares the LORD, "plans to prosper you and not to harm you, plans to give you hope and a future. Then you will call upon me and come and pray to me, and I will listen to you. You will seek me and find me when you seek me with all your heart. I will be found by you," declares the LORD, "and will bring you back from captivity."

Jeremiah 29:11-14 (NIV)

We have been looking at these verses all week and drawn some great principles from them. Let's remind ourselves of them.

- God has plans for you. You don't have to settle for yours or other people's plans.

- His plans are to do you good and involve health, wealth and a big future.

- He wants to daily reveal to us the true potential we have within; that which He packed in us, like Jeremiah, before we were born.

- He is not looking for superstars – just faithful, agreeable people who will say "Yes!" even when they feel totally unable in their own ability.

The Bible is jammed full of people that were unlikely but chosen by God. To name just a few, there are:

- **Moses:** On the run, had a speech impediment – God used him to be a spokesman and deliverer a whole nation from national captivity.

- **Gideon:** Found hiding in a wine press with nothing positive to say – God uses him to lead armies into battle, totally outnumbered.

- **David:** Was a shepherd boy, overlooked and despised by his own family – God saw a king, not just any king, the king of all Israel.

- **Rahab:** A prostitute – God used her to lead the children of Israel through a vital part of their journey.

The point is, God has plans for you too! Don't worry about what you think you can do – if He calls you to a purpose, He has equipped you for it; that's grace.

We should also know that, according to today's text, when we pray, He listens. That's a great thought for today. Know in your heart that when you pray, He listens. He may be running a universe but He will take time to stop and listen to you. It also reveals that He is there to be found by us – all we need to do is seek Him with all of our hearts. He is not hiding, not to be found, but to see if anyone can be bothered. Be bothered! Seek Him and He promises you will find Him. Finally, He promises to bring us out of captivity; whatever captivity it may be, His plans are freedom!

Don't get itchy ears, love truth

For the time will come when they will not endure sound doctrine, but according to their own desires, because they have itching ears, they will heap up for themselves teachers; and they will turn their ears away from the truth, and be turned aside to fables.

2 Timothy 4:3-4 (NKJV)

We again hear the apostle Paul giving his son in the faith, Timothy, some good advice concerning people and their love for God's truth. He says that there will be people who, instead of loving and applying the truth of God's eternal Word, will rather run here, there and everywhere looking for people who teach what they like. Though this was written so many years ago, it is still so relevant for today.

Sadly, I often see Christians chasing after something new that tickles their ears rather than letting the Word of God in its entirety to do the transforming work it was sent by Him to do.

In my experience, one reason people turn their ears from truth and heap up ear-tickling messages is because they don't want to change something that really needs to be changed. It is easier to find a cheap, fluffy message that validates or backs up the wrong they are doing instead of come face to face with the truth that will convince them to change. We live in an incredible media-based age where there is certainly no shortage of Bible teachers, conferences and multimedia resources and that's not a bad thing, unless you're heaping up junk and starving yourself of foundational truth. Make sure that what you are listening to is based on and backed up by God's Word, Champion, and is not just 'pleasing to the ear'.

When was the last time you read the Bible and said, "Ouch!" We all need to be doing that every now and then. If it's been a while, then maybe we need to check that we have not developed a case of 'itchy ear' syndrome? Fables can't help or change you but truth can, so let us make sure that our ears and our hearts crave the solid meat of the truth and not fluffy candy-floss that's nice but has no power to change you or cause long term good.

Love truth and let God's Word do what it was sent to do – transform you!

You're going to find that there will be times when people will have no stomach for solid teaching, but will fill up on spiritual junk food — catchy opinions that tickle their fancy. They'll turn their backs on truth and chase mirages. But you — keep your eye on what you're doing; accept the hard times along with the good; keep the Message alive; do a thorough job as God's servant.

(The Message)

What was sent to crush you, can actually redefine you

No weapon formed against you shall prosper, and every tongue which rises against you in judgment you shall condemn. This is the heritage of the servants of the LORD, and their righteousness is from Me," Says the LORD.

Isaiah 54:17 (NKJV)

If you look at the meaning of the word used here, *"weapon"*, among other things it means *article or object.* God's promise to you today is that no article, object or thing that is sent against you, because you're living for Him, will prosper. Notice that it does not promise that things won't be sent but it does promise they will not prosper or accomplish in what they were sent to do.

Life is very much like a game-show. We have one in the UK called *Bring on the Wall.* In it, contestants stand on the edge of a swimming pool and, as lights suddenly flash, a wall comes at them with the intention of knocking them into the pool and out of the game. Cut into every new unique wall that comes at them during the competition is a unique body shape and, if the contestant can shape himself to fit it, he goes through the wall and is not crushed or knocked out of the game by it. If he gets through the wall, it does not ruin him; in fact, the wall actually defines him as a winner, leaving him in a better position in the game than he was before.

Listen, just like that show, when you choose to live for God you will get wall after wall that may come at you but none of them have to crush you. Rather, each one of them can actually redefine you. The art is to be able to reshape yourself to go through each new and varied one. Think of David. His future as a king and national leader was the other side of a very real wall, a wall of a man called Goliath. This wall did not crush him as the Philistines intended it to; rather, it redefined him as a leader in the sight of all who watched. All he had to do was follow God's plan for getting through it and reshape himself from that of a shepherd boy to that of a covenant warrior.

Listen, Champ, your wall, or current challenge, may be different to mine but God has promised us both that they will not crush us, as they were sent to do, but rather redefine us. Spend some time with God and find your way through it, knowing that, after this one, there will be another and you will reshape and beat that one too.

Champion's Prayer:

Father, help me today with the walls and challenges I may face. Help me to see and hear Your ways for getting the other side of them. Help me to be flexible enough to get past every challenge that may come my way – Amen.

"Bring on the wall!"

"No weapon forged against you will prevail, and you will refute every tongue that accuses you. This is the heritage of the servants of the LORD, and this is their vindication from me," declares the LORD.

Isaiah 54:17 (NIV)

A life lived on purpose will always attract differing walls of opposition, especially when the purpose being lived is all about what God is wanting to do in the world. The walls will always come to stop, or crush, what God is doing or intending to do through you but let us remind ourselves concerning what God says the end results that these walls, or momentary challenges, will have, *"they will not prosper or prevail!"* Instead, our faith shall prevail because this is our heritage as servants of the Lord.

The Bible is full of people who came up against walls of opposition on their individual pilgrimages of faith but each one chose to see them as walls of opportunity. That choice is ours as we face walls that may be standing in our way – will we see them as opposition sent to crush or stop us, or as walls of opportunity sent to redefine us and bring us into a greater measure of success and reputation?

Nehemiah had to deal with the very physical walls of Jerusalem. No one else would take responsibility for them but he did and, in taking on those broken down walls with a big heart for their restoration, he redefined himself in the sight of the people as more than a cupbearer to the king. He was now a national leader, even in the sight of his enemies.

Will you take on a wall, a kingdom task, for God that others are ignoring and moaning about the condition it is in?

Think also about Joshua and the walls of Jericho; they too were very real walls that stood before him and what God had next for Israel. He did not reverse in fear but went forwards in faith. The walls that were there to stop him actually crumbled before him and defined him as a man of faith, a man who had the guts to trust God in seemingly impossible situations.

It's all about perspective – how you choose to look at the walls that are in your life today. Yes, they could well be walls of opposition but, at the very same time, they could well be walls of great opportunity that, when you find your way over or through them, will leave you redefined in the sight of those who are watching. It's how you look at it really. I am choosing to look at them as challenges that contain the potential to make me more than I am now, so "Bring on the wall!"

If God is for me, and He is, who can be against me?! How about you?

What was sent to ruin turned out really well

Joseph said to them, "Do not be afraid, for am I in the place of God? But as for you, you meant evil against me; but God meant it for good, in order to bring it about as it is this day, to save many people alive. Now therefore, do not be afraid; I will provide for you and your little ones." And he comforted them and spoke kindly to them.

Genesis 50:19-21 (NKJV)

W e have been speaking about defining moments and how 'walls' or things sent to crush or ruin us can actually be the things that can redefine us and leave us in a better place than where we were before. As we have seen, it certainly worked that way for David, Nehemiah and Joshua. Sometimes the timing is the thing that makes it a little more confusing but it is then that we have to believe in the bigger picture of what is presently happening, not the current moment we find ourselves in.

It was certainly this way for Joseph. When you read through his life, it looks like he gets hit by one stinking wall after another but none of the walls crushed him. Rather, they only ever redefined and often repositioned him for God's bigger picture plan. If he lived and chose to judge everything by the individual moments he experienced, it would have given him a nervous breakdown! No, he trusted God that each wall-like moment and each individual victory was a part of a bigger plan that would one day make complete sense.

And it really did. The text that we read this morning is from the moment when Joseph is now Prime Minister, second in charge in the nation, and his brothers are now bowing before him begging provision, not knowing who he was – including the ones who actually started his confusing, roller coaster journey to latter-day success by throwing him in a pit to die then selling him on as a slave.

This moment is where Joseph speaks out of the bigger picture that he knew God had been painting the whole time: *"But as for you, you meant evil against me; but God meant it for good, in order to bring it about as it is this day, to save many people alive."*

The bottom line is, when God is in it, you will win it, Champion. What a picture of grace – the one they did so much bad to ended up being the one who would save them. Don't judge everything by the walls or challenges you may be facing today but trust God that you are in a moving picture that will one day make a lot of life-giving sense.

Blessed are the flexible, for they shall not be broken!

The disciples were amazed at his words. But Jesus said again, "Children, how hard it is to enter the kingdom of God! It is easier for a camel to go through the eye of a needle than for a rich man to enter the kingdom of God."

Mark 10:24-26 (NIV)

L et's continue to talk about walls. Sometimes getting through the wall at hand is about daring to re-shape yourself for what is currently needed.

We have been speaking about walls that God says will not prosper, specifically those sent to stop us or crush us. Our challenge is always to get to the other side of them, right? Sometimes that is about simply finding the ladder to get you over them or digging a tunnel that will get you under them. But, at other times, it is about looking at the shape you need to be to get through them!

Referring back to the game-show I mentioned a couple of days ago, called *Bring on the Wall*, success for the contestants is based on their ability to reshape themselves to the fast approaching cut out that is coming toward them. Their flexibility to reshape for each new uniquely challenging wall is what gives them the success they need every time.

We need to always be flexible enough to reshape ourselves to take on the position needed to get through the wall at hand. Maybe today that position is prayer or praise or maybe standing in faith?

Today's text confused me for many of my younger years – I would sit there as a kid thinking, "How can a camel get through the eye of a sowing needle?" Then one day, I found out Jesus was referring to one of the many gates into Jerusalem, one of the gates that would get the traders and salesmen of the day through the surrounding walls of the Jerusalem and into the city so they could trade. It was so narrow that they would have to unpack their camels to get the camels through, and then repack the camels the other side. That made so much more sense to my over active imagination!

Hey, Champion, to go where God is leading you next may mean you need to unpack, or shed, some stuff – some baggage you no longer need! We should be ever shedding stuff on our pilgrimage with God: attitudes, habits and stuff that won't do us any good where we are going next. Lighten your load; go through the wall that is at hand into the next chapter of your God-ordained adventure. You won't even miss the stuff you leave behind because of the sudden lightness you will experience!

Defining moments always leave you with a choice

So he asked Jesse, "Are these all the sons you have?" "There is still the youngest," Jesse answered, "but he is tending the sheep." Samuel said, "Send for him; we will not sit down until he arrives." So he sent and had him brought in. He was ruddy, with a fine appearance and handsome features. Then the LORD said, "Rise and anoint him; he is the one." So Samuel took the horn of oil and anointed him in the presence of his brothers, and from that day on the Spirit of the LORD came upon David in power. Samuel then went to Ramah.

1 Samuel 16:11-13 (NIV)

David had a choice to make in this moment he had with God's prophet. His life had just been totally redefined, anointed and empowered. If you take time to read the story line leading up to this point, you'll see it was a powerful day for the young shepherd boy David where everything suddenly changed in a moment. Hours before, he was sitting, unnoticed by man, on a hillside tending sheep; suddenly, his whole life is redefined to being that of a future king.

The prophet did three things for David that day that revolutionised his life. He brought the word of God to him and it was that which redefined him. He anointed him with oil and he gave him the certain promise of a God-empowered future.

All of these three things have happened to each of us too: His Word revealing our true identity and potential has come to us in the vehicle of the Bible; His Spirit has been poured upon us as anointing oil was upon David that day and the commission has been given to go and live like we have never lived before. These three things created a powerful defining moment for David to experience a call to a brand new, bigger life. All that was left to do for this new life to start was for David to make a decision – a simple decision that we to also have to make when God gives us a defining moment: "Do I go back to what I knew, to that which previously defined me, or do I go forward into the life that God has called and qualified me for?"

He could have ignored the word, the anointing and the sending and gone back to the hillside to the sheep and spent the rest of his days doing what he had always done. But no, he chose to live forward from this moment.

We too must choose to live forward in what God has spoken over our lives, and know that the anointing has broken every yoke or restriction on us too. As we daily, like David did, step out into what God has called us to do we will know the empowerment of the Spirit to live that great big life God promised. David had all of the 'man-made wheel clamps' taken off the car of his life that day and, as you read on, you see that he responded by putting his life in gear and moving forward into his future. He never stayed parked up and neither should you.

His Father is our Father

Do not be like them, for your Father knows what you need before you ask him. "This, then, is how you should pray: "Our Father in heaven, hallowed be your name…"

Matthew 6:8-9 (NIV)

One of the most important things to grasp concerning your Christianity is the simple, yet profound truth that you have a heavenly Father who adores you. You may know the exact dimensions of Noah's ark off by heart, be able to recite the books of the Bible backwards and even be able to name the major and minor prophets in alphabetical order but if you don't understand this simple truth, your relational foundation with God will always be more wobbly than it could or should be.

Champion, you have a heavenly Father who adores you!

In these verses, Jesus is reminding us of something very powerful and that is, "His Father is now our Father". Notice how Jesus uses the words *"your"* and *"our"* instead of the words "mine" or "my". What He was saying in choosing to use these specific words was, "He is now your Father too!"

This thought of Jesus saying *"our Father"* really caught my attention so I started to look through the Bible to see when *"our Father"* was first, or most often, used. I looked real hard but only found it used in the context of people having a heavenly Father in common when Jesus used it. There are other times in the Old Testament when *"our father"* was used but it was always regarding two children sharing an earthly father (like Esau and Jacob), not the sharing of a heavenly one.

It was only used by Jesus because He was the one who qualified us to stand again as sons and daughters of a living God and heavenly Father. His perfect work at the cross was what removed every barrier that stood in our way and re-positioned us as heirs to the Father and joint heirs with the Son so that we too are now children of God.

Now if we are children, then we are heirs – heirs of God and co-heirs with Christ, if indeed we share in his sufferings in order that we may also share in his glory.

Romans 8:17 (NIV)

Wow, that's a thought worth pondering – His Father is now your father also. You have a heavenly Father who adores you! God bless, go ahead and enjoy that thought.

How much more is God?

Or what man is there among you who, if his son asks for bread, will give him a stone? Or if he asks for a fish, will he give him a serpent? If you then, being evil, know how to give good gifts to your children, how much more will your Father who is in heaven give good things to those who ask Him!

Matthew 7:9-11 (NKJV)

Yesterday, we considered the incredible truth of God being our heavenly Father. When the reality of this truth continues to drip-feed into your spirit, a great confidence and authority starts to manifest and you will find yourself walking through life with a whole new stride!

I am conscious, when you mention the title 'father', that it can cause different reactions in people; the reaction often depending on what a person's experience of a natural, earthly father was. For one, the name 'father' will cause a smile, to another, a sense of a key person being absent and to another, sadly, the thoughts of cruelty and abuse. Many of us would have experienced so many different things from the person we knew or know as our earthly father. So when we come to a point of being told that God is our heavenly Father, not everyone smiles.

But the truth is, you do now have a heavenly Father and all of us have the potential to understand Him as a great father because we all have an internal picture of what the perfect father is or should be. For the person who had a good dad, He is all that your dad was and so much more; for the person who had a not-so-good, or even a terrible dad, He is everything you imagined a great dad to be. You see, you must have had an ideal of what a perfect father was for you to judge that yours was no good, right? He is everything you imagine that perfect father to be and so much more.

I have a really great earthly dad who always did his best for me and my brother and I also believe that, in my own way, I am a great father too. I do my very best for my five kids and love them so very much but I am so aware that, even after my best day of fathering, I am nowhere near as good a father as God is.

In today's verse, it compares the love and care of a human father to the love and care of a heavenly one and asks the question, "How much more is God?" The answer is simple: "So much more!"

Whatever your experience of a natural or earthly father, I encourage you to open up the gates of your heart to a heavenly one who truly adores you and really is 'so much more'. Whatever your ideal of a perfect father is, either because you experienced one or dreamed of one, He is all of that and **so** much more. Let Him love on you today.

That's what great fathers do

Therefore do not worry, saying, 'What shall we eat?' or 'What shall we drink?' or 'What shall we wear?' For after all these things the Gentiles seek. For your heavenly Father knows that you need all these things.

Matthew 6:31-32 (NKJV)

We have been taking time to consider, again, the life-changing truth that God is our heavenly Father and also that, knowing Him as your heavenly Father, who adores you, is the most fundamentally important building block to your walk with Him. So God is your heavenly Father. What can or should you expect from Him? Here are a few things I think a child can expect from a great dad so we should be able to expect them from an extraordinary, divine one.

Fathers Protect

I believe that it's in the very DNA, or fundamental wiring, of a father to protect their children; whether in a bear, a lion or human, the instinct to protect your children in every way is not something that has to be taught. Have you ever seen a father's posture change when harm is around? They position themselves in front of their kids and get ready to protect them, right? I know I do! You need to know that God is very protective of you. When sin came to take its owed payment from us God, in Christ, stood in front of it and us and took the hit for us. God's love is that love that is, among other things, always protective *(1 Corinthians 13)*.

Fathers Provide

Again, I believe this characteristic is in the natural DNA of any father. They will always live to provide for their kids, even if it means they themselves experience self-lack or suffering. A father's delight is to know his family are safe and taken care of. This is also a characteristic of Father God. One of the biblical names that He uses to reveal Himself to us is *"Jehovah Jireh"* – this name means 'God the provider, the one who provides'. Our text this morning reminds us of this as, with any loving parent, Father God knows what we need and has already made plans to make sure we have what we need. I love to watch my kids living with confidence under my care, knowing that their dad will make sure they have what they need. I have, thankfully, never had to watch them panic or worry concerning this but rather see that they have a confidence in their provision.

We too can live confident, knowing we have a heavenly Father who is committed to providing for us, a Father who is both willing and able. Even if your natural father did not provide well for you, your heavenly Father will.

When my father and my mother forsake me, then the LORD will take care of me.
Psalm 27:10 (KJV)

That's what great fathers do (cont'd)

And you have forgotten the exhortation which speaks to you as to sons: "My son, do not despise the chastening of the LORD, Nor be discouraged when you are rebuked by Him; For whom the LORD loves He chastens, And scourges every son whom He receives." If you endure chastening, God deals with you as with sons; for what son is there whom a father does not chasten? But if you are without chastening, of which all have become partakers, then you are illegitimate and not sons.

Hebrews 12:5-8 (NKJV)

L et's continue to consider what we can expect from God as our heavenly Father. We have established that He is there as our protector and provider – let's now look at another great and very important characteristic of a great Father.

Great Fathers chasten (discipline)

This is the one most likely to cause the greatest reaction in people, again because of bad experiences they may have had. But we need to define what chastening really is so that we can understand that chastening is an important part of parenting. A great parent is a parent that will love a child enough to chasten them, not just let them get away with anything. As well as being protectors and providers, fathers should be a figure of loving discipline. Come on, very few of us *never* heard this statement when we were young: "Wait till your father gets home!" That was the ultimate sentence spoken by mothers who had been taken to the edge, right?

Great fathers chastise, they don't abuse – these are two very different things. Chastisement means **to discipline or to child raise**, not to abuse. This part of understanding great fathering can be the hardest one to talk about if the hand behind the chastisement you have known was not driven by love but by something else. When God, as our Father, disciplines, or chastens, there is nothing but love for us behind it, a love that will deal with something potentially harmful in us while it is still the size of a seed.

A great father will have the courage to deal with the seed-like form of bad or harmful behaviour instead of visiting it when it is in prison or hospital, fully grown, later. Chastening is actually a demonstration of love – it may not be fun but what is behind it could save your life or mean the difference between a great life and a difficult one. *Hebrews* teaches us that if we understand that a part of God's fathering in our lives is to discipline us when needed, we are indeed children but if we refuse to allow Him to correct us, we are actually illegitimate (the *King James* version actually uses the word "*Bastards*").

I don't know about you, Champion, but I don't want to be illegitimate in any area of my life. I'd rather be a son who knows that all that God does to me is for my good. I trust the hand that chastens me, knowing that it is only ever fuelled by love – you can trust Him too. *Proverbs 3:12.*

He turns scarlet red to majestic white

"Come now, let us reason together," says the LORD. *"Though your sins are like scarlet, they shall be as white as snow; though they are red as crimson, they shall be like wool."*

Isaiah 1:18 (NIV)

Here's a very topical thought. The last couple of days, we in the UK have awoken to a carpeting of white snow that covered everything. I looked out of my bedroom window and everything in my back garden was covered with a lovely white layer of snow. Snow has a way of making everything look so clean, fresh and pure, doesn't it?

Areas in my garden that were dirty with mud and muck were now covered with this new pure blanket. Areas that were messy to look at normally were now covered in a majestic white. In fact, every part of the garden, the good, the bad and the ugly, were now covered with the purity of snow. It made me think of these verses in Isaiah that speak of our salvation that comes to us through Jesus alone.

- Though we were once messy and bloodstained like crimson in His sight, we are now pure white through the perfect work of Christ.

- The shedding of the redness of His blood has produced for us the whiteness of our eternal innocence (righteousness by faith).

- He took our stains and mucky bits and washed us majestically clean.

It's good also to remember the law only **covered** sin but grace has removed it as far as the east is from the west. This is good because we will never be different because of a thaw! All remains this way in His sight for ever.

When God looks out over the garden of your life today, He does not see a muddy backyard full of rusting junk. He sees a white, grace-covered paradise. The first statement made is worth some thought as well, *"Come now, let us reason together,"* – God is reasonable! He does not want to be a dictator in our lives but rather have a relationship with us where we can feel welcome to come and reason with Him concerning the issues we may face. When we reason with Him, He shows us what we do not see and our lives are blessed.

Champion's Prayer:

Thank You today, Lord, that because of Jesus I stand pure and white, all of my sins have been forgiven by Your one-time sacrifice. The landscape of my life is now completely different because of what You did for me and thank You that I have a relationship that is reasonable – Amen.

You say it best when you say nothing at all

Then some stood up and gave this false testimony against him: "We heard him say, 'I will destroy this man-made temple and in three days will build another, not made by man.'" Yet even then their testimony did not agree. Then the high priest stood up before them and asked Jesus, "Are you not going to answer? What is this testimony that these men are bringing against you?" But Jesus remained silent and gave no answer.

Mark 14:57-62 (NIV)

In this account, Jesus has been arrested and is being falsely accused by people whose stories could not even hold water. He had been dragged before a kangaroo court of false testimonies and made-up tales. Like any TV courtroom scene, accusations and allegations were being fired at Him from every direction and He found Himself right in the middle, although innocent of all the charges and lies. In the middle of this trial of errors, we see Jesus choose to say one of the greatest things of all. He said nothing at all. He knew what we all need to discover that, in a battle of words, often silence is the winner.

The greatest statement He could make to the false things being said about Him was to say nothing. Why? He did not need to justify the lies. He needed only to stand confidently in the truth of what He knew was real. As we make the decision to live for God, we too will be falsely accused and, just like Jesus, we will have the option to fight back verbally. Maybe we will find ourselves or our reputation being defamed or set up too. We may have the potential and opportunity to verbally give the best defence ever given but we need to ask ourselves if it will match the power of silence? Remember, one of the greatest statements Jesus ever made was to say nothing.

Sometimes, the use of words just tries to justify something that does not qualify justification. Truth does not need to be justified to everyone, just confidently rested upon, "Time will tell your story". You see, truth is like a beach ball that is being held under water in a swimming pool. It is only a matter of time before it comes back up to the surface. The pressure working for it is greater than that working against it!

Make the decision not to always fight your own corner when you don't need to. Try not to get into a verbal wrestling match when silence is clearly the best contender.

Sometimes, like Jesus knew, and a UK singer once sang, "You say it best when you say nothing at all". Think about that.

You say it best when you say nothing at all (cont'd)

The high priests let loose a barrage of accusations. Pilate asked again, "Aren't you going to answer anything? That's quite a list of accusations." Still He said nothing. Pilate was impressed, really impressed.

Matthew 15:3-5 (The Message)

Let's think again about the power of silence and look at these verses using the modern *Message* translation, looking again at the account found in the book of *Mark*. In not speaking, He impressed Pilate and, more importantly, was actually fulfilling what Isaiah the prophet had prophesied concerning Him, validating His identity and the truth of who He was to those who had ears to hear and eyes to see.

He was oppressed and afflicted, yet he did not open his mouth; he was led like a lamb to the slaughter, and as a sheep before her shearers is silent, so he did not open his mouth.

Isaiah 53:7 (NIV)

Jesus knew exactly what He was doing and was able to trust His Father God in the midst of it. A good leadership lesson is that, when we know what we are doing, there is no reason or purpose to justify it to everyone. I am sure you have learned, as I have, that speaking when you don't need to or just shouldn't, can get you into the position where you find yourself digging yourself out of a hole you never needed to be in. Have you ever dug your way out of pointless holes? You can't change them but you can stop yourself from digging others.

If He had got himself into a conversation or debate concerning the what and why of all He was doing, He would have stepped out of Isaiah's prophecy concerning who He was and positioned Himself in a place where He could jeopardise the redemptive plan that would be carried out. By not verbally justifying who He was, or His actions, He more clearly showed that He was the One whom God had chosen to redeem the world, according to Isaiah's prophetic word. His silence was the fulfilment of the scripture and the Jews who were there watching would know this and see prophetic fulfilment unfolding before their very eyes.

Leadership Lesson:

As we lead in life for God, let's be wise with our speech. Have different responses for different people, depending on who they are in your life and the situation at hand. Remember, different people can handle knowing different things. What can they handle? Don't give them what they can't! And certain people deserve to know certain things and others don't but need to wait and see. So, be wise with your words!

Do you want to be amazed at what comes out of your mouth?

Therefore settle it in your hearts not to meditate beforehand on what you will answer; for I will give you a mouth and wisdom which all your adversaries will not be able to contradict or resist.

Luke 21:14-15 (NKJV)

We have spoken about the power of "saying nothing at all" but what about when you have to say something? We know that, according to *Ecclesiastes*, there is a time for everything, "a time to be silent and a time to speak". What about those times when silence won't serve you best and you need to say something and you know that what you say could have a serious effect? Jesus gives some great advice concerning this in the Gospel of Luke

Jesus gave this promise to His disciples as He spoke to them on the subject of the signs of the end times. He spoke of people betraying them and setting them up with loaded or trick questions intended to incriminate or defame them and their God. He told them not to worry about it but rather, when they found themselves in one of those awkward moments, to open their mouth and listen to what comes out. The promise He made to them is still valid for us today. Why? Because His Spirit, the spirit of wisdom and revelation, lives now in us and is not silent but still speaks.

When we dare to take our minds out of gear and listen for Him, it is amazing the answers and responses we suddenly have to give that appear seemingly from nowhere. Consider this promise and its implications for you today.

Jesus promised that He would give 'the mouth (courage, eloquent ability) and the wise answer (truth for the moment)' to those who would dare to not premeditate responses but simply trust Him in those moments for the perfect answers. Not only will He give you the perfect answer but an answer that will not be able to be contradicted or resisted. Now that is a great response.

So remember, sometimes it is better not to speak, "to say nothing at all" and at other times, when words are needed, why not let His wisdom become the 'appearing seemingly from nowhere' words you use? As you do, you will leave your hearers unable to contradict. Why? That is what truth does when it is spoken with wisdom!

Make up your mind right now not to worry about it. I'll give you the words and wisdom that will reduce all your accusers to stammers and stutters.

Luke 21:15 (The Message)

Covenant people just can't lose

"Is not the whole land before you? Let's part company. If you go to the left, I'll go to the right; if you go to the right, I'll go to the left." Lot looked around and saw that the whole plain of the Jordan toward Zoar was well watered, like the garden of the LORD, *like the land of Egypt. (This was before the* LORD *destroyed Sodom and Gomorrah.) So Lot chose for himself the whole plain of the Jordan and set out toward the east. The two men parted company.*

Genesis 13:9-11 (NIV)

Another great truth to realise in your faith walk is that covenant people know that God is with them so they cannot lose! God had blessed Abram so much that there was no room left for him and Lot, who God had also blessed, I believe, because he was journeying with Abram, he was getting the overflow (think who you will journey with!). So they came to a point where they needed to split up to each have enough room.

Look at Abram's confidence as he says to his nephew Lot, "You choose first, I will have what's left." Wow, how many Christians today would fight for what looked the better option instead? Not Abram – he knew he was walking in covenant and wherever he went, God would bless him richly.

So Lot looks around and chooses what looks the much better of the two options – the one that was apparently green, fruitful and well watered. Little did he know he was actually walking into what would later be hell on earth, Sodom and Gomorrah. There's another a good lesson here about the need for spiritual discernment and walking by faith and not sight, right?

So, Lot went his way and soon needed the help of Abram to get him out of the trouble his choice had brought into his life. But Abram happily goes the other way. It does not speak of what his choice looked like – no well-watered gardens in sight. But guess what, when you read on you see that Abram is blessed, blessed and then blessed again.

We too should have this bold confidence because we have a better covenant established by God's own Son. We to need to walk knowing that, as we walk with faith and obedience, we too can leave the choice to others instead of fighting over things and we'll see blessing and future in the route we take because we are destined to reign.

Champion's Challenge:

Next time you find yourself in a moment where the first choice is being fought for and God reminds you of this devotional, step back and let them choose first knowing, as Abraham, that you can't lose because you are in covenant with God.

How are you responding to 'The Book'

Ezra opened the book. All the people could see him because he was standing above them; and as he opened it, the people all stood up. Ezra praised the LORD, the great God; and all the people lifted their hands and responded, "Amen! Amen!" Then they bowed down and worshipped the LORD with their faces to the ground.

Nehemiah 8:5-6 (NIV)

Nehemiah had rebuilt the walls and indeed the city and culture of Jerusalem as well. We now see the priest, Ezra, take the stage to lead the people according to God's Word. Ezra opens the book and gets an incredible response from the people. They all stand up and begin to shout praises to God. They shouted, *"Amen! Amen!"* which, as we understand it today, would be equivalent to "So be it, let it be done for us". The people then lifted up their hands and it must have looked like a football match. Finally, they went into worshipping, hitting the ground and bowing down in worship and all that had happened, so far, was that the Book was lifted up and opened. What a great picture of a proper due response to God's Word.

What were they responding to? The Book, God's Word and, remember, they only had a few books of the whole Old Testament. Today, we have the fully finished, completed version and the New Testament as well. How much greater should our response be than theirs because we get to read the end and find out that our Saviour has come and we are redeemed from the law and are now under grace! I personally think our response to the opening of the book should be a lot louder then theirs was.

Champion, make sure you are responding to God's Word correctly. Don't let it become 'just another book in your library'. Make the decision that you are going to honour His Word above all others in your life today. Believe God's promises and live out His instructions for a great life. Let us all be inspired to have a fresh celebration in our hearts concerning 'the book' and begin to read it with expectancy and *"Amen"* it with all your heart. It's our turn to hear it and respond, "So be it, let it be for us". Imagine what your church service would look like this Sunday if everyone clapped when the pastor opened his Bible? Maybe you're the one to start off a new response?

God's words are life-changing. Just one of them could redefine your life forever. It is not just another book; it is the breakfast of Champions.

Champion's Prayer:

Father, I thank You that Your Word is powerful. It is not just another book. I approach it again with faith and expectancy, waiting to hear You speak to me through every page. I honour my Bible as Your living words; speak to me today as I read it – Amen.

Dress for where you're going

Finally, be strong in the LORD and in his mighty power. Put on the full armour of God so that you can take your stand against the devil's schemes.

Ephesians 6:10-11 (NIV)

These verses speak about wearing the right garments for the moment you're going into. They remind us that, if you're going into battle, make sure you wear the suit of armour you need for that battle. I want to challenge you over the next couple of days concerning what you're currently wearing in life and ask you whether or not it's what you should be wearing for where you say you want to go next.

We all wear stuff naturally, which is good, because otherwise we would be nudists, getting arrested! But the truth is, we also all have the potential to wear other stuff too. Just as we choose what we are going to wear in a natural sense, we also have a choice what other non-clothing-related stuff we wear. For example, stuff like guilt, depression, sarcasm and unforgiveness to name just a few can all be worn by a person. The truth is, none of these things suit you anymore now that your life is in Christ! So it's time for you to look in the mirror and ask yourself, "Does what I am wearing in life suit the season I am in?" and, "Is it what I need to wear for where I am saying my life is going next?"

These are good questions that could really help you to redress your life for the success that God has for you next. Obviously, we have to be honest with ourselves: if you find you're still wearing some of the stuff you used to wear years ago, that used to really suit the person you were but not the one you are now, then let the Holy Spirit help you redress your life so that you wearing what you need and what suits you for who you are today.

You would not go into a battle with swimming shorts and flip flops, even if you had just come from the beach! You would change what you had on to fit where you were going next. This is what we always need to be doing with our walk with God.

So, tomorrow we will begin to look at your wardrobe – see you there, get ready for a spring clean!

Champion's Prayer:

Father, today I put on the full armour that You have provided for me to wear. Forgive me for so often running into battle with the wrong clothes on and then blaming You when I got hurt. Today, I dress for the battles ahead knowing that I am destined to win – Amen.

Does what you are wearing compliment you?

But the father said to his servants, 'Quick! Bring the best robe and put it on him. Put a ring on his finger and sandals on his feet. Bring the fattened calf and kill it. Let's have a feast and celebrate. For this son of mine was dead and is alive again; he was lost and is found.' So they began to celebrate.

Luke 15:22-24 (NIV)

As we discussed yesterday, let's ask some important questions about what you are wearing in life. More specifically, we should ask this – is what you're currently wearing in life complimenting the decisions and resolutions you have made recently in your life?

In our text today, we read the account of the wayward child, specifically, the part when he returns home after coming to his senses. In brief, he had been raised in a great home with a great father. Foolishly, he then decides to go and see if the 'grass on the other side is greener', loses everything and ends up in a pigsty desiring to eat pig food. While in the pigsty of his own foolishness, he is wearing the clothes that would be suited to living with pigs. They must have been so filthy and so very smelly! When he came to his senses and makes some resolutions, he comes back to his father's household. His father welcomes him with love and adoration – his lost son had returned. Notice what he does next: he re-clothes him! He takes away his old pig-dung-smelling clothes, replacing them with the garments of a king's son.

Why was this change of clothes so important? Because the clothes he was wearing associated him with where he had been, not where he was now or where he was going next. Those clothes always would have reminded him of who he used to be and the dumb and filthy things he had done. They would have also always reminded the father who wanted to forget and move on.

This is a great picture of our lives, that we were also once clothed in garments that were filthy and sin-stained but when we came back to the Father, He took our old garments, washed us clean and clothed us in His righteousness. We need to constantly remember what we are now wearing – garments of white. As we do, it will affect where we choose to go in life. When we remember we are no longer wearing mud-stained clothes, we will be more likely to keep away from muddy puddles. The thought of rolling around in pig waste while wearing a white suit should have a whole new impact in your reasoning.

The prodigal son clothed himself in garments that complimented the resolutions and decisions he had made. We would be wise to do this also – don't wear what associates you with where you came from, wear what declares where you are at today! *Isaiah 1:18 (NKJV)*

Wear the right size clothes (they are the ones that fit you now)

So Elijah went from there and found Elisha son of Shaphat. He was ploughing with twelve yoke of oxen, and he himself was driving the twelfth pair. Elijah went up to him and threw his cloak around him. Elisha then left his oxen and ran after Elijah. "Let me kiss my father and mother good-bye," he said, "and then I will come with you." "Go back," Elijah replied. "What have I done to you?" So Elisha left him and went back. He took his yoke of oxen and slaughtered them. He burned the ploughing equipment to cook the meat and gave it to the people, and they ate. Then he set out to follow Elijah and became his attendant.

1 Kings 19:18-22 (NIV)

Welcome back for some further fashion advice! Here we have another garment-related account: the account of when the prophet Elijah hands over the mantle of spiritual authority that was on his life to a young, up-and-coming prophet called Elisha.

Elisha is busy working in the field with a heart full of desire to be a prophet for God then, seemingly without warning, the prophet Elijah comes to him and throws his garment, or mantle, around him and says, "It's time for you to wear this now". We then see Elisha struggle slightly with the hold of his past before boldly stepping into his future, burning everything that could make him, or allow him, to go back.

He had a choice concerning what he would wear. He could have shrugged the garment off and said, "It's far too big for me, I wear stuff that is a lot smaller." Rather, he chose to make the bigger thing that God was calling him to his new size. You know, it did not take him long to grow into it either. God called him to wear bigger things; he responded and his life grew.

I believe that God is constantly wanting to grow us to a new size and, as we dare to dress in the larger clothes He offers, we will keep moving into the bigger things He has ordained for us. Your life should be constantly outgrowing things as you daily walk with God. Like a snake shedding its skin each year, so we should be shedding skin on a regular basis, testifying that our lives are getting bigger and constantly outgrowing what once fitted or contained us.

Champion, dress for where God is leading you. Don't be afraid to put on that bigger responsibility when it is offered to you, like Elisha; wear the clothes that fit your future, not your past. I see young people today wearing skinny jeans – I don't get them! Maybe I am jealous because I can't get any to fit me. But I know, in God, I do not want to wear skinny anything, I want to always have the right size on and the right size is that you have further room to grow and develop.

Go through your 'life wardrobe' and throw out the small stuff you don't fit into anymore.

Know when to change your clothes

David noticed that his servants were whispering among themselves and he realised the child was dead. "Is the child dead?" he asked. "Yes," they replied, "he is dead." Then David got up from the ground. After he had washed, put on lotions and changed his clothes, he went into the house of the LORD and worshipped. Then he went to his own house, and at his request they served him food, and he ate.

2 Samuel 12:19-21 (NIV)

Some clothes are to be worn for certain moments of your life, not for the rest of your life.

Welcome to this account of one of the worst moments in King David's life. It was the moment when the son he had produced in sin had died. David had spent much time pleading for the life of this child. In these verses, we join him in the moment when he discovers 'it's all over'. This is, indeed, a very sad moment but what David does next can inspire us all concerning rising up out of moments of loss and great pain. Again, this is a garment-changing account that we can learn a whole lot from.

David had probably been wearing sackcloth and ashes or another outfit of mourning but, when the moment arrived for David to stand up and move on, notice what he did. David washed, anointed himself and then he changed his clothes. He took off the garments that smelt of the horrible moment he had known – a moment so very painful – and he put on new garments that determined how he would live from this moment. A great lesson to learn is that he wore the clothes that were right for the moment or season he found himself in but was also courageous enough to change that outfit when it was the right time.

Grief is a very real moment filled with pain. Even if you have the eternal hope in Christ of a reunion with the one you have lost, the moment of earthly separation can be so painful. But then there comes a day, as it did for David, when you need to get up and change what you are wearing; where you allow God to take the garments of heaviness and give you fresh clothes. When you wear any clothes longer than you should, they start to smell. There are clothes like grief we have to wear at certain times but we should never keep them on longer than necessary – have the courage to let God re-clothe you.

And provide for those who grieve in Zion, to bestow on them a crown of beauty instead of ashes, the oil of gladness instead of mourning, and a garment of praise instead of a spirit of despair.

Isaiah 61:3 (KJV)

Prosperity works best when it has a Godly purpose

For the sake of the house of the LORD our God, I will seek your prosperity.

Psalm 122:9 (NIV)

Why are you seeking prosperity?

I have discovered that prosperity is a great thing when it has great purpose attached to it. When people seek prosperity but have no purpose for it, other than self-gratification, it is then that it so often all goes wrong. There is nothing wrong with prosperity, it just needs a good purpose to give it meaning. It functions at its best when it has purpose, especially when it has a Godly one.

What better purpose is there for seeking prosperity than for the house of God? To me this is the greatest reason to seek it. The house of the Lord, the 'local church', is God's masterplan for changing the world one life at a time. When we bless it, we bless far, far beyond its four walls.

When you purpose in your heart that you will seek prosperity with the intention not only to enlarge your life but, primarily, to bless God's house, you set yourself up to be blessed indeed. God will position you where you need to be for that desire to be fulfilled on an ongoing basis.

Prosperity needs a purpose, a reason for being. God will release wealth and prosperity when you have the establishment of what He values embedded in your heart and desires. Always remember, we may work hard and have brilliant entrepreneurial capabilities for creating great success by our skills but at the end of the day, without God, we really would be nothing.

Then you say in your heart, 'My power and the might of my hand have gained me this wealth.' And you shall remember the LORD your God, for it is He who gives you power to get wealth, that He may establish His covenant which He swore to your fathers, as it is this day.
Deuteronomy 8:17-19 (NKJV)

Remembering this fact will enable us to walk with humility and humility always attracts the blessing and increase of the Lord. Are you seeking prosperity today? You may have a list of "Whys?", all good and valid, but do yourself a favour and make sure you have 'the house of the Lord' on that list too. In fact, make sure it's at the top.

Champion's Prayer:

Father, my whole life is Yours including what I can do and what I have. Thank You for Your blessing upon my life to get wealth, thank You for Godly increase today. Help me to always stay focused and keep the purpose to my prosperity You and Your kingdom – Amen.

Who is chasing who?

When the LORD was about to take Elijah up to heaven in a whirlwind, Elijah and Elisha were on their way from Gilgal. Elijah said to Elisha, "Stay here; the LORD has sent me to Bethel." But Elisha said, "As surely as the LORD lives and as you live, I will not leave you." So they went down to Bethel.

2 Kings 2:1-2 (NIV)

I believe one of the greatest gifts that God gives to us are great relationships: some are for friendship that walk alongside us; others are for mentorship, sent to empower, challenge and inspire. I also believe that many people, sadly, do not get from this second group of God-arranged relationships what they could because they have no chase or pursuit in them. Why? Often because they see things the wrong way round – they want to be pursued rather than pursue, they always want to be followed up rather than follow.

In this morning's text, we read about Elisha pursuing the prophet and spiritual leader Elijah. He knew that God had put into Elijah what he needed in his life and he was not going to deal with that in a polite manner – he went after Elijah. When you read through this account, it looks like he is almost stalking poor Elijah. As you read on, you hear Elijah turn and say to Elisha another two times, "What do you want? What must I do to shake you off?" Even the large company of prophets following Elijah turned three times to Elisha and said, "Leave the poor guy alone!" but he could not and would not be put off.

What a lovely picture of a man taking a God-ordained relationship in his life seriously. He knew who and what he needed and would not let up. Hey, you can call him a nutcase or desperate but read the end of account. He got what he wanted. Not just that – he got a 'double portion' of it. Champion, please understand, Elisha getting a double portion was all about the spirit of pursuit that was in him – he would not have got anything if he had waited politely for Elijah to call him.

One thing that surprises me, as I watch and work with leaders, is the lack of determined pursuit in people's hearts. You meet with people and they tell you what they want and how bad they want help and assistance, then nothing! No further calls, emails, no pursuit. It's time to look at things more correctly – it is not the job of your Elijah to chase you, it's your responsibility to go after them.

Every great leader will make time for those that they see are serious – are you serious? How are you relating to the leaders you have been given and the ones you desire input from? Are you in hot pursuit or are you sitting there, waiting for them to pursue you and chase you up? Chances are, they never will because they are in hot pursuit themselves – they are pursuing God but I know they can always make room on the bus for someone who REALLY means business.

WHO ARE YOU CHASING?

Churches need good leadership and good follow-ship

Then they answered Joshua, "Whatever you have commanded us we will do, and wherever you send us we will go. Just as we fully obeyed Moses, so we will obey you. Only may the LORD your God be with you as he was with Moses. Whoever rebels against your word and does not obey your words, whatever you may command them, will be put to death. Only be strong and courageous!"

Joshua 1:16-18 (NIV)

A lot of emphasis, these days, is put on the need for good leadership in the church but the reality is the church does not just need good leadership and good leaders but also good follow-ship: people that can follow well.

It's easy to point the finger at leaders that have made mistakes or not led well but what about followers taking responsibility for how well they have followed leadership? I think this is a really interesting thought that has the potential to produce a whole lot of good and very healthy, effective churches – if we dare to think about it.

In our text this morning, we read about some great followers – the followers of Joshua. This is the second time Israel had been given an opportunity to inherit the land God had promised. As you know, the first time did not go so well.

Why did it all go wrong that first time when Moses was leading? If you read about that account the problem was not actually with the leaders – Moses, Joshua and Caleb – it was with the followers. They were the ones that caused the nation to not enter in. This time, under the leadership of Joshua, things are very different. He had followers who were for him and for the vision that was given to him, followers who were sold out for the journey of God that was before them. I believe it was their good hearts and great attitudes that caused this second attempt to gain the Promised Land to be a success.

Just as leaders are meant to empower followers, so followers have the potential to empower their leaders. It is a powerful thing for a leader when his or her people come alongside them with a 'we can do it' attitude. Read it again: these guys were even willing to take care of the negative followers themselves to make sure that success happened.

We are all leaders in life but we are all often followers too. How good are you at being a follower? Do you empower the leaders in your life and give them courage to go for it like Joshua's followers did? Good question, right?

Would you get your leader a glass of water?

At that time David was in the stronghold, and the Philistine garrison was at Bethlehem. David longed for water and said, "Oh, that someone would get me a drink of water from the well near the gate of Bethlehem!" So the three mighty men broke through the Philistine lines, drew water from the well near the gate of Bethlehem and carried it back to David. But he refused to drink it; instead, he poured it out before the LORD. "Far be it from me, O LORD, to do this!" he said. "Is it not the blood of men who went at the risk of their lives?" And David would not drink it. Such were the exploits of the three mighty men.

2 Samuel 23:14-17 (NIV)

L et's stay on the theme of being a good follower.

King David is known as one of the greatest leaders in history; his courage, integrity and passion caused *"mighty men"* to gladly follow his lead. Much has been recorded concerning his leadership skills and abilities but here we see recorded the incredible potential of some of the men who were following him – their follow-ship is nothing short of incredible and ever amazes me.

In this account, David makes a casual statement about the best glass of water he had ever tasted. I don't believe he was hinting – his surprised reaction later tells us this clearly. It was just a casual statement, that's all, but to his followers it became a mission, even when it was potentially 'mission impossible'. They then sneak off and risk life and limb to get a glass of water for David their leader. Talk about getting carried away! Some may think this was right of them, some may think this was wrong but the fact is, it is an amazing picture of the desire-based commitment that David's followers had to his leadership. Maybe that's why they won so many battles together?

In this account we also see the picture of what made David's leadership so easy and desirable to follow. He sees what they have done, the risk they took not for God but for him and he chokes up, then uses what they have brought him for an offering to God. He says "Guys, this is too expensive, it cost too much for me to drink." He then uses it to worship God.

Sadly, in many churches in our land, there are followers that would not go to the church kitchen to get their pastor a glass of water if he was coughing his heart out. Some would even smirk! Again I want to put to you, a successful church is not just about good leaders but good followers – when there are both in the church, any battle can be won. In the gospel of Mark, chapter one we read the account of Jesus calling the disciples to *"come and follow Me"*. Today, He is still looking for followers. The question is, are you waiting for Jesus or are you ready to follow passionately the leader He has positioned in your life to lead you in His ways? *(Mark 1:16-18.)*

Hope this challenges you – it does me!

You are complete

For in Him dwells all the fullness of the Godhead bodily; and you are complete in Him, who is the head of all principality and power.

Colossians 2:9-10 (NKJV)

People who do not know God as their Creator and Lord strive daily to find completeness and wholeness. They regularly start new relationships looking for it, buy more stuff, attend more courses and, normally when they have done all of this, they still feel incomplete! This should never be the case for us – we should live from a revelation of our completeness and wholeness that we are complete in Him. It is our union with Christ, and that alone, that has taken away from us all incompleteness and made us complete in every way.

We should not strive, as those who do not know God, to be complete – rather realise that we already are, in Him. The whole worldly system of advertising works on the basic premise of convincing people they lack something or need something else to be all they are meant to be. Magazines, adverts, TV and billboards daily send out the message to the consumer: "Buy this and you will be complete and acceptable." Don't get me wrong, it is nice to buy stuff but our buying stuff should never be fuelled by the thinking that our completeness is found in the obtaining of that stuff.

Christ alone has made us perfectly complete, by His death, burial and resurrection, and each of us should start each new day knowing that we are already complete in Him. When you understand this, even the greatest advertising campaigns lose their grip on you. This is especially true when it comes to relationships in your life. You should never strive for them, thinking you will find your completeness in them – this can be so dangerous.

The healthiest relationships I have witnessed are always when both people entered in knowing they were already complete in Christ. If you go into any kind of relationship feeling incomplete, you can often begin to try to draw from the other person what they cannot give you, that which only God can. Yes, two become one when they are married but that always works best when it is two complete people becoming one new one.

So think about that today – where do you need to stop trying to draw completeness from? Again, find it in Christ alone. What a wonderful way to start the day: complete!

Champion's Confession:

Thank You, Jesus, that I am complete in You, that I am not lacking or insignificant in any way, I am a person who is loved with a destiny that is great. Thank You that in You I lack nothing but stand complete!

Use what's in your hand

Then Moses answered and said, "But suppose they will not believe me or listen to my voice; suppose they say, 'The LORD has not appeared to you.'" So the LORD said to him, "What is that in your hand?" He said, "A rod." And He said, "Cast it on the ground." So he cast it on the ground, and it became a serpent; and Moses fled from it. Then the LORD said to Moses, "Reach out your hand and take it by the tail" (and he reached out his hand and caught it, and it became a rod in his hand), "that they may believe that the LORD God of their fathers, the God of Abraham, the God of Isaac, and the God of Jacob, has appeared to you."

Exodus 4:1-5 (NKJV)

Often, when God asks you to do something for Him, you look at what you presently have in your life and wonder, "How is that ever going to happen?" In this account, we see the great Moses feel the same. God had just called him to go face to face with Pharaoh, to command him to release the whole nation of Israel who were the slaves of the land. Moses, along with his speech problem, thinks, "Okay, what tools are you giving me, God, because what I have and what I own right now in my life is not enough to pull that task off?" Look at God's response to him.

Moses was probably looking for some military equipment or, at the very least, a helicopter! God's response was, "What's in your hand?" In that statement, God said a whole lot to Moses and to us. First of all, you have everything you need to do everything that God has called you to do in your life now. Don't wait for a 'divine download', just let Him empower what you already have and are and then watch with amazement at what you can do. Moses had carried that rod around for years leading sheep with it but he never saw it the way God did. I bet he never imagined it could do tricks and part oceans at crucial moments. We need to realise that, like Moses, we too sometimes underestimate everyday things in our life and we all need to dare to see everyday things with the same potential and imagination as God does.

The truth is that it was just a rod made of wood but when God empowered it then it was able to assist Moses to deliver a nation. When you allow God to use the everyday things in your life, you too will be amazed at what they are really able to do. Stop looking at what you think you have not got and begin to commit to Him daily what you do! Look afresh at what God has already given you in the light of its potential with God's touch on it. He has blessed each and every one of us with different gifts, abilities and talents. Bring them again to Him today and let Him turn what looks to you like a stick into something that impacts lives and situations.

Remember the account of the disciples when they met the crippled man at Gate Beautiful? He asked them for money but they responded, *"Silver and gold have we none but such as we have we will give to you"*.

Don't spend your life looking at what you don't have but let God do something supernatural with what you do have.

Let's give Jesus what He is looking for

I tell you that He will avenge them speedily. Nevertheless, when the Son of Man comes, will He really find faith on the earth?

Luke 18:8 (NKJV)

This great statement ends with a big old question mark, meaning that a response is desired. I want to challenge you, as this challenged me, by asking, "How will you answer that question in your life — **will He find faith?**"

If we hold this question in context, we see that it follows the parable of the persistent widow, a story relaying the truth of what happens to a person when they refuse to sit down but rather make the choice to just keep on keeping on for what they need and believe is rightfully theirs. Notice in the parable that Jesus did not rebuke the widow for being annoying; on the contrary, He portrayed her favourably for getting what she persisted for. In this verse, does He ask, "Will I find good management?" Does He ask, "Will I find incredible wisdom?" No! Both of those are very important and are necessities when building something well but they are not what He asked if He would find. He wanted to know if He would find faith: people trusting Him and His promises in a child-like yet dynamic, mountain-moving way.

We all have a percentage of our life which represents our potential, what we can do and what we are capable of with the talents and abilities He has blessed us with. But we should also all have a percentage which is God's bit, a piece that says we are trusting in His involvement, a bit that says, "If God does not turn up and help in what we have planned, we have had it." When we create a percentage that has His name on it, we actually unroll a red carpet of faith inviting him to join in with what we are doing and He will always turn up when faith is released. There will always be things in life that seem beyond our natural power and capabilities and it is with these things we are called not to down-size our dreams, to 'be reasonable' but to put our faith in God and believe that He is able to take care of us and cause the breakthroughs we need.

Don't have your life all worked out based on what you can produce or achieve by your own ability but rather have a big slice called faith where you daily declare, "I am believing God for the impossible!" It is then that we see our lives change from natural lives to supernatural ones.

What are you believing Him for these days? What impossible thing are you presently trusting Him for? If the answer is "Nothing" then start to believe again and unroll the red carpet of your faith, because it is faith that He is actually looking for.

Persistent faith always pays off

However, when the Son of Man comes, will He find [persistence in] faith on the earth?

Luke 18:8b (Amplified Bible)

Again, let me underline or contextualise this verse. It follows the parable of the persistent widow that was used by Jesus as an example concerning persistence in prayer. He says that He is looking for faith in our lives. We need to be found not just living in what we know to be humanly possible but also with arms expectantly stretched forward to that which can only come from Him as a product of believing.

Have persistence in your faith. The lady in the parable got what she wanted because she knew what was rightfully hers to ask for. Know what is rightfully yours in Christ and don't be scared to be persistent in both your prayers and thanksgiving regarding it because God is not offended when we say, "You said . . ." Also, because she had the gumption to stand there till it happened or was released to her. Remember, Jesus was using the parable of this woman to make a point, which was that we need to have faith that does not sit down and shut up when others do but keeps going till the manifestation occurs.

Don't let time stop you believing for what you know God wants you to have. What if the persistent widow went home after the first delay or denial? She would not have received what she had come for and rightfully deserved. The fact is, sometimes the things we are believing or asking for do not come by next-day delivery. When we have persistent faith, we are willing to stand in faith for as long as it takes, knowing that even the patience we develop in the wait is Godly gold in our lives.

Don't be put off by other people's stories. This woman may have heard stories of how other people did not get anything when they asked the judge or were left disappointed but she made the decision that she would not live in other people's experiences. Don't let other people's negative stories make you quit. Remember, faith allows each of us to be writing our own stories – stories of how God did incredible things through our everyday lives for His glory.

Will He find faith? Will He find persistent faith? Will He find people who know what is rightfully theirs and are not afraid to remain standing till they get it? The stand you need is simply the stance of faith!

Hey Champion, keep standing in faith knowing that our God is not like the corrupt, uncaring judge of the parable but rather a Father who loves us with incredible passion and is so for us.

PERSISTENCE!

What's your story?

Now faith is the substance of things hoped for, the evidence of things not seen. For by it the elders obtained a good testimony.

Hebrews 11:1-2 (NKJV)

Faith enabled the elders or 'believers of old' to obtain a good testimony – 'a good story to tell' – and that same faith will enable us to do the same in our generation too. The elders, the disciples, always had a good story to tell of what they had experienced a living God do through their everyday lives. These were stories of miracle provision or of people healed and restored and of God making a way when there seemed to be no way.

The good news is that you and I can have some good stories too. All you need to do is what the disciples did which was to daily engage with God and His promises by faith, in other words, simple childlike trust. Hear what God says He can do in that situation you're facing and then choose to agree with Him, even if your current situation or circumstance seems to disagree in every way.

Imagine all the stories, or testimonies, the disciples had and imagine what it was like when they got together or had coffee and shared the incredible stories of what they saw when they walked with Jesus and of what they continued to see once He had risen from the dead and empowered them by His indwelling presence.

Good news! We have the same Spirit living in us and we too, daily, come across seemingly impossible hurdles and apparent dead ends, don't we? Just like them we also have a choice concerning how we are going to respond. Let's dare to start responding more by faith because then we can also have some great stories in our lives of what God has been doing each and every week.

Champion, declare this week a week of releasing your faith in a greater way. Let it be a week of realising that, no matter how big the challenge may seem, if God is in it, you can win it. Ask Gideon, Moses, Joshua, David or any of the other elders that went and got themselves a story! This week, go get a story of what God did for you and through you then find some people to listen and inspire them.

Food for thought:

Salvation is when you give God ownership of the countertop of your life; discipleship is when you let Him into the chipboard of it and let Him do what he needs to.

Called to cause trouble!

*But when they did not find them, they dragged Jason and some brethren to the rulers of the city, crying out, "**These who have turned the world upside down have come here too.**"*

Acts 17:6 (NKJV)

What a great reputation! I personally believe that this is the reputation of the Spirit-filled God-lover. We are not called to fit into everything that society and life expects us to or deems normal but rather we are called of God to be people who turn the world upside down for Him. Poor old Jason got into mega trouble for housing some 'followers of Jesus'. Would we get someone into trouble if we went to stay with them this week? Would Christ, in us, turn something upside down when we 'passed through'? What a great challenge.

Whatever the realm of life that God has called you to function in, make sure that when you look in the mirror before leaving your house, you see someone called of God to turn things upside down or, put another way, right side up.

How?

Simply make the decision that wherever you find yourself you are going to:

- Stand up for Jesus and His kingdom and not shrink back or hide.

- Live for the truth of God's Word. Let it be what determines your absolutes, not the so called wisdom which comes from an ever-changing and confused society.

- Remember, you are only on this planet once. Live in such a way that your life has a unique flavour. Stand out. Have definition and don't settle for bland!

What we believe, God's truth, should make us stick out in the crowd. It should be constantly turning wrong thinking and behaviour upside down and, let's face it, it is destined to cause trouble.

These men who have caused trouble all over the world have now come here,

Acts 17:6 (NIV)

The Gospel is not a sedative meant to quieten you down but rather it is a divine stimulant, meant to fire you up. It's an empowering license to live passionately for a cause that changes people's lives and lasts for eternity. Come on; let's get the Church its world-changing reputation back.

Realise that Jesus, the revolutionary, lives in you and have a world-shaking day. How? Let Him out!

How's your appetite this morning?

Blessed are those who hunger and thirst for righteousness, for they will be filled.

Matthew 5:6 (NIV)

I'm not referring to your appetite for food but your appetite for God.

The Bible says, *"Blessed* (empowered to prosper and be happy) *are those who hunger and thirst for righteousness"* because it's a great thing to stay hungry for God and for what He loves.

Here are a couple of thoughts to get you thinking about your appetite this morning.

How hungry are you exactly? Do you want a 'Scooby snack' or a banquet? God is busy setting up a banquet for you and me but so often we settle for a *Kit Kat* or mere snack. Champion, get hungry – you will never out-eat His provision!

How about this one: does your appetite for God get others motivated? When a lady is pregnant, she can get some very strange cravings but also knows how to mobilise everyone in her life and world to get her the things she is craving for (I have personal experience of this!). Does your hunger for God and His righteousness motivate and mobilise others in your world to get hungry for Him too?

Does your hunger for Him get you doing things you would not normally do? Natural hunger mobilises a person and so does spiritual hunger. When you have an appetite for something, it 'gets you moving'. You get up out of the armchair and go out to get what you are wanting or craving. Whether it be a curry or kebab, you do something about that appetite. When you are hungry for God, it is the same. You get up out of the armchair of apathy to go get what you say you are desiring. Thank God for appetite – it stops you starving to death.

The promise of God to the hungry is as it says at the end of the verse: *"they will be filled."* How about you, do you want to *"be filled"* by God?

Then it's simple. Simply maintain and cultivate a great daily appetite for Him and I promise you will not be disappointed! He is not trying to tease you – He is trying to get you hungry so He can satisfy you with more than you ever imagined.

For He satisfies the thirsty and fills the hungry with good things.

Psalm 107:9 (NIV)

Stay hungry for Him, Champion, and for what He loves.

Run to win and get your crown from God

I have fought the good fight, I have finished the race, I have kept the faith. Now there is in store for me the crown of righteousness, which the LORD, the righteous Judge, will award to me on that day – and not only to me, but also to all who have longed for His appearing.

2 Timothy 4:7-8 (NIV)

What a great closing statement to a life well lived; a life lived for the purposes of God and His kingdom. The Apostle Paul puts into words what should be in the heart of each of us. They are words that stir me concerning how I am running my race and living my life for God. How about you?

Let us, as Paul did, set our hearts to:

- Fight the good fight of faith with perseverance, determination and courage.

- Finish our individual race because it's no good running half a race. Set your eyes on the finish line. Like an athlete, pace yourself to get there and finish in style too.

- Keep the faith. You may witness others bail out or quit for other lesser races and give their lame excuses but let us keep to the faith that saves us to the uttermost.

There is an eternal crown!

Paul had confidence concerning the crown of reward that awaited him for the race he had run with his life. When we spend our days on God and His purposes, we too can know there is a crown that awaits us on the other side of the line. Notice he said that this crown is awarded to spiritual athletes by God Himself – wow!

Finally, consider again the crown you are living to receive. So many people are giving their strength to run races to receive temporary crowns that will last a mere moment in the light of eternity. Crowns of fame and man's applause will disappear like smoke. We run and we fight to receive a crown that is eternal and that will never fade or rust. People give their lives to get crowns that they can see here, in this temporary chapter. Let us give our lives to gain our crowns for the chapter that has no end: eternity.

What will we do with our crowns? We'll probably use them for worship and cast them at the feet of Him who is crowned above all others, Jesus. Run your race well for God, Champion. Fight well. Keep the faith even when other around you don't!

RUN!

You do not run alone!

Therefore, since we are surrounded by such a great cloud of witnesses, let us throw off everything that hinders and the sin that so easily entangles, and let us run with perseverance the race marked out for us.

Hebrews 12:1 (NIV)

I have never been a long distance runner but I imagine that any runner who runs long distance or cross country races must, at times, feel very alone. Even if others are taking part in the race, each runner faces their own personal challenges and they have to deal with their own thoughts of quitting. A runner must overcome what is termed 'the wall', that moment when they think they have nothing left to give and feel their bodies begging them to stop. The runner endures pain as his or her body, with every new stride, gives its all to run the best race possible and all this is done alone.

Most often, it is not until they cross the finishing line that they hear the cheers from the people who were supporting them and have been waiting for them to round the final corner. It would have been nice to have had some people cheering during the lonely bends of the race they had just run.

Christianity is a race that we all run together but at the same time alone. Though we run towards the same finish line, we all run a race that belongs to us personally. The race can get lonely and be full of challenges and we too can, at times, hit a wall and really want to stop but it is then that we need to realise that we are not alone. The balconies of heaven are filled with the cheers of "Come on, you can do it!" shouted from the believers who have gone before, those who ran their race to the finish and now cheer us on to both run and finish well as we carry the baton of the Gospel that they once held and ran with.

If you are tired and at a loss for energy in your race of faith, hear the great crowd of witnesses again today – Paul, John and Peter – as they shout from the balconies of Heaven, "Come on, don't quit, you can do it". Take a breath, cast off the stuff that has slowed you down and run the race that is marked out for you.

Do you see what this means – all these pioneers who blazed the way, all these veterans cheering us on? It means we'd better get on with it. Strip down, start running – and never quit! No extra spiritual fat, no parasitic sins. Keep your eyes on Jesus, who both began and finished this race we're in.

Hebrews 12:1 (The Message)

Keep your eyes on the One in front

Keep your eyes on Jesus, who both began and finished this race we're in. Study how he did it. Because he never lost sight of where he was headed—that exhilarating finish in and with God—he could put up with anything along the way: Cross, shame, whatever. And now he's there, in the place of honour, right alongside God. When you find yourselves flagging in your faith, go over that story again, item by item, that long litany of hostility he ploughed through. That will shoot adrenaline into your souls!

Hebrews 12:2-3 (The Message)

Because Jesus both ran and finished His race, we can now run and finish ours. We can be certain that, though our race seems tough at times, we will never have to run a race like He had to run and we will never experience the same amount of physical and emotional pain that He faced when He set His heart to cross that finishing line of redemption victoriously. It was His race that fashioned the very track of salvation that we who believe run upon today; a track of grace. It was His well-finished race that established for us an opportunity of having a finishing line that we could both run towards and cross.

When running a long-distance race, apparently it is always good to set your gaze upon someone in front, especially if they are a gold medal winner, and just keep running towards them with every new step. Make them your marker and the one who sets your pace. Jesus is our perfect marker so keep your eyes on Him, Champion, and, as you do, you can guarantee you will finish your race victoriously as he finished His.

Don't look to the left – the law – or the right – man's opinion – and don't look to see what other runners are doing. This can cause you to trip. No, keep your eyes on the winner and run in step with Him. Imitate Him and watch how He handled the hurdles of life and then jump them in the same way. Observe how He carried on when it would have been much more comfortable or easier to quit and do the same. Keep close to Him, avoid distractions and finish well.

He received a crown for a race run well and so will you and I. Keep your eyes on Him who began, ran a perfect race and then finished!

Champion's Prayer:

Father, help me to run my best race for You, help me to keep my eyes locked onto You and not be distracted by what is happening to the left and the right. Thank You that I run this race knowing heaven cheers me on and the crown I will receive will be better than any crown this world could offer – Amen.

You are blessed so begin to act like it!

Christ redeemed us from the curse of the law by becoming a curse for us, for it is written: "Cursed is everyone who is hung on a tree." He redeemed us in order that the blessing given to Abraham might come to the Gentiles through Christ Jesus, so that by faith we might receive the promise of the Spirit.

Galatians 3:13-14 (NIV)

Good news, Champion. If you have placed your faith in Jesus as Lord and Saviour, you are not cursed today! This verse tells us plainly that Jesus redeemed us – 'purchased us out of' the curse – and has led us into an inheritance of blessing. His purpose in positioning Himself on the tree and settling the curse for us was to position **us** so that blessing and goodness could be our daily experience.

He **became** the curse (past tense) so that we should not have to **be** cursed (present tense). He that knew no sin and was above any reproach that could attract a curse, positioned Himself where we stood in life. He took every curse upon Himself and settled it once and for all. Every curse was settled by His loving substitution. So think about it, if He took it all and we connect to His perfect completed work by faith, what is left for us? The answer is the blessings of God because they are ours today in Christ!

Two things to remember:

- Every curse was paid for by His sacrificial act of love. No curse has authority over you when your life is positioned in Him. He paid the bill completely. No curse is greater than His finished work. Curses no longer have a landing pad on your life!

Like a flitting sparrow, like a flying swallow, so a curse without cause shall not alight.

Proverbs 26:2 (NKJV)

- As with everything in God, our connection to participate in this great daily reality is simply faith. Believe the truth, confess the truth and see the fruit of truth manifest in your life.

Why not start to speak the truth again over your life today? Go on, Champion, speak out these powerful words, "I am blessed in Him and no curse can come upon me. Today, I expect again the manifestation of blessing in and through Jesus Christ, my Lord. Amen".

BLESSED!

Delighting in His word will prosper you

Blessed is the man who does not walk in the counsel of the wicked or stand in the way of sinners or sit in the seat of mockers. But his delight is in the law of the LORD, and on his law he meditates day and night. He is like a tree planted by streams of water, which yields its fruit in season and whose leaf does not wither. Whatever he does prospers.

Psalm 1:1-3 (NIV)

This is a great Psalm that promises so much to the person who will commit to delight and meditate not in the wisdom of the ungodly but "*in the law of the LORD*". As we have established many times in this devotional, we are no longer under the law but under grace and positioned in Christ by our faith in His grace, not our works. So how does this Word, or promise, apply to us today?

Two ways: firstly, we may no longer be under the law contained within the Old Testament as it was fulfilled by Jesus but we should still daily remain under the teachings of its truth and wisdom, living to daily apply the incredible principles of God found within each of its pages. The Word, the Bible, will always do your life good and cause your life to flourish as you submit to it. Why? Because the Bible is a living book and is jammed full of God's thoughts and ways and, when you clearly understand the covenants, what's relevant now to your life and what's not, and know how to apply the truth of His word to your life, it will always cause an outbreak of life and blessing in every part you expose it to.

If we change the word *"law"* for '**Word of God**', it holds the same power of promise for us today. God's Word is good for your life when you daily delight in it and mediate on it – your life will consistently experience incredible blessing and flourishing and go from strength to strength.

Another thing to consider is Jesus Himself. The Bible refers to Him as the *"word of God made flesh"* (*John 1:14*). Because Jesus is the Word of God made flesh, it means that as we choose to behold Him daily, we are beholding the Word of God. As we daily gaze upon Jesus, delight in Him and think and muse on all He has done for us, we are actually delighting and mediating on the Word of God as He instructed us to. And, as promised, that will cause your life to flourish and prosper so you will be like that promised tree that is planted by the river, ever bearing fruit.

Make sure you are delighting and meditating on both the living words within the book and the living Word that is the person – as you do, you will be blessed!

Seeds become harvests

For who has despised the day of small things?

Zechariah 4:10a (NIV)

W hat a great question to start the day with.
According to the dictionary, to despise is to 'regard with contempt, loathe, to hold as seemingly insignificant'. A great key to remember is to never look at small things or beginnings as insignificant but rather, by faith, always dare to see their possible future potential. Because the bottom line is that everything that is one day great starts as something that is seemingly small –every mighty oak tree starts its journey as a small acorn.

We all want the great 'oak trees' and the successes that come with them but we need to understand and always commit to the process of getting them. This process is seen in *Genesis 8:22* and is called seedtime and harvest. To actually understand this principle you need to take it from being two words or components to being three: 'seed – time – harvest'! Every great thing, whether it be a church, business or project, starts seemingly small, like a **seed** in your hand. Then comes **time** – this is the one we often try to remove so we get straight to harvest but it is in this component that things gain their strength and root themselves for permanence. Then finally comes **harvest** – this is when we see before us what we first dreamed of when we held that seemingly insignificant small seed.

Seeds produce Harvests

This reality can work both positively and negatively in our lives and, when we understand that fact, we can begin to manage, remove and design some of the harvests we experience in our life. Everything starts as a seed – great ideas and dreams but also deceptions, delusions and habits. They all start as seemingly small thoughts and things.

One of the keys to being a leader in life is to be a *seed spotter* – someone who can recognise things that have the potential to produce harvest and manage them when they are still seeds. In a positive context, this would be to nurture and protect its growth and, in a negative context, this would be to get rid of delusions and deception and habits when they are still small and manageable. Remember, if you don't deal with the seed you will deal with the harvest!

Even the devil understood this principle – notice that when he came after both Moses and Jesus to destroy them, he came after them as babies, or seeds. Why? Because he knew that would be a lot easier than dealing with the harvest that their fully grown lives would produce. He did not succeed and Jesus became that grain of wheat that caused an ever increasing harvest to be triggered, of which we are a part today *(John 12:24)*. What seeds need to be managed in your life today?

Thoughts are like seeds

Casting down arguments and every high thing that exalts itself against the knowledge of God, bringing every thought into captivity to the obedience of Christ.

2 Corinthians 10:6 (NKJV)

We spoke yesterday about not despising the day of small beginnings and noted that every mighty oak tree starts its journey as a tiny acorn. When we understand that everything big in our lives, whether positive or negative in context, starts small and seed-like, we can begin to determine and manage some of the harvests our lives are continually growing.

Thoughts are like seeds – they start so seemingly small but can produce so very much. The greatest multi-million pound companies in existence today started as a single thought in the mind of an individual; a thought that the owner had the choice to act on and allow to germinate or to disregard. It's the thoughts we allow to germinate that are what determine the future harvests and destinations of our life. Again, this can be positive or negative because thoughts have the potential to contain and carry both.

Today, our church is experiencing incredible growth and success and we have planted out other churches and ministries and, in some ways, it is like an oak tree sustaining the life of many others. I look around and am amazed at what God has done and is doing but I am also reminded where it all started.

A thought came into my mind, just over thirteen years ago, as I was driving home from a meeting. A simple thought that could have been easily ignored, "Start a church in Portsmouth". I allowed that thought to stay in the ground of my mind and then germinate in my heart, believing it to be a God thought. That thought was the acorn of the tree which now is called **Family Church** – that was a positive thought!

Thoughts are so powerful, they can take you where you have never been before or destroy you! Think of King David and the whole mess he got himself into with Bathsheba. He ended up committing adultery, had an innocent man killed and produced a child in sin that would sadly die. Where did that journey of pain for him and the others involved start? With a single thought on a roof top *(2 Samuel 11)*. Whilst he should have been at war with the men, he was at home and looked over the balcony to see something he shouldn't have: a UFO (undressed feminine object). There, in that moment, a thought came; he had a choice as to what to do with that thought. Sadly, he chose to let it germinate and a pathway of pain was created. God's grace was greater than his sin but still, it never needed to happen.

Our text today gives us some good advice concerning the seeds of thought – bring every one of them under what God says is true and right then we can be certain of great things that bless others being the produced from our thought life. Think about what you're thinking about!

Today is a great day

For who has despised the day of small things?

Zechariah 4:10a (NIV)

This is the day the LORD has made; let us rejoice and be glad in it.

Psalm 118:24 (NIV)

We have been looking at the subject of not despising the *"day of small things"* or beginnings but daring to look at them through the lenses of faith and wisdom, to see the 'future harvest' contained in the 'present seed' of what could be just a seemingly-small thing.

Notice the verse from Zechariah speaks of not despising the *"day of small things"*. The day you are currently in is a great day when you choose to live and see things by faith. Every mighty oak tree comes from a small acorn; every conquered mountain starts with one small step taken in the right direction. When we commit to live in God's never-failing principle of seed, time and harvest, we sign up for living in one of these three individual seasons – at any given time we can be in any one of the three.

The time of small beginnings, when the seed is all we see, is when you have not got any harvest to see or experience but it is a vital time. The big tomorrow you're dreaming of is dependent upon your faithfulness in this moment of time. Then there is the day, or time, when you wait – remember, the Bible says that we are to imitate those who, by faith and patience, inherit promises, those who know how to believe and wait, not just those who know how to believe. Then comes the day of harvest, or manifestation of what was originally dreamt of. This is where we behold what we have spent time sowing and waiting patiently for. This is a great day but, face it, every day is a great day when you know you are living in the system of 'seed time-harvest'.

Too many people are not happy unless they see harvest or touch the oak tree. God wants us to be bigger than this and be people who do not despise the day when things are seemingly small. Don't despise the day you are in. If you are living by God's principle of 'seed – time – harvest' then today, when you sow the seed and wait, is a great day, not just tomorrow when you see the harvest.

Close your eyes and imagine the harvest that will be then open your eyes and smile at the seemingly small seed that will produce it. You never see annoyed, frustrated farmers sowing their seeds because they know how it works – they sow, they wait, they harvest. Let's learn from them when it comes to growing things in our world. Don't despise the day of seemingly small things – you will one day walk through the orchards your deeds, faith and patience have produced.

Your words are seeds

Death and life are in the power of the tongue, and those who love it will eat its fruit (harvest).
Proverbs 18:21 (NKJV)

We have been speaking about not despising small things but rather walking conscious of the big harvests that can be produced by seemingly small seeds. Let's again remember that words are another thing in our lives that we can compare to seeds. They too are seemingly small things and the tongue is, indeed, a seed dispenser, daily casting and sowing seeds, or words, into our world and the world of others.

As with all the other examples we have looked at, this too has a negative or positive reality depending on the seeds we choose to speak! *Proverbs* teaches us that Death and Life are in the power of the tongue. Wow! Those are two very big and very different harvests. Which one do you want? Then sow the seeds that will produce it.

Remember, as it is naturally, so it is spiritually; every seed bears fruit after its own kind. Put carrot seeds in the ground and carrots will grow; you don't end up with cabbages. You will never get a different harvest to the seed you choose to sow and it is that way with our words, the seeds of our mouth. If you want to set yourself up for a harvest of life, not death, then speak words of life; govern what rolls off of your lips on a daily basis. You do have the power to shut the gate!

It's not just about our world – our words have great impact in the life of others so make sure your words are always seasoned with grace, faith and hope. Words that build up, not tear down, cause people to keep going and not quit.

Those seemingly small seeds called 'the words you choose to speak' have power in them to produce – what will you use yours to produce today?

Food for thought:

Make sure you celebrate your harvests with the people who dared to sow alongside you when the fields were empty and your vision yet unproved.

A greater righteousness

For I say to you, that unless your righteousness exceeds the righteousness of the scribes and Pharisees, you will by no means enter the kingdom of heaven.

Matthew 5:20 (NKJV)

If you are not experienced concerning the new covenant you have, that which was established by Christ for you, these are daunting verses that would seriously make you think, "How on earth can I match the Pharisee or their righteousness?" It would also leave you thinking, "I have no chance of entering the kingdom of God – I cannot equal the religious performance of the Pharisee and Scribe, can I?"

Good news (the gospel)

If you have placed your faith in Jesus as your Lord and saviour, you have not just equalled it but have actually abundantly exceeded it.

Remember

The key is to remember that there are two covenants, or agreements, which represent two types of righteousness: man-made and God-made. We do not stand as the Pharisee did, and still sadly does today, in a mere man-made, performance-based righteousness. Rather, we stand with a righteousness which is inherent, achieved and given to us as a gift by God. Our righteousness is the result of faith and faith alone; faith placed in the perfect, redeeming, finished work of another man – Jesus. It is based in the fact that everything He came to do and achieve two thousand years ago He did; and not just did but completed perfectly.

Today, our righteousness far exceeds that of the Pharisee because it is the righteousness of Christ given to us. It qualifies us to enter into the kingdom because it is based not on our daily varying performance or ability but on the perfect performance of Jesus to justify. When we stand in this righteousness, we stand secure, forgiven and accepted.

He has qualified and done all the work for you to stand before Him and to enter into His kingdom with your head held high again today. Thanks be to Jesus, our righteousness revealed.

Champion's prayer:

Thank You, Father, that the righteousness You have given me in Christ exceeds that which religion can produce. You have given me as a gift what I could never earn or achieve in my ability. Thank You, that today, I stand accepted in Your presence – Amen.

His goodness will change your mind

Or do you despise the riches of His goodness, forbearance, and longsuffering, not knowing that the goodness of God leads you to repentance?

Romans 2:4 (NKJV)

Here's a lovely little nugget of truth to start the day with. It is the goodness of God that leads a person to repentance. Think about that. It's God's goodness and kindness that causes true repentance in our lives and not the use or abuse of fear, shame or guilt.

What is Repentance?
The New Testament word used here for repentance is also the one most commonly used throughout the New Testament. It is the Greek word *metanoia*, which means 'to change one's mind or thinking'! This is a very different meaning to the Old Testament Hebrew word used for repentance: *nacham* which means 'to be mournfully sorrowful'.

The type of repentance that God wants from us is the New Testament type. Yes, we may feel sorrowful when we have done something wrong but it should never stop there. We need to move on to do something about it by daring to change the way we think. Why? Because it is when we change the way we think that we will change the way we live in a way that lasts.

A sorrowful response needs to be the porchway, or entrance, into something much larger – namely a change of thinking toward that specific area of our life being high-lighted by God at that moment. What should it be that inspires us to 'repent' to 'change our thinking'? According to *Romans 2:4*, it is the goodness, or kindness, of God. Wow, imagine that God remains so good and kind toward us that, in response, we desire to change our thinking to bring it into alignment with His truth and His ways for our lives.

Today, don't have the expectation of fear, shame and guilt coming from your Heavenly Father; rather, a never-ending waterfall of His goodness and mercy. When it comes, let it cause repentance that changes you beyond a momentary emotional response. Respond to His goodness with *metanoia* by changing the way you think because then you will change the way you live!

It's like a person who makes apple pies; they have the potential to re-create the same pie each and every day by using the same ingredients, heat and oven. What if the pie does not taste good? Then they need to change the ingredients and the pie will taste different. In the same way, God gets us, by His goodness, to change the ingredients of the pie of our life, in other words, the way we think, and, as we do, the flavour of our life changes.

'Tis the Season to be Mary

(Sounds like a well-known Christmas carol, doesn't it?)

Now it happened as they went that He entered a certain village; and a certain woman named Martha welcomed Him into her house. And she had a sister called Mary, who also sat at Jesus' feet and heard His word. But Martha was distracted with much serving, and she approached Him and said, "Lord, do You not care that my sister has left me to serve alone? Therefore tell her to help me." And Jesus answered and said to her, "Martha, Martha, you are worried and troubled about many things. But one thing is needed, and Mary has chosen that good part, which will not be taken away from her."

Luke 10:38-42 (NKJV)

Jesus arrives at the house of His friends Mary and Martha, the sisters of Lazarus. He is there to spend quality time with them. He was not there for a party; He just wanted to spend time with them. He knew that the cross and its torment lay ahead and maybe He was just popping in to be with friends as He prepared for the hard time that He knew lay before Him.

We are then introduced to two different ladies with two very different temperaments. First let's look at Mary. The scripture says that straight away she stopped what she was doing to sit at His feet and hear His words. Next, we meet sister Martha whose response to her visitor was to hit the kitchen and start preparing a meal which was a very common thing to do in middle eastern culture.

The problem was not with her hospitality but with the distraction she allowed it to cause in her life. She then gets all bent out of shape when she sees Mary sitting at His feet, apparently doing nothing, and eventually shares her opinion, underlining firmly that she felt someone in the room was being very lazy.

How surprised she must have been when Jesus then commended Mary's apparent laziness and suggested Martha learn from Mary and do the same. Was Jesus telling Martha off for serving rather than sitting? No, I don't think so. What He was communicating to her was that there is a time for both. We too can learn so much from this account. There is a time for us to be busy like Martha but also we need to be able to sit at His feet like Mary.

Should you be more like Mary or Martha? I think the answer is that we need to be able to be both but always know when the moment is right to be whichever is appropriate or fitting for the season or moment at hand.

SIT!

Keep the main thing the main thing!

A woman by the name of Martha welcomed him and made him feel quite at home. She had a sister, Mary, who sat before the Master, hanging on every word he said. But Martha was pulled away by all she had to do in the kitchen. Later, she stepped in, interrupting them. "Master, don't you care that my sister has abandoned the kitchen to me? Tell her to lend me a hand." The Master said, "Martha, dear Martha, you're fussing far too much and getting yourself worked up over nothing. One thing only is essential, and Mary has chosen it—it's the main course, and won't be taken from her."

Luke 10:38-42 (The Message)

There is a time for being a super-servant like Martha. Great churches are built by faithful 'Martha-type' servants that serve with a passion long after others have gone home. Jesus was not rebuking this servant-hearted way of living but He was just gently reminding her not to let her hard work become a distraction that took her away from what is essential.

What was essential for Martha that day should always be essential to us. What is it? It is taking time to sit at the feet of the Lord and let His every word wash all over you. This is what Jesus regarded as essential and so should we. This should be essential to us, first of all, because He deserves our undisturbed attention whenever He wants it. And also because, when we learn to sit, we discover and receive the wisdom and strength to serve like He has called us to.

I don't know about you, Champion, but honestly, I find it easier to be like Martha than Mary. I know other people who have a problem getting away from Jesus' feet and they don't do anything. This isn't right either but I suppose it comes down to how you are wired. One thing I have resolved in my heart is that I am going to take more time in my daily life to sit at His feet as Mary did. Why? Because this lovely account in *Luke* gives me revelation that it is God's will for my life and that I will actually be a better servant, like Martha, if I do.

A thought for you to chew on today:

How about you – are you a stronger Mary or Martha? Which sister do you need to emulate a little more in your life? If spending time is the essential thing, then that makes it the main thing. Commit with me in the midst of a busy world to keep the main thing the main thing!

Champion's Challenge:

Ask yourself who you are most like at this moment in your life, Mary or Martha? Think about what you need to do to correct the picture. If you are too much like Martha, create some time to sit again at the feet of the master.

Dead things can live and bear fruit

Now it came to pass on the next day that Moses went into the tabernacle of witness, and behold, the rod of Aaron, of the house of Levi, had sprouted and put forth buds, had produced blossoms and yielded ripe almonds.

Numbers 17:8 (NKJV)

Here we read about the very unusual account of God showing the people of Israel that Aaron was to be the High Priest among them. God instructs Moses to get twelve leaders to put their rods in his tent of meeting, which they do. When they return, Aaron's rod has sprouted, put forth buds, blossomed and yielded fruit all in one night! This sign and wonder clearly demonstrated to Israel who God's hand was on to lead them as their High Priest.

We can learn a couple of things from this account: firstly, it is symbolic of the fact that God's chosen instrument will always be someone that has God's life within them, someone whose life is budding and bearing good fruit (not just gifting).

But what I really want to draw your attention to is how God can cause life to flow from something that was seemingly dead – that's His resurrection (restored life) ability. That rod looked just like the other eleven, like a dead stick! But when God got involved that dead stick became a living testimony. When you read on you find out that it became one of the items contained in the Ark of the Covenant.

It's God that brings life out of death. He alone can make seemingly dead things find new life and fruitfulness. We read in the Gospels about how Jesus caused Lazarus to blossom and bud again when he had become a "dead thing", but that is also a picture of each of us, isn't it? When we came to Jesus we were dead – dead in our sins (*Colossians 2:13*) – but in His presence life supernaturally returned and, like Lazarus, we came to life; like the rod of Aaron we began to sprout, blossom and bear fruit.

Thank God for His resurrection life! Never underestimate what God can cause to live again even when you or others may have written them off as lifeless. It's God who causes lives, marriages, dreams and ministries to begin to live again – not just live but bud and bear fruit when they seemed so very dead.

Notice the rod had no connected place to claim its life source from, only God. That's the same with the dead things we see live again – there is no other reason for it except GOD!

Believers or Disciples?

Go therefore and make disciples of all the nations, baptizing them in the name of the Father and of the Son and of the Holy Spirit.

Matthew 28:19 (NKJV)

"Go into the world and make disciples" – I was challenged again by this verse at one of our annual Empower Conferences. One of the speakers preached on this verse and inspired us concerning the great challenge found within it, how that, like so many other truths in the Bible, the power can sometimes be 'lost in our translation'.

He then threw out a big challenge that I want to throw out to you now: "Are we busy getting people to be disciples or just believers?" In all our doing, are we inspiring people to just believe in Jesus and that's it, or to be disciples, followers of Him, in their daily lives? The truth is, before we look at 'them' we need to dare to look at ourselves and apply this worthy challenge to where we are presently at with God.

Are we just believers? Jesus never told us to make, or merely be, believers but rather disciples. Why? Because there can sometimes be a big difference between the two. Think about it, you can believe in something and actually then do nothing about it. To believe in something takes no real effort, just decisions. But to be a follower or disciple of something or someone means you daily commit to be transformed into their likeness and live out a life that looks like theirs.

Compared to being a disciple, being a believer can be really easy but it is not enough to change a world. Believers see their world changed; disciples do as well but they also change the worlds of others.

Jesus is looking for people who, yes, believe in Him, but then take it further and leave their comfort zones to become disciples: followers of Him. Don't get me wrong, both go to heaven – because all you need to do to be saved is believe in Jesus – but not both live a life that is the adventure Jesus invited us all to experience. Disciples step out of their own saved worlds for the benefit of others.

How about you, Champion, are you a Believer or are you a Disciple? Are you a daily follower of Jesus, living out His life for all to see? May we, like Paul, be able to daily say to those around us, "Follow me as I follow Christ."

Forget former things

Forget the former things; do not dwell on the past. See, I am doing a new thing! Now it springs up; do you not perceive it? I am making a way in the desert and streams in the wasteland.

Isaiah 43:18-20 (NIV)

Here's a thought for you. It will cost you your future to live in the past and that is a far too expensive price to pay, isn't it? If those former things were negative then it is time to forget and move on. If those former things were positive, it is time to give thanks for them and move on to the even greater things that God has for you next.

Make sure that you spend your life living for what God is doing now, not forever wandering down some memory lane that leads you nowhere you really want to be. Memory lane is great to visit every now and then but it is not where we should choose to live! To live there would cost you the weekly rental payments of your present and your future.

Isaiah instructs us to *"not dwell on the past"*. Where are you dwelling today? Are you living in a moment that was or a moment that is unfolding? For a lot of you that are reading this today, the past you need to leave behind or choose not to live in is a good one but just because it is good does not mean that we make it our place of residence.

So, let's stop living in past failures or indeed victories and set our faces forward today to be a part of what God is doing **right now**. Remember, even yesterday is your past now.

What makes us step out of the moments that have gone with confidence and passion? When we have a revelation of the next bit of the verse, where God tells us that He is doing a new thing and He invites us to be a part of it, whatever it is and whatever it may look like. Get hungry for the new thing that God is doing and that will cause you to let go of the old thing. When you chose to not live in your past but be ever moving on, you're released to do what He promised to do and that is to turn your apparent wastelands into fruitful places.

Interesting wording, *"wasteland"*. The good news is that when you daily follow Jesus, He will take all the things that you thought were waste and turn them into things that bring life to your future or the lives of others.

Champion's Challenge:

Get yourself a bit of paper. Write on it some things from the past you are tired of carrying; maybe people you have not forgiven, habits or guilt from things done in your past. Say goodbye; get a match and set light to it or screw it up; put it in a bin and walk away. It's time to move on!

Trade in your old for His new

This is what God says, the God who builds a road right through the ocean, who carves a path through pounding waves, the God who summons horses and chariots and armies – they lie down and then can't get up; they're snuffed out like so many candles: "Forget about what's happened; don't keep going over old history. Be alert, be present. I'm about to do something brand-new. It's bursting out! Don't you see it? There it is! I'm making a road through the desert, rivers in the badlands."

Isaiah 43:16-21 (The Message)

As we established yesterday, God's desire for us is to move on from the past. Whether that past to you is a platform of failure and pain or one of victory and accolade, we still need to move on into the realm of what is next! We need to daily resolve that we will not live our lives desiring to be in moments that have passed but rather to be a part of the God moment that now is. Ever had a postcard from somewhere real nice that had the classic message written on it, "Wish you were here"? It is great that the sender thought of you but the truth is, you are not there and you will never be there for that sunset moment when the postcard photo was taken. The good news is that you can be a part of the 'what God is doing' postcard of today.

The Bible and the history books are like catalogues of great moments that happened that you were neither at or a part of. Plus, you don't own a Tardis or a time machine so you cannot go back to them! There is the good news though, God doesn't want you to be living in them: if He did, then He was quite able to position you in both the time and location of their actual happening *(Acts 17:25-27)*. The truth is **God wants you alive today, to live for what He is doing today**.

These verses say, "Look, I am doing a new thing." So today, trade in your desires to be back in a moment that has been and gone for the honour and excitement of being in a moment that, like an artist, God is painting right now.

If you 'make the trade' in the future, when people say, "Did you hear what God did in 2011?" you will be able to say, "I know, because I was there when it happened!" If you keep your heart set on moving with the God who does new things, you can say that about every year of the rest of your life because our God is always doing a new thing or a next thing somewhere.

In your life today, God is getting set to do a new thing. Can't you feel it bursting out?

Perceive, know and give heed

Do not [earnestly] remember the former things; neither consider the things of old. Behold, I am doing a new thing! Now it springs forth; do you not perceive and know it and will you not give heed to it? I will even make a way in the wilderness and rivers in the desert.

Isaiah 43:18-19 (Amplified Bible)

Concerning the new thing that God is doing and causing to *"[spring] forth"* in your life, He asks us to do three things to relate to it: *"perceive"* it, *"know"* it and *"give heed"* to it.

Perceive it
According to the dictionary, to perceive is to 'recognise, discern, envision or understand'. We need to make sure that we are at a point in our daily spirituality that we are able to sense and perceive what God is doing in a person's life or any given situation. It would be a shame to miss the wave of something God was doing because our senses, or ability to discern 'new things', were numb – maybe numbed from carnality or distraction. Make sure your 'taste buds' for spiritual things are sharp and able to know the flavour of our God doing something new in your day.

Know it
Know when God is bringing a change of season. Jesus said to a crowd, mentioned in the Scripture below, that they knew how to discern natural changes like weather and then He rebuked them for not being able to sense or know when a spiritual change of season was at hand. Let's make sure we do not fall into the category of the ignorant but stand with those who can feel the wind of change when it blows.

He said to the crowd: "When you see a cloud rising in the west, immediately you say, 'It's going to rain,' and it does. And when the south wind blows, you say, 'It's going to be hot,' and it is. Hypocrites! You know how to interpret the appearance of the earth and the sky. How is it that you don't know how to interpret this present time?"

Luke 12:54 (NKJV)

Give heed
Finally, He wants us to give heed to it – another way of putting that would be to be aware of it or live in accordance with it. Let's make sure we understand when God is doing something new and that we are passionate to be a part of it, and not bound to a previous moment. Choose to live in accordance with what He is doing today and not just what He once did.

Biblical mathematics (have correct division and subtraction)

Be diligent to present yourself approved to God, a worker who does not need to be ashamed, rightly dividing the word of truth.

2 Timothy 2:15 (NKJV)

Here we see Paul calling God's people to diligence, to become people who are not ashamed when it comes to understanding and correctly interpreting the truth of His Word – people who know how to divide it in the right way.

A major key for rightly dividing the Word of God is reading it in the correct context. Always take the time to understand the context of what was being spoken – for example, who was being spoken to and when? The most important context to establish is whether it was spoken before Jesus died, the perfect redeeming work of the cross, or after. You must always divide the Word with the understanding that there really is an Old and a New Testament; more specifically, there is an old and a new covenant. This we can never afford to forget if we want to walk in victory.

There is an old and a new covenant and we are called to live in accordance to, and find our identity in, the new, not the old. Fact: the old was replaced by the new; it was replaced by God, not man, because it was not good enough. That is why a place was sought by God for a second covenant! The first was not able to make a man righteous and justified because it was based on the performance of man. The second, new covenant is able to make a man righteous because it is based solely on the perfect performance of Jesus. To walk in victory, you need to correctly divide the old and the new covenants and subtract what is no longer relevant to your walk with God because of what Jesus has fulfilled and finalised on your behalf.

Think about it. If you are trying to live in two very different agreements, you will never completely or effectively live in either. Everything changed when Jesus died – the old covenant based on us fulfilling the law daily was fulfilled and replaced and the new covenant establishing us as righteous because of what Jesus did on our behalf began. Let us not spend our lives trying to add up what will never make sense.

Subtract from your walk with God what is no longer relevant to your life now that it is 'in Christ', and live wholehearted in what is relevant, the new. The fact is, a person is saved and regenerated by placing their faith in the grace and unmerited favour of God and that alone.

By grace are we saved!

Draw an accurate line in your Bible

Study and be eager and do your utmost to present yourself to God approved [tested by trial], a workman who has no cause to be ashamed, correctly analyzing and accurately dividing [rightly handling and skilfully teaching] the Word of Truth.

2 Timothy 2:15 (Amplified Bible)

Yesterday we looked at the importance of being someone who rightly divides the Word of God – a person who knows the difference between the old covenant and the new covenant, who knows how to subtract that which is no longer relevant because of what Christ Jesus has achieved on their behalf.

To divide the Word of God, the truth, correctly, you must have an accurate line in your understanding of the Word that allows you to perceive correctly when the old stopped and the new started. This line is, of course, the cross of Christ. Everything changed when Jesus shed His blood, died and rose again! We do not throw our Old Testament away but we must determine to daily live by the revealed truths of the covenant we find in the New Testament. Don't get me wrong: both Jesus and the plan of God for redeeming mankind are throughout the whole Bible.

I have heard it put well this way: in the Old, Jesus is concealed (there to be found if you are looking), He is present in so many types and shadows throughout every book of it; yet in the New He is revealed – revealed as the Saviour and Redeemer of the world and of your life. I regularly read both the Old and the New Testaments, yet I live and build my life in accordance to the realities of the New Testament. I am no longer fashioning my walk with God according to a replaced, obsolete, old covenant based upon law but a living and present one based on grace and a finished work.

The Old Testament can teach us so much but the law, or the covenant it represented, could never, and can never, save us – in fact, in itself, it continually pointed to the One who would, and did: Jesus.

Rightly divide the Word of truth by accurately knowing where one covenant stops and another begins, by knowing when things stopped being down to man's imperfect performance and started being down to Jesus' perfect one – perfect enough to perfect all who have believed. Enjoy both parts of the Bible but know accurately in your heart which part saves you and leaves you complete. We present ourselves to God approved when we present ourselves to Him positioned in Christ, living out of all that He achieved for us by His death, burial and resurrection.

Draw that important line and don't rub it out. Then you will divide the Word of truth correctly, getting from both sides what you were meant to.

Don't just be a citizen – be an ambassador

Once, having been asked by the Pharisees when the kingdom of God would come, Jesus replied, "The kingdom of God does not come with your careful observation, nor will people say, 'Here it is,' or 'There it is,' because the kingdom of God is within you."

Luke 17:20-22 (NIV)

Looking around at the condition of the world, I am ever aware that this is the moment for something that represents God well to arise. I'm not talking about religion, that will be of no help at all, but rather God lovers, kingdom-minded, sold-out people! People of all nationalities, cultures, denominational histories, that have the same King, kingdom and cause in common. People who want to represent God's kingdom well in the lives they live beyond two hours on a Sunday morning. People that carry God's kingdom wherever they go because they have realised they are now citizens of it and that it now lives in and manifests through them.

Citizenship of the kingdom of God becomes yours only when you believe in Jesus and are born again.

In reply Jesus declared, "I tell you the truth, no one can see the kingdom of God unless he is born again."

John 3:3 (KJV)

So it is a citizenship right that, like so many natural ones, is yours by birth. But there is a difference with this citizenship – though you are born into your first one (natural one), this new one, the kingdom, is born into you. This residency is an internal one.

Our cities need people who are not just citizens or passport holders, entitled to heaven after death but ambassadors who live it out – there is a difference. I am very much a Brit. I have a British passport and am also very British in how I act – wherever I happen to find myself in the world, the way I live out my life, wherever I am, reveals me as one, not just my legal documents. In the same way, may I not just have the passport or legal documents for God's kingdom but live daily like a citizen of it.

What are we doing when we are 'doing Church'? Hopefully, we are birthing, raising up and mobilising kingdom-minded people – people who know their true citizenship is of an eternal kingdom to which they truly belong, one for which they live with all they are.

The Kingdom is our message

When Jesus had called the Twelve together, he gave them power and authority to drive out all demons and to cure diseases, and he sent them out to preach the kingdom of God and to heal the sick.

Luke 9:1-3 (NIV)

When people encounter us, they should experience and hear the sound of the Gospel, the good news of the kingdom of God. Every other kingdom our lives might represent should be secondary to the one that reigns and will always remain when others fail.

Notice that the message the first disciples were sent to preach was the message of the kingdom – we need to make sure that it is still our message today. Don't worry, it does not leave Jesus out or rob Him of anything because wherever there is a kingdom, there is a king, and as we share the message of the kingdom, we share the message of its King and His rule and reign at the very same moment.

The message of the kingdom is a powerful message that releases people from contained living, from imprisonment through what they have known, from things that may have negatively defined them thus far on their life journey. The truth is, people always live out of what they have been exposed to through their life until something comes from outside of the 'containing bubble of their experience' offering something new. The kingdom of God comes like a pathway with new, bigger and better options for all of humanity – but remember, you always have to leave somewhere to go somewhere new. That's why Jesus said that we have to repent and 'think different' to see and enter His kingdom.

I love mission trips because they take people outside of everything they have known and experienced thus far in their lives to a bigger place of world experience. When they have seen and felt new things they can't often go back to what they knew previously. It's too small now because their lives have come into a bigger place. People who have experienced abuse or man-made religion remain contained by its effect and impact until another option to live differently comes in like a pathway to break them free and take them to a better way of living.

That is what the Gospel does: it comes into places of containment and imprisonment and sets people free to live in a bigger place, offering them a pathway to a bigger and better experience of both life and love.

So remember, we are to preach the kingdom and, as we do, lives will be set free and liberated. The message we share is the invitation and new pathway for people to know a better life, a life bigger and better then they have ever experienced.

Be His ambassador in your world

All this is from God, who reconciled us to himself through Christ and gave us the ministry of reconciliation: that God was reconciling the world to himself in Christ, not counting men's sins against them. And he has committed to us the message of reconciliation. We are therefore Christ's ambassadors, as though God were making his appeal through us.

2 Corinthians 5:18-20 (NIV)

In these verses, we see three very powerful things that should radically affect the way we see ourselves today.

First, we are to realise that each of us are ministers and He has given to each and every one of us the ministry of reconciliation. Next, we see that each of us are His messengers and He has committed to us a very important message for the world. He actually desires that our lives would be a living message, a living epistle or letter of divine invitation of reconciliation to a lost world.

Lastly, God says that we are ambassadors. What a privilege that God has called you to be a person who has the honour of representing Him and His kingdom wherever you go. When an ambassador goes somewhere, he carries a number of things from the king or kingdom he represents:

- His word or message (God has given you His message to share).

- His authority (God has given you His authority to bind and loose where ever needed).

When we go into our daily worlds again today, whether they be your work place or community, we need to remember that God has called us as ambassadors and that, in every place we find ourselves, we are to be His representatives, letting people know the goodness of our God and how incredible His kingdom really is.

We are to carry His Word and represent Him in every place that He sends us which actually is the whole world (The Great Commission). But a good place to start today is your world, that world or circle of influence that is unique to you.

This week, walk again through the world He has sent you to, armed with the knowledge that you have been called an ambassador by God and that you carry a life-changing message. You are His ambassador; represent Him well.

A never-ending story

I tell you the truth, anyone who has faith in me will do what I have been doing. He will do even greater things than these, because I am going to the Father.

John 14:12 (NIV)

These great words, spoken by Jesus, endorse the fact that we can live expectant of great things happening through our lives in our generation. These promises were not just for the original disciples, to whom they were first spoken, but for all those future disciples who would put their faith in Jesus, through all the generations that were yet to come, including ours!

The reality of the book of *Acts* is that it is an ongoing masterpiece with no real ending to it. Its chapters recording the exploits of the early believers may end in the Bible but they don't end in history because of the ongoing outworking of what God has continued to do though believers ever since. Why? Because the book may be called *Acts of the Apostles* but it would be better named the *Acts of the Holy Spirit, a record of the Spirit of God moving through the lives of those who believe in Jesus* (maybe that title is too long, right?). But that is the truth – the same Spirit that was in them is in those who believe in Jesus today. Who knows what chapter we're up to, but it's the same story!

Can I share with you one of the two greatest compliments ever given to me – given by my son, Ethan, when he was nine years old. We were driving to church one day and I asked if he loved God. He replied, "Yes, Dad, and I love you, Dad." He then stopped and thought and then said, "You know, Dad, I was thinking – if ever they were to add another book to the Bible, you would be in it!" Wow, what a compliment and my hope is that what he said would be true. Hey, why not?

The same Spirit that was given to the early Church has been given to us. They saw incredible things when they let Him flow through their lives and those things were recorded in a book so, if He is the same Spirit that is now in us, why shouldn't we see great things too? Though what we see may never be recorded in a book called the Bible we can know it is being recorded in heaven.

Remember, Jesus said that greater things will you see. Get expectant, get ready to see some of those greater things happening.

This is your chapter, live it!

That's how to talk to your giants

David said to the Philistine, "You come against me with sword and spear and javelin, but I come against you in the name of the LORD Almighty, the God of the armies of Israel, whom you have defied. This day the LORD will hand you over to me, and I'll strike you down and cut off your head. Today I will give the carcasses of the Philistine army to the birds of the air and the beasts of the earth, and the whole world will know that there is a God in Israel."

1 Samuel 17:45-46 (NIV)

Here, David gives us a lesson on how to talk to giants.

We have spoken about speaking to mountains in this devotional so now let's look now at how to speak to giants or, in other words, those situations and things that stand in front of you, threatening and intimidating you, whose sole purpose it is to create a life-freezing fear within you.

Look how David approached Goliath. What gave David the confidence to approach this giant with such authority? Yes, you guessed it. He had been basking in the bigness of his God.

The Israelites, on the other hand, had been basking in the bigness of this giant for many days. He had come before them daily and threatened them with intimidating statements. When you read this chapter, you see that they had become experts concerning this giant. They knew his size and how much his spearhead weighed. They had spent days basking in his bigness which had produced fear and caused them to totally forget how awesome their covenant God was.

But David was different and he wasn't having any of it! He was a shepherd boy who spent years staring into star-filled heavens, worshipping God and he had spent years basking in the bigness of God so that, when this moment arrived, there really was no competition. His G.O.D. was B.I.G! He just ran at the problem from his correct, godly perception and dealt with it in no time at all.

Champion, when, like David, you make it your habit to bask in the bigness of God and not become an expert concerning the giants of life, you too can run at any giant as David did, tell them their destiny and then take them out. Remember, we are in covenant with the same God that David trusted in. In fact, we have a superior Christ-based covenant with Him! Stop studying the giant but rather let God's bigness get into your heart!

Hey, Champion, why not go tell a giant what you, and your covenant God, are going to do to it?!

Breaking the grip of the Egyptian

Then God said to Moses, "Go and speak to Pharaoh king of Egypt so that he will release the Israelites from his land."

Exodus 6:10-11 (The Message)

When you look at God's intention for the children of Israel in the book of *Exodus*, you see that His desire was to totally liberate them from all of the cruelty, abuse and debt that had held them captive during their slavery in Egypt for so many years.

He sends Moses down to Egypt to speak to the people responsible for the debt and captivity; he comes with a very simple message from the Lord, *"Set my people free"*. You know the rest of the story – Pharaoh is having none of it and refuses outright to release those he held in slavery so God gets more and more persuasive with a number of plagues until, finally, after the death of Pharaoh's first born (amazing what it takes some people!), he then releases the children of Israel.

If you read the whole account, you also notice that they did not leave broke. Why did God instruct them to borrow gold and precious things from their captors prior to leaving? Because God had a better long-term plan in mind. Those borrowed things would actually turn out to be the years of unpaid wages they were due when God supernaturally cancelled the debt.

God's plan for them was freedom and this freedom included their wealth and financial futures; His plans for you are the same. When I read about the Egyptians of that time, they are representative or symbolic to me of debt! Debt holds you as a slave, against your will, making you serve it, never saying thank you and eating everything that should be yours to enjoy. I can feel some of you nodding!

I believe we are at a moment where God wants to lose the hand of the Egyptian again; by this I mean 'liberate His people from the life draining grip of debt'. God's plan for liberating the children of Israel was very unique – no one could have imagined how or what it could have looked like. Even Moses had trouble understanding it at the beginning of the master plan! It may have been a strange and unusual plan, but it worked!

Why not find out God's unusual plan for your freedom from debt? Remember, these plans are not all the same but rather unique plans that take into consideration such things as: who you are, what and how much the debt is and where your faith presently is. But don't doubt for a moment God has a plan – why not ask Him what it is? You will love it when His plan comes together.

Complete freedom was His agenda

And Moses stretched out his hand over the sea; and when the morning appeared, the sea returned to its full depth, while the Egyptians were fleeing into it. So the LORD overthrew the Egyptians in the midst of the sea. Then the waters returned and covered the chariots, the horsemen, and all the army of Pharaoh that came into the sea after them. Not so much as one of them remained.

Exodus 14:27-28 (NKJV)

We talked yesterday about God setting His people free from the captivity of debt and we compared debt to the Egyptians that were in the day of Moses. After God's people leave Egypt, we read of how the Egyptians responded to the release of their captives: they were not happy. Yes, they had released them but there was always an unseen agenda to kill or recapture them. Basically, a plan to bring them back into the grip of their cruel captivity. The good news is that God had an agenda too and His agenda was complete and lasting liberty from every grip the Egyptians had on them, both present and future.

So you read on and suddenly Pharaoh's hardness of heart returns and he changes his mind and wants to reclaim what he had liberated, switching to this other agenda. When he switched, so did God. They pursued the children of Israel into the Red Sea but only God's children came through. In that one moment, God drowned every pursuing Egyptian so that His people could be debt free and liberated from anything that could pursue them later.

Again, I want to say I believe this is God's plan for the debts that have held us and threaten to pursue us in these days. God wants to free you from the grip of what has governed you for so long. It's not right that what you do, what you give and what you dream of achieving with your life should be controlled by 'Egyptian-type' realities. Remember, just as with the children of Israel and the decisions they had made earlier on, most of the time it was us that caused the debt; but in His grace, He will be the one who leads us out in freedom, restoring liberty in our lives.

Like the children of Israel, are you ready for God to do something, to lead you somewhere you have not been before? Are you going to follow His leading with a smile of faith and not a grumble of unbelief?

Get ready to leave Egypt!

Champion's Prayer:

Father, today I make the choice to be free. Thank You, that as I choose to walk in the steps of freedom You provide so I know You will drown the things that have kept me captive. Freedom is Your only plan for me, thank You for freedom – Amen.

You have to get Egypt out of you

"Why has the LORD brought us to this land to fall by the sword, that our wives and children should become victims? Would it not be better for us to return to Egypt?" So they said to one another, "Let us select a leader and return to Egypt."

Numbers 14:3-4 (NKJV)

We have looked at how God miraculously freed His people Israel from the grip of Egyptian rule and finalised it so that Egypt, the captor, had no further claim on His people. We compared Egypt to things like debt and saw how God's desire is to liberate us in such a way that our lives are free from their life-sapping grip.

In today's verse, we see the sad reality that God could take His people out of Egypt but He couldn't take Egypt out of some of His people. Here we see the moment in their God-ordained journey where they are beyond the incredible miracle of the parting of the Red Sea and are experiencing incredible provision and miracles on a daily basis. They are standing on the edge of their promised land, facing a moment where there are another couple of challenges that simply need to, again, be overcome by their faith and, remember, God had promised they were stronger than these obstacles too.

Instead of joining in with their leaders with shouts of, "God is with us, we can do it!" some of them chose to reflect back to their captivity in Egypt and actually managed to deceive themselves that they were better off there! How crazy is that? They were now living in the divine freedom of God and merely facing another momentary challenge that God would give them incredible victory in.

This underlines for us the sad reality that some of them had never actually left Egypt in their hearts. The truth for us also is that if you don't leave something in your heart and put it well and truly behind you forever, you will always give yourself an option or reason to return.

God wants you to be liberated from the debts and stuff that bound and restricted your life. When He liberates you, leave in such a way that there is no route for you to return. Burn your bridge so that, in those challenging times, you don't have even the desire to move back to former things but ever forwards in faith, trusting Him for the promised better days.

Face the fact: where He has delivered you from was not really that good, was it?

Where does your help come from?

I lift up my eyes to the hills – where does my help come from? My help comes from the LORD*, the Maker of heaven and earth. He will not let your foot slip – he who watches over you will not slumber;*

Psalm 121:1-3 (NIV)

The first three verses of this Psalm start with a question and then the Psalm ends with a statement of persuasion and a declaration of faith!

Have you ever asked yourself the question, "Where does my help come from?" Or maybe, "Where will my help come from in this situation I am facing right here, right now?" The answer given in this Psalm is your answer too, Champion. Your help, whatever that help needs to look like, comes from the Lord. He is, and will always be, the source of your help so don't look to the hills with question marks but rather look to your Lord with an exclamation mark of persuasion, for He fails not!

Think about it, those are some great qualifications God has, *"Maker of heaven and earth."* When I think about that, it makes Him totally overqualified to help me with my current situations. He who threw the stars into space cares for me and has appointed Himself my Helper and strong refuge in time of need.

Another great part of this promise is, *"He will not let your foot slip!"* Remember, the steps of a righteous man, which is what you are through faith in Christ, are ordered of God. Where you are walking at the moment may feel a bit slippery but He will keep your foot from slipping.

Finally, notice He is your never-sleeping help! He that watches over you does not slumber so He has your back, Champion, and never takes His eyes off of you. Thank God that He does not nod off but is constant and continuous in His help and assistance. He alone offers an infallible 24-7 service. Today He is your help!

Again, let the confidence of David be yours and, even when you are in the midst of stuff, even stuff that may feel like a valley of death, don't turn your eyes to the hills but look further upwards and turn them to the God who has promised He will save the day!

Champion's Prayer:

Father, I thank You today that You are my helper. Forgive me for looking to other things and other people. I lift my eyes to You; You are my very present help in time of need. Thank You that today, and every day, You are all I need. Help me with the things I am facing. Thank You that You never sleep or slumber and are always there to answer my every call – Amen.

How to avoid a great crash

Therefore everyone who hears these words of mine and puts them into practice is like a wise man who built his house on the rock. The rain came down, the streams rose, and the winds blew and beat against that house; yet it did not fall, because it had its foundation on the rock. But everyone who hears these words of mine and does not put them into practice is like a foolish man who built his house on sand. The rain came down, the streams rose, and the winds blew and beat against that house, and it fell with a great crash.

Matthew 7:24-27 (NIV)

In this parable, Jesus compares a wise builder, the man that builds on the rock of God's Word and wisdom, to a foolish builder, the man who builds on other stuff. Notice that Jesus does not call the second man ignorant but rather foolish. It would be very different if he was ignorant. That would mean he was unknowing or unaware of God's Word and wisdom. No, Jesus chooses the word *"foolish"* and this is a different thing altogether. This man was not ignorant of God's Word and ways – rather, he knew them but chose to build according to what he thought would work better. This can always be a very dangerous thing to do.

At the end of the account, we see that, actually, he did not know better and everything he thought to be 'better wisdom', or a more practical way of doing it, was actually nothing more than shifting, unstable shingle.

The truth is that storms affect both the saved and the unsaved. The storms of life beat against the lives of the righteous and the unrighteous but these storms do not have to cause a major crash in your life. You do not have to see everything you have built destroyed in one single moment. All you need to do is take Jesus' advice and build your life in accordance to the truth of His Word and as you do, you then daily position yourself on the *"rock"* that is referred to. The waves and storms may still come but the life you build will remain and not fall.

Don't be foolish, neither be ignorant. Rather be wise, build how God tells you to and you too can avoid the crash!

Champion's challenge:

Take a moment to look at what you are building your life upon. If you are building on things other than God, make the wise decision to change those foundations before the storms and the waves begin to come. Make sure that He is the sure foundation you are building your life upon.

You need two healthy trees, not one

But the fruit of the Spirit is love, joy, peace, longsuffering, kindness, goodness, faithfulness, gentleness, self-control. Against such there is no law.

Galatians 5:22 (NKJV)

O K, let's talk about character and the need for a commitment to its development today.

As we daily walk with God, we should be experiencing two things ever developing and growing in our lives. We should be experiencing the gifts of the Spirit developing in and through our lives and also the fruit of the Spirit.

These are two very separate things and a healthy Christian always has the right amount of both! Remember, when we talk about the gifts of the Spirit as they are revealed in *1 Corinthians 12,* we are talking about things that are given as gifts by God – we did nothing to get them. But when we speak about fruit, we speak of things that are developed in our lives as we daily submit to and walk in accordance with God's ways.

If the gifts and fruits of the Spirit were conifer trees standing at the front of the house of your life, would you have two healthy ones or would one be looking not so healthy? This world does not need to see any more gifted Christians, rather more God-gifted Christians who have great character too – people living lives where the fruit of the life of His Spirit now within is seen and experienced too.

Recently, again we have seen too many headlines concerning celebrities and football players who have cheated on their wives and lived in ways they should not have, lifestyles not fitting well with their influential public roles. Often, these are young men who have been thrown into a fickle industry where, very quickly, they have fame, money and anything they want. Sadly, many times we see that they do not have the character to carry the gift, or opportunity given, and it all blows up into yet another embarrassing headline. Sadly, we have seen this happen in ministry too, which does the advancement of Christianity no favours at all.

True success needs to be judged more holistically. Just because someone can kick a ball, sing or speak well does not mean they are successful! If the rest of their life has no character and is a mess, then they are merely people with messed up lives who do a good job performing on the stage or kicking a ball on the pitch. If you want true success, Champion, then be committed to developing both the gifts God gives you and the fruit that it is down to you to grow. Don't worry, if you have the desire to, then the Holy Spirit will help you all the way!

Live to be a person with two healthy trees – gifts and fruit, talent and character. God can use that sort of person time and time again!

Don't let your gift take you where your character can't keep you

The purposes of a man's heart are deep waters, but a man of understanding draws them out. Many a man claims to have unfailing love, but a faithful man who can find?

Proverbs 20:5-6 (NIV)

These verses ask the question, "Who can find a faithful man?" Faithfulness really is a character thing, something that dwells within the unseen wiring of a person's life. Let's further consider the topic of gifts and fruit, talents and character.

As we said yesterday, too often in the headlines we experience the reality of people who are highly gifted or talented one day finding themselves in a place where they can no longer exist or remain because the character part of their life was not strong enough, or developed enough to keep them safe in their moment of success.

When you have strong gifting, you will find that opportunities and success are never far away. But, be aware that often, within that opportunity or success, there is not just stuff that can profit you but also stuff that has the potential to destroy you – especially if you have little character. These opportunities can take you from being a person with a long future destiny to being someone who, like a shooting star, has a mere moment of fame or success.

So what is it that keeps you safe from some of the side effects of fame and opportunity? The answer is simple: your God-developed character. It is this that enables you to say no when you need to and to walk away when you know your integrity is on the line. Remember, the compromises and things that come to ruin you are rarely ugly but often very good looking – they sound 'kind of right' and smell real good.

Champion, always take time to sense what is going on in your spirit, in other words, what God is saying to you. When suspicious opportunities arrive, always have the courage to follow God; this could well save you and your future success.

Your character is all about what happens in the real, inside you; it finds its strength in what you truly believe and what you value. Let God's Word and ways continue to influence and impact the development of your character then purpose to always live true to it, especially when the offers are really good but not really God! In doing this you will set yourself up for long and continued success!

It's your character that 'gets you out of there'

One day he (Joseph) went into the house to attend to his duties, and none of the household servants was inside. She caught him by his cloak and said, "Come to bed with me!" But he left his cloak in her hand and ran out of the house.

Genesis 39:11-12 (NIV)

Think about this crazy moment in the very colourful life of Joseph. After being abandoned then sold as a slave by his brothers, he is purchased by Potiphar. Potiphar sees 'the hand of the Lord' on him and promotes him to the top job so that Joseph is in the position of ruling over everything he owns. This man had given Joseph so much and such great opportunity. Then along comes what could have been 'one of the perks' if he was a man of no honour or character – namely Potiphar's immoral wife. With hubby away, she comes to seduce this handsome, young, key employee using the language of "You deserve it and no-one will ever know". What a great moment for Joseph! If he had no character, he could have had a ball and made a great ally at the same time! But Joseph **did** have character and it says that "Joseph got up and ran!" That was his character leading his life.

Why did he run? Maybe because he was conscious of his own inability and weakness and did not want to see what would happen if his character was further chipped away at? Yes, she still set him up and accused him of rape and he was imprisoned but then one day the truth rises to the top and he rose again with it. Why? When you live with strong character and determine to be true to it, then you always set yourself up for great future. Despite those challenging moments, you give God something He can mega-bless and always work with!

Listen to the great character within his response to this lady offering him apparent 'success':

"No one is greater in this house than I am. My master has withheld nothing from me except you, because you are his wife. How then could I do such a wicked thing and sin against God?"

Joseph is a great role model. Let's build lives that are sustained by great character. Hey, whenever your character is being tested, you can always do what he did – RUN!

But the fruit of the Spirit is love, joy, peace, longsuffering, kindness, goodness, faithfulness, gentleness, self-control. Against such there is no law.

Galatians 5:22 (NKJV)

Champion's Challenge:

Take some time to look again at the fruits of the Spirit. Be honest and see which one may need some more work then allow God to work on it, remembering that everything He does brings life.

You can build on character

Therefore select out from among yourselves, brethren, seven men of good and attested character and repute, full of the [Holy] Spirit and wisdom, whom we may assign to look after this business and duty.
Acts 6:3 (Amplified Bible)

Here's another great verse that's very relevant to the importance of character development.

Here, we see the early Church come to a point where they needed some staffing changes involving delegation. Some issues had arisen and some practical things to do with people-care were not running as well as they should so the disciples decided to enlarge their leadership team to make sure all was done well.

Notice that, when they wrote the job description, right near the front was the need for good character then came *"full of the [Holy] Spirit and wisdom"*. They knew, as many employers have discovered ever since, that talent and gift are good but they can often be of no use if a person does not have good character. For example, you can be super-gifted but if you don't turn up on time where you said you would or when you're needed to be, what use is your great gift and talent to the moment?

Of course, the best deal is to have people who are gifted and talented **and** who also have character and integrity so that they do what they say and don't do what they know they shouldn't. But if I had to pick one or the other, I would go for character every time. You can teach people talents and skills but character is something they have developed and it enables you to release responsibility knowing things will be done as they should, when they should – even when you're not looking!

If the disciples used this principle, and most employers do also, do you think God does? I do. I think when God is looking for someone to use, He looks for the person of character first, the person He can trust to do what He needs to be done over the person who can do it when they eventually get there in an 'all-singing, all-dancing' way.

Let's live to give God both – our talents and skills but, first of all, let's give Him good, solid character!

Champion's Prayer:

Father, today I stand before You, a person desiring both gifting and character. Thank You for the gifts You give but also I ask You to help me to be developing the character that I need for the life You have given me to live. Let the fruit of Your Spirit ever be growing and flowing out of the garden, bringing glory to You – Amen.

He has to take you out to bring you in

Abram believed the LORD, and He credited it to him as righteousness. He also said to him, "I am the LORD, who brought you out of Ur of the Chaldeans to give you this land to take possession of it."

Genesis 15:6-7 (NIV)

Here we see God remind Abraham that He, God, was the Author and the Finisher of Abraham's faith journey, that He had led him out in order to bring him in so that he could possess the land!

Here, we are reminded of something very simple, yet very powerful, when it comes to walking by faith with God: you can't be in two places at once. God is a God of movement and change; He loves to keep us journeying into the greater things He has for us. But before He can bring you into somewhere new, He has to get you to leave somewhere old. Until Abraham left Ur, he could not arrive in Canaan and that bit was not down to God but down to him. It's the same for us – if we want to arrive somewhere new, we have to be ready and prepared to leave somewhere old. If we want Him to bring us in, we need to let Him first lead us out.

This could be relevant to a number of things in your world. For Abraham, it was a physical location move. Yep, that could be for some of you also but it may be other things, like ways of thinking, circles of friendships or other differing opportunities. I think that if we are given the choice we would, because of our insecurities, prefer to rather remain **and** arrive at the same time but that is not how it works. Like Abraham, we need to exercise our faith in leaving to position ourselves for the arriving God has in store and then, indeed, the possessing too.

Where is God wanting to lead you next? Are you ready to leave so that you can arrive? Remember, the promise of the Lord is to bless your going out and your coming in, in that order.

The LORD shall preserve you from all evil; He shall preserve your soul. The LORD shall preserve your going out and your coming in from this time forth, and even forevermore.

Psalm 121:7-8 (NKJV)

Champion's Prayer:

Father, I thank You that in order to bring me into something new, You have to lead me out of somewhere old. Grant me the courage to follow You when it does not make sense to my understanding. Father, please lead me out of where I need to leave, bring me into what You have for me next and cause me to possess that land for Your glory – Amen.

Your life is ripe for harvest now!

Do you not say, 'There are still four months and then comes the harvest'? Behold, I say to you, lift up your eyes and look at the fields, for they are already white for harvest!

John 4:35 (NKJV)

Do not live your life always thinking, "I will do that in a few months time." For many things, the greatest time to do is **now**. Procrastination is not a friend to your life, don't treat it like one. Sometimes we do have to wait, sometimes God makes us wait or take time to journey towards something, like we might in a pilgrimage, but at other times, it can just be us not being motivated. We find it easier to file what needs to be done in that place called 'I will do that later'. These are the things I want to bring a challenge to this morning. Jesus told His disciples, in reference to the harvest of men's souls, not four months but now!

Live with a sense of *carpe vitam*

Most of us have heard of the Latin phrase *carpe diem* which means 'seize the day' or, more literally, 'harvest your day'. I love the sense of seizing, or harvesting, my day but my day is not enough – there is so much more to be harvested. That is why I found the Latin word for 'life' and changed the quote to *carpe vitam* – seize your life!

There are many well know proverbs around today that each contain an element of wisdom, like, "A stitch in time saves nine" or ,"The early bird catches the worm". But have you ever heard this one, "You don't know what you've got until it's gone"? This one is the one I really want to re-write because I don't think it suits our lives and destinies as followers of Jesus – it's simply not big enough, or good enough, for God lovers. I have officially changed it in my world to this: **"Know what you have and fully appreciate it while you still have it."**

Think about that today. What, or who, do you have that you're not making the most of or that you could appreciate a whole lot more while you still have it or them? Here's some common ones.

- **Health** – if you have health, enjoy it, max it, use it to the full.

- **Youth** – this has a shelf life; whatever you have left of it, use it and fully appreciate it.

- **Relationships** – no one promised that those who are in your life now will always be there. Don't live in fear of this reality but do live in present day appreciation of who is in your world.

Champion, know what you have and make the very most of it now, not in four months. In so many ways, your life is so ripe for harvest right now!

Harvest your relationships

Do you not say, 'There are still four months and then comes the harvest'? Behold, I say to you, lift up your eyes and look at the fields, for they are already white for harvest!

John 4:35 (NKJV)

Our key thought: know, enjoy and love what you have while you have it – don't wait until it is gone to appreciate it! We ended yesterday on the thought of relationships. Relationships are a gift in your life; always make sure you are appreciating or getting the most out of each of them. The sad fact is, as we said yesterday, not everyone that is in your life now will necessarily be there in the same way in a few years time. This is so worth thinking about. I hope that thought does not cause fear but rather a motivation that, in turn, will deliver you from the chance of any regrets 'later on'.

Parents

Make the most of every stage of your children's life and development. When they are through certain stages, they are so often done with them and those stages are never repeated. Like flowers in a field, take the time to smell the daily scent of who they presently are in this thing called life. Remember, their lives are not like DVD players so don't live with your finger on fast forward or you will miss important moments. Don't live as if there is a rewind, thinking you'll be able to see it all another time when you're not so busy – you won't! Keep your finger on play and enjoy 'real-time' life playing out before you.

Kids (however old you are)

However many parents you have left, and no matter what age they are, make the choice to live in such a way that you *carpe* the juice out of those relationships because the sad heritage for kids is that we all say goodbye to our parents one day and that is the right way round. Hopefully, there is the assurance of reuniting with them in the next leg of eternity. Again, it's not about living with fear or regret but purposing in our hearts to get the most out of these relationships – not in four months time but now!

As many of you know, a number of years ago my mum died of cancer. It was so fast; she went into a hospital with back pain and four weeks later died in a hospice. I loved my mum – she was a great mum and an inspiration and mentor to my faith in God. I remember sitting in that hospice day and night in those last few days, trying to get as many moments as I could with and from her. The reality is, the moments were always there for many years previously; it was not that I did not want them, I was busy. Thinking back, maybe too busy? Maybe, if I had that chance again, I would be less busy, who knows? Make that phone call, arrange that visit, forgive, love, they're worth it! Whether it's children, parents or friends, make the most of who is in your world today!

Be ready for your moment

Do you not say, 'There are still four months and then comes the harvest'? Behold, I say to you, lift up your eyes and look at the fields, for they are already white for harvest!

John 4:35 (NKJV)

We have been looking at living outside of procrastination, living with a desire to harvest and seize what is in our worlds now. Too many people are waiting for that one day that will come. We too need to remain in faith concerning the yet unseen of God in our future but also be the people that grab each new day with both hands and determine to get the most from it.

We looked at relationships yesterday. Today I want to challenge you concerning opportunities. I believe God brings and offers opportunities to us all at different times in our life and we have a choice to grab them passionately or let them pass us by. Live in such a way that, with wisdom, you seize opportunities, especially those which are authored and sent by God.

At different times in the Bible, you see God turn up and offer something to someone then you get to witness those who *carpe* the God-offer and those who don't. Think of Elisha and that moment when Elijah walked across the field and offered him his mantle (his job). God's intention was clear, the choice was now his. He chose to burn his plough and step into his God given opportunity; he could have chosen to keep on ploughing and ignore it. What about the disciples? They were fishing; they never saw Jesus coming but He had been watching them. Suddenly a God-opportunity comes out of nowhere. Jesus says to them, *"Drop your nets and follow Me, and I will make you fishers of men."* Again, they had the choice to say, "No thanks, we like fishing!" but they too seized the moment and stepped into their destiny.

Sadly, a negative example would be the rich, young ruler who thought he was ready for his moment but, when the cost was explained, he really wasn't. God will always bring opportunities to you – some small, some large, some bigger than you could have ever imagined. Make sure you are ready for the 'no warning' offer of God when it comes. Let us all make the choice, like the wise virgins, to 'live ready'. Not just for the second coming of Christ but for those divine opportunities that suddenly come that need us to respond with faith, not fear.

I personally believe He prepares you for these moments when you are not even noticing. I believe He had been working on the heart of Elisha prior to Elijah's arrival; He had been working in the hearts of the fishermen before the one-time offer came; He is working on our hearts now concerning future moments and opportunities that will come.

Just as King David was prepared for his opportunity with Goliath while defeating lions and bears, so what you are getting victory with today is setting you up for golden opportunities that God is going to bring to you in your tomorrows. Live ready because they come to us all!

God's three-part life restoration plan

"At that time I will gather you; at that time I will bring you home. I will give you honour and praise among all the peoples of the earth when I restore your fortunes before your very eyes," says the LORD.
Zephaniah 3:20 (NIV)

W hat a great bunch of restoration promises!
God made this three-part promise to His people many, many years ago. We read in the Old Testament that it was a promise originally spoken under an old 'law-based' covenant. I believe that it is still a valid promise for you and me today if we will dare to claim it and we should be even more excited about it than those it was originally spoken to because we receive it knowing that we have a new and even better agreement or covenant with God. One based on faith and grace.

There are three distinct promises of restoration in this verse.

- *"I will gather you; at that time I will bring you home"* – you will be redeemed and restored.

- *"I will give you honour and praise among all the peoples of the earth"* – you will be re-established.

- *"I restore your fortunes before your very eyes"* – you will be prospered.

Wow! This is a three-part plan you do not want to ignore. This is one of those promises that are worth learning inside out and upside down – make it such a part of you that you can recite it in twenty different translations and even Hebrew! Notice what the first step is: God says, "He will bring you back to Him". Listen, if you want the other two, you have to first experience this one because it is the one that is most important to God.

If you have been away from Him, or drifted a bit in your relationship and seen stuff in your life go wrong, realise that first God restores 'you and Him' and then He will restore everything else. Don't try and bypass step one, let God *"bring you home"* then watch Him re-establish your life, your name and then, as it says so well, watch as He restores your fortunes or, as it says in the Amplified, *"reverses your captivity"*.

The reverse of captivity is **freedom** and that is God's intention for your life. But remember, first, He wants you back home!

Have deep-rooted confidence

Therefore do not cast away your confidence, which has great reward. For you have need of endurance, so that after you have done the will of God, you may receive the promise.

Hebrews 10:35-36 (KJV)

In *John 10:10*, Jesus reveals the devil as a thief. He was, and will always be, exactly that: a stinking thief, ever intent and hell-bent on stealing things from God's people.

What is he wanting to steal from you and me? The answer is simple: every single thing that God has so richly given us. **Our peace**, that peace that passes all human understanding and guards our hearts in Christ. **Our joy,** that force that surpasses mere happiness that keeps us strong in even the hardest of times. **Our revelation of righteousness**, oh, how he ever longs to get us back into the grind of performance and dead works!

But I personally think the one he really wants is our confidence. Why? Because *Hebrews* says it is of great reward. He wants to snatch from under you your confidence in the most fundamental things like: knowing who you are, your God-given identity, what you can do, your God-given potential. And what you can have or expect, your God-given hopes and expectations.

Your Godly confidence is of great reward because when, with confidence, you endure and just keep on going, you will inherit and come into possession of all that God has promised you. If the devil can get you to cast away your confidence, then he can stop you inheriting or walking in all that great stuff God has for you. Don't let him!

Have you ever stopped and watched people walking around the shops? You can tell by how they hold and carry themselves those who have confidence and those who don't. Those with confidence have their heads lifted and their shoulders back and they walk with steps that say, "I belong here".

That's how God wants you to walk through this day; His word should cause you to lift your head up, put back your shoulders and face the day and all it holds with courage and boldness because, as with Joshua, so it is with you. GOD IS WITH YOU!

Confidence does not need to be loud; it needs to be silently deep rooted *(Isaiah 30:15)!* Often, quiet confidence has more power than loud confidence, that confidence that resides deep down, that says quietly, yet firmly, "I know God is for me and His promises over me are "Yes!" and "Amen!" I know that things may seem strange now but they will turn around for my good!"

Remember, there is a thief out there. Don't let him take what belongs to you, what you can't afford to lose!

The grace of the Father qualifies the undeserving

The son said to him, 'Father, I have sinned against heaven and against you. I am no longer worthy to be called your son. But the father said to his servants, 'Quick! Bring the best robe and put it on him. Put a ring on his finger and sandals on his feet. Bring the fattened calf and kill it. Let's have a feast and celebrate. For this son of mine was dead and is alive again; he was lost and is found.' So they began to celebrate.

Luke 15:21-24 (NIV)

Here we see the powerful moment of reunion between the child who went astray and the father who had so eagerly awaited his return.

This was a parable that Jesus used to reveal to the Pharisee the true heart of His Father towards those who had gone astray and lost their way. On the son's return, instead of walking back into extreme discipline, judgement and deserved punishment which, when you read what he had done, was a valid entitlement according to the law, we see him walk back into the welcoming arms of a father whose heart was set on restoration and reinstatement.

Notice the son is not deceived or deluded concerning what he deserves. He flat out says, "I am not worthy, I deserve nothing, not even of what was mine through birth". Now notice the father's response: he totally ignores his son! Why? He knew the work that was needed to be done had been done in the life of his son and that the son's humble return confirmed the reality of this. Instead, he turns to his servant and orders that his son be re-clothed with a robe, righteousness, a ring, authority and sandals, evidence that he was a son, not the slave as he had set his heart to be.

Think about it: the son deserved nothing; all he had done had disqualified him of any right or inheritance. Yet the father lavishly showered him in grace – undeserved, unmerited, unearned favour – and it was grace that restored the boy's life and gave dignity back to the one who was not worthy of it.

This is our common story. We all, like sheep, had gone astray yet, like this returning son, when we approached God the Father, desperate for help, we also did not receive what we deserved. That's mercy. But rather we received what we never dreamed possible. That's grace.

Remember, Champion – you being established and repositioned as a righteous heir and son or daughter is all about His grace and mercy, not your ability. Make sure you ever love Him for that.

Enjoy His grace again today and remember, by it, we all stand!

GRACE!

Don't be an ugly brother

Meanwhile, the older son was in the field. When he came near the house, he heard music and dancing. So he called one of the servants and asked him what was going on. 'Your brother has come,' he replied, 'and your father has killed the fattened calf because he has him back safe and sound.' The older brother became angry and refused to go in. So his father went out and pleaded with him.

Luke 15:25-28 (NIV)

L et's continue to look at the parable of the wayward child this morning and take a look at another character in the story line, namely the older brother.

I am sure you have heard about the ugly sisters in the story of Cinderella, right? Well here's the story of the ugly brother, a story that Jesus told to display how ugly some religious people's attitudes can be when it comes to others returning to God and needing grace. There is no record of him being an outwardly ugly person, his ugliness was contained in his attitudes and reasonings concerning what other deserve.

His younger brother had gone off the rails, thrown everything away, and then returned hoping to be a mere servant in his father's household. To the older brother's amazement, his brother is restored to full sonship and not employed as a servant. The father puts on a big party and, when the older brother hears of this celebration of restoration, instead of getting all excited and joining in, he gets a big, fat, ugly attitude. Despite the father going to him and trying to reason, he chooses to stay positioned in his bad attitude concerning the grace being used on his brother rather than the judgement and harsh punishment he deserved.

Let us learn from this parable. May we choose never to be an 'ugly brother' but rather always have rejoicing in our hearts for those who are returning home, even if we know – or think we know – what they have been doing while away from the Father.

It is not our place, and we have no right, to judge people coming to God or coming back to God but rather we should display that *1 Corinthians 13* type love that always hopes and believes the best.

Always remember that we all stand because of the mercy and grace of God, given to us in Jesus. So, when considering the returning journey of others, let us always purpose to remember that well-known saying, 'There, but for the grace of God, go I.'

Bless you – give applause today to those desiring and being courageous enough to make a comeback.

Want to increase the size of your world?

The world of the generous gets larger and larger; the world of the stingy gets smaller and smaller.
Proverbs 11:24 (The Message)

Here's some great wisdom for those wanting a life that just continues to get larger and larger as the years go by, ending up somewhere that is incredibly bigger than what you ever imagined in your wildest dreams.

The key is real simple. Here it is: choose to live generously! Do you want your world and life to get bigger and bigger or smaller and smaller? How are you going to choose to live to make that desired life a living reality?

Today's verse does not say your 'finances'; it says your *"world"*. Obviously your world, or life, is more than your financial success, right? Your world involves your health, relationships, influence and so much more. In every section of your life, you have the opportunity, daily, to be generous; the choice to be generous or stingy belongs only to you!

Generosity can be manifested through every bit of who we are and the life we daily live; with our words we can be generous, encouraging people, or stingy, never speaking words of life or hope but rather gossip and criticism. With our time we can be generous or stingy. We can spend it on ourselves or choose to spend it on, and for, others too. With our finances and the resources of our life we can be generous, giving and lending where we can or we can be stingy and live a self-benefiting, self-preserving existence.

In every single section of what makes your world unique to you, you have the choice to be generous or mean. I don't know about you, but I don't want the inheritance of the stingy, a life that gets smaller and smaller as time goes by.

Finally, this really isn't a matter of faith but one of choice: it may take faith to be as generous as you really want to but the choice to be generous, rather than stingy, is the daily, first step.

Hey, Champion, give something away today. I dare you! Imagine, if everyone that reads this devotional deliberately gave something special away to someone else today, that would be a fun wave we would create together and send into the ocean of life. Money, time, encouragement: you choose. One or all of them – but be generous, knowing that, as you do, God promises your world will get bigger and bigger.

BE GENEROUS!

What are you devising?

Also the schemes of the schemer are evil; he devises wicked plans to destroy the poor with lying words, even when the needy speaks justice. But a generous man devises generous things, and by generosity he shall stand.

Isaiah 32:7-8 (NKJV)

Let's stay a little longer looking at the subject of being generous people. Yesterday, we saw that the promise of God to those who choose to be generous rather than stingy was an ever-enlarging life. Today's challenge is: what are you devising in your heart and what will what you are devising cause you to do? All of us continually devise stuff, the problem is that some devise wicked or selfish stuff while others devise generous stuff that causes blessing and profits the life of others.

A generous man devises generous things

To devise is to plan, to plot, to secretly arrange. This really is the calling of the believer to be a person that is continually plotting and planning the blessing of others. This is also a real fun way to live.

We used to have a man in our church that I nicknamed the 'ten pound angel'. I knew who he was but no one else did. Every Sunday, he would get some crisp, ten pound notes and then pray about who he should give them to. Then he would spend Sunday morning hiding the ten pound notes in people's Bibles and bags. He caused a real stir as, each Sunday, people would discover a tenner, or sometimes more, in their Bible and, you guessed it, a lot of the time it came at a moment when it was really needed. But no one knew, except God. I used to love watching this man creep around church hiding tenners, knowing that he had spent the morning praying and devising generous things to bless others. Note: he did this as well as tithe, not instead of!

The promise to those who choose to live a life that devises generous plans for others and not wicked or mean ones is that you will stand. Do current news headlines of lack and recession worry you? Then take this promise personally – it clearly says that it's the generosity of the one who devises good to others that will cause him to stand, even when there is a recession or when others may fall. Get devising: remember, generosity is not just financial. You can be generous with many things: time, energy, encouragement, the list goes on and on!

Champion's Challenge:

Like the 'ten pound angel' in my church, devise something good for someone in your church or world, not someone you always do good for but someone random that God puts on your heart. Devise a blessing then do it!

Take control of your heart activity

Peace I leave with you, My peace I give to you; not as the world gives do I give to you. Let not your heart be troubled, neither let it be afraid.

John 14:27 (NKJV)

When walking by faith, you have to control the activity of your heart. When you are walking towards a God-given promise, as we have previously said, most times without a clue how God is going to do what He has promised, a lot of different emotions can happen in the internal world of your life. Your heart is a very important part of your life. Naturally, if it fails, then nothing else really matters. So it is also with our unseen heart: that place of emotions where reasoning occurs, that place where either faith or fear can reside.

Today's verse is all about peace – more specifically, the peace of God, that peace which is more powerful and superior than any other. Notice Jesus said that, like His righteousness, He gives it. This means we do not have to fear that its continued presence is down to our performance. It is a gift given to remain continually. Notice what Jesus says next, "Because you now have His peace, you can, and should, now take control of the activity of your heart."

Make sure the activity is not fear-based but rather faith-based. When there is faith-based activity in your heart, then you ward off the side effects that come with such things as fear, things like anxiety and worry that actually have the potential to shorten your days.

Jesus specifically speaks of not letting your heart do certain things. Wow! That means that you actually have a controlling role concerning its daily activity.

Okay, firstly Jesus says, "Don't let your heart be troubled or upset". Remember, we walk by faith and not by sight which means we should not be moved or distressed by what we may see. Rather, we should be stable, despite the changing landscapes, because of what we believe. Secondly, He says, "Don't allow your heart to be afraid or scared". Again, according to Jesus, **you** have the right to chose this, not your circumstances. Choose to banish the things that strive to produce fearfulness – you cannot afford to be full of fear, rather be full of faith.

Okay, it's down to you! Christ is in you, which means your peace is going nowhere on your journey of faith. But now you must choose what you are going to let your heart do during the inevitable ups and downs of the journey.

The day of the donkey

The disciples went and did as Jesus had instructed them. They brought the donkey and the colt, placed their cloaks on them, and Jesus sat on them. A very large crowd spread their cloaks on the road, while others cut branches from the trees and spread them on the road.

Matthew 21:6-8 (NIV)

Let us remind ourselves again that the vehicle Jesus chose to enter the most significant city of its time, Jerusalem, was not a golden chariot or a fine black stallion but rather a very simple, everyday donkey. It was the back of this often overlooked, common creature that was chosen to carry the greatest package ever carried, humanity's hope: Jesus.

It's very interesting when you study the word donkey – one translation says, *"beast of burden"*. How fitting that this beast of burden would get to carry the one who would, in turn, carry the sins and burdens of the whole world.

Why did Jesus not choose a chariot or a stallion? Maybe because He never came as the Pharisees expected, a saving messiah to come riding into town on a golden chariot, but rather as His Father in heaven wanted Him to – with meekness and authority, born in a manger. And maybe He didn't choose a stallion because stallions can have big egos and He did not need an ego to carry Him on this very important journey. Maybe, when the applause and shouts began, a stallion would have thought it was all about him and would rear up in pride causing the rider, that very important package, to be thrown off?

No. This moment of entry was all about the rider, Jesus, and the vehicle He chose was perfect because it spoke of His humility, meekness and servant heart. Let's face it, donkeys are not known for their fine looks but they are known for their faithfulness and steadfastness. When you want a package to leave one place on time and arrive safely at another, you can rely on a donkey.

Today, Jesus is still wanting to go places and is looking for a lift. He is wanting to go into your cities, colleges, neighbourhoods and He is looking for a suitable vehicle, a vehicle that will be faithful. How about you? Will you bear your back, your life, to carry Him? Will you be a donkey or vehicle He can use?

It's the day of the donkey, the faithful, not the stallion, the superstar.

Loosed for a purpose

Now when they drew near Jerusalem, and came to Bethphage, at the Mount of Olives, then Jesus sent two disciples, saying to them, "Go into the village opposite you, and immediately you will find a donkey tied, and a colt with her. Loose them and bring them to Me".

Matthew 21:1-2 (NKJV)

L et's stay on the theme of the donkey.
Notice what Jesus said to His disciples when He commissioned them to go and get Him a vehicle for entering the great city of Jerusalem, *"Loose them and bring them to Me"*. The story records that the disciples found the donkey tied up, just as Jesus had said and, indeed, loosed it and brought it to Him. That day, everything changed for that donkey – probably all it had known up to that day was walking around in circles tied to a pole, stopping every now and then to eat hay and look at a world she could not go into because of her captivity.

Here's a thought: Jesus never loosed the donkey because He liked donkeys and wanted to release it so it could enjoy its freedom or to take it to a donkey sanctuary – He loosed it for a purpose. It was given its freedom so that it could carry the presence of God, Jesus, where He needed to go. Wow! What a day that was for that donkey; from being bound to a pole to being a carrier of a move of God – Jesus.

You have probably worked out my comparison, right? Each of us is like that donkey. We were tied up to sin and stuff, bound and not free then Jesus sent His message of freedom and liberated us from the captivity we knew. But you need to understand that, like that donkey, it is not just about your freedom. It's great that you're set free but what now? The best bit is that Jesus wants to ride upon your life, as He did that donkey, to bring His message of freedom and spirit of life to the other places where it is so needed; He has a purpose for you.

I don't want to be a free donkey, running around a field doing my own thing. I am so grateful for the freedom He has given me, grateful enough to offer that freedom back to Him for His plans and intentions. How about you?

It was for freedom that Christ has set you free but that freedom also had a kingdom-transporting purpose to it.

Will you be freed, or freed and brought to Him for His purposes?

It's about the next generation, too

As they approached Jerusalem and came to Bethphage on the Mount of Olives, Jesus sent two disciples, saying to them, "Go to the village ahead of you, and at once you will find a donkey tied there, with her colt by her. Untie them and bring them to me."

Matthew 21:1-3 (NIV)

We have been looking at this great account of Jesus sending His disciples to loose a donkey for the purpose of carrying Him into Jerusalem. We saw how He chose a donkey over a stallion as He is looking for faithfulness, not ego. We also considered how, like the donkey, we have not just been loosed to be free but rather that we would also have the privilege of carrying Him to all the places He now wants to go.

One other thing that I notice when I read this account in *Matthew* is that Jesus sent the disciples to loose and bring to Him not just the donkey but her young colt also. When I thought about this, I saw something very significant relating to us and the next generation which is following us.

God is not just looking at releasing faithful carriers for this generation through us but He is also passionate about the next one too. I believe true success is when we allow Him to loose our lives and use them for His kingdom purpose but also that we bring the next generation to Him too; that we take the time to raise them up to love and serve Him as we have decided to do. Again, it's that timeless principle of 'monkey see, monkey do'. When we allow the next generation, the colts, to watch us carry and serve the Lord, we will inspire them to do the same in their generation. We then raise up an army to follow in our tracks.

Jesus wants us and them. It's our responsibility to let the children and young people in our world find Jesus and His purposes while they are young, raising them up in the way they will go so when they get old they don't depart *(Proverbs 22:6)*.

We should be protecting them from all the religious cobwebs we had to beat our way through to find Him, carrying them on our shoulders so they can see further than us. Whether you are a parent, grandparent, children's or youth worker, remember, and be inspired today, that your influence over those 'colts' in your world is powerful. Make sure that you are influencing them toward Jesus, just as you are running after Him for yourself. We are God's masterplan for this moment; they are His masterplan for the moments that follow ours.

Faith leaves the how to God!

Trust in the LORD with all your heart, and lean not on your own understanding; in all your ways acknowledge Him, and He shall direct your paths.

Proverbs 3:5-6 (NKJV)

When learning about faith, with the desire to let it ever develop further in your life, you soon discover that it is simply a matter of trust. Not a matter of trust when you know how everything is going to happen, rather an issue of trusting when you have no understanding, or idea, of how God is going to make what He has promised you come about. Being human, we always want to know the **how** or, put another way, the specific route to the destination that God has promised us. But most of the time, that is not how God operates because He is wanting us to operate in faith. Faith itself is all the substance we need and does not need to be accompanied with physical evidence *(Hebrews 11:1)*.

When you study the life of Abraham, you see how God operates when it comes to faith. When you gain the understanding of this, it enables you to understand how to walk by faith with Him.

At the start of Abraham's journey, God steps into his settled, secure world and says, "I have so much more for you". When Abraham enquires concerning the route to this great destination all God says is, "Leave where you are at and go **that** way". No map, no 'sat-nav.' No co-ordinates, no idea of what was around the corner, or where the next corner was! Yet Abraham chose not to lean on his understanding but rather trust the promise and the Promise Giver.

As he stepped forward toward the promise, the route began to be revealed: at every bend he experienced the favour and goodness of God and one day he arrived at the place God had promised.

If you are waiting for the route, a map, or for that moment you fully understand what God is asking you to do, my friend, you may have a long wait. God is looking for those in this generation that will receive the promises He gives and walk in accordance to them, even when the 'how' cannot be understood or does not make sense to your understanding. That's faith.

What has God promised you? What is delaying you setting off on the journey towards it? Are you waiting for God to release the 'how'? How is God going to make that happen, how is God going to provide, how is God going to open those doors we would need open? There is never any shortage of 'hows' with the faith walk but faith is to entrust the 'hows' to the God who has promised you a greater destination.

God is looking for faith-filled obedience

Then God said, "Take your son, your only son, Isaac, whom you love, and go to the region of Moriah. Sacrifice him there as a burnt offering on one of the mountains I will tell you about."

Genesis 22:2 (NIV)

L et's stay with Abraham and see once again that faith is simple trust, even when you do not understand the 'how'. In this account, God has asked Abraham to sacrifice the promised son whom He had given to him. This doesn't make sense, does it! God promised him a child supernaturally and now He is just going to take him away. Worse than that, He expects this father, who loves the kid so much, to sacrifice his only son. We then see Abraham, in obedience, do exactly what God asks, even when the child is asking, "Where is the lamb?" He keeps building the fire and, eventually, we see him standing over the child with a knife.

I believe Abraham knew he would end up with his son and that God would not take from him, permanently, what He had given. We see a glimpse of this faith when we hear what Abraham said to his servants as they ascended the mountain, "Wait for us, we will return". He knew God and His goodness well enough to know he would return with the child but what he did not know was the 'how'. How was God going to do this?

As he stands at the moment of no return, with all that was precious to him on the altar, God says, "Stop." and shows him the lamb in the thicket. He then says, "There is My provision for this sacrifice, release your son". We understand now, many years on, that an agreement was being made spiritually, that just as Abraham was willing to sacrifice his only beloved son so, many years later, God would do the same for us.

But in that moment, Abraham could have chosen any number of 'hows'. How's this going to happen, how's it going to work out? Rather, for our example, he chose to have faith, to trust in God and not lean on his own understanding.

How about you, will you put your future on the altar? Maybe something that represents your security and safety? Do you trust deep within that God only has your best at heart and though this moment, or what He is asking, does not make sense, you will end up at a great destination?

As Abraham had an individual faith walk with God, so do each of us and God still asks for what is precious to us to see if faith and trust are just words in a song we sing or, indeed, our deliberate, purposed way of life.

Let me end by saying this: read the end of the stories of people that chose to trust God – Joseph, Abraham, Joshua and so on – the journey was full of 'hows' but the promised destinations were always arrived at.

I hope you enjoyed this devotional and that is has been both a blessing and a challenge to your life and walk with God. Maybe you just got hold of it and are looking through before starting. Long ago, I made the decision never to take for granted that everyone has prayed a prayer to receive Jesus as their Lord, so am including that as my finale.

If you have never asked Jesus into your life and would like to do that now, it's so easy. Just pray this simple prayer:

Dear Lord Jesus, thank You for dying on the cross for me. I believe that You gave Your life so that I could have life. When You died on the cross, You died as an innocent man who had done nothing wrong. You were paying for my sins and the debt I could never pay. I believe in You, Jesus, and receive the brand new life and fresh start that the Bible promises that I can have. Thank You for my sins forgiven, for the righteousness that comes to me as a gift from You, for hope and love beyond what I have known and the assurance of eternal life that is now mine.
Amen.

Good next moves are to get yourself a Bible that is easy to understand and begin to read. Maybe start in *John* so you can discover all about Jesus for yourself. Start to pray – prayer is simply talking to God – and, finally, find a church that's alive and get your life planted in it. These simple ingredients will cause your relationship with God to grow.

Why not email me and let me know if you did that so I can rejoice with you?

response@greatbiglife.co.uk

If you would like to order more copies of this devotional or want to contact us, you can do so at:

Great Big Life Publishing
Empower Centre
83-87 Kingston Road
Portsmouth
Hants
PO2 7DX

Telephone: +44 23 9266 2257

Email: info@greatbiglifepublishing.com
Web: www.greatbiglifepublishing.com

For more information about Andy Elmes or the ministries of Great Big Life, Family Church or Synergy, here are the links you will need:

Great Big Life – greatbiglife.co.uk
Family Church – family-church.org.uk
Synergy Alliance – synergy-alliance.org
Synergy Christian Churches – synergychristianchurches.org

To sign up for the free midweek devotional – breakfastofchampions.co.uk

If you have enjoyed reading Andy's thoughts and would like to listen to some audio resources, we have many different CD sets available where Andy speaks on a variety of different subjects, most being recorded during the regular meetings at Family Church. Go to the Great Big Life website (greatbiglife.co.uk) for more information on these resources and others.

If you're going through something,
remember, you're halfway through a
testimony, don't blow it!

(Maureen Elmes, 1940-2006)

Are you an Author?

Do you have a word from God on your heart that you're looking to get published to a wider audience?

We're looking for manuscripts that identify with our own vision of bringing life-giving and relevant messages to Body of Christ. Send yours for review towards possible publication to:

Great Big Life Publishing
Empower Centre
83-87 Kingston Road
Portsmouth
Hants
PO2 7DX
info@greatbiglifepublishing.com